DOMINION

DR. CHRISTIAN
HARFOUCHE

DOMINION

Global Revival Distribution
Pensacola, Florida

Unless otherwise indicated, all scriptural references are from the King James Version of the Bible, Cambridge © 1769.

Verses marked NKJV are taken from the New King James Version. Copyright © 1982 by Thomas Nelson, Inc. Used by permission of NavPress Publishing Group.

Verses marked NEB are taken from The Word: The Bible from 26 Translations, ISBN 0935491015, © 1991-2004 Mathis Publishers, Inc., Gulfport, MS 39506.

Verses marked Wuest are taken from The New Testament An Expanded Translation by Kenneth S. Wuest. © Copyright in 1961 by Wm. B. Eerdmans Publishing Company.

Verses marked Amplified are taken from the Amplified Bible ® Copyright © 1954, 1958, 1964, 1987 by The Lockman Foundation. Used by permission.

Verses marked Moffatt are taken from The Word: The Bible from 26 Translations, ISBN 0935491015, © 1991-2004 Mathis Publishers, Inc., Gulfport, MS 39506.

For emphasis, the author has placed selected words from Bible quotations in italics and/or parenthesis.

Dominion
ISBN 1-888966-73-4

Published by:
Global Revival Distribution
4317 N. Palafox St.
Pensacola, FL 32505
www.globalrevival.com

Cover & interior design and book production by:
M.E.D.I.A. Group
421 North Palafox Street, Pensacola, FL 32501
Cover illustration is protected by the 1976 United States Copyright Act.
Copyright © 2006 by M.E.D.I.A. Group, Inc

Copyright © 2006 Dr. Christian Harfouche. All rights reserved. Reproduction of text in whole or part without the express written consent by the author is not permitted and is unlawful according to the 1976 United States Copyright Act. Printed in the United States of America

It is one thing to write about miracles - many writers can. But.....it is another to write with a pen in hand - when that hand has felt the power of miracles.

Christian Harfouche is truly one whom our Almighty God has chosen - chosen to anoint with the giftings of being able to manifest HIS miracles -

Under this mighty anointing, Christian inspires the reader to rise up - You can be mightily used by God to lay hands upon the sick, speak the Word, and experience, "These signs shall follow them that believe." Mark 16:17a

As Christian says, "You are the walking revelation of Jesus Christ!" If you ask anything in my Name, that will I do that the Father may be glorified in the Son.

**–Dr. Morris Cerullo, President
Morris Cerullo World Evangelism**

"I have known Dr. Harfouche for many years. His life and ministry are a Godly example to all of us. He has been in ministry over 25 years and is one of the finest teachers on faith and miracles that I have known. I know that his book will be a blessing to everyone who reads it and I would recommend it to anyone."

"Dr. Harfouche, Maggie and I want to thank you for your friendship over the years. In your over 25 years of ministry, you and Robin have truly demonstrated integrity, godliness and the love of God. Your teachings on faith and tithing are some of the best I have heard. It is a privilege and an honor to call you friends."

**–Dr. Norvel L. Hayes
Norvel Hayes Ministries**

"Congratulations on passing the 25 year mark for a fruitful and productive ministry. In the Bible, the number 25 is for the word grace - five times over. You have been gifted, enabled and graced for a signs and wonders ministry. Christian and Robin - In old Testament days, 25 years were spent in acquiring knowledge and learning. The next 25 years were spent in abundant fruit bearing. I predict according to Job 11:6 (NKJV), that your ministry will start doubling in results."

–Dr. Dick Mills
Dick Mills Ministries

"The miracle and prophetic ministry of Dr. Christian Harfouche has profoundly impacted our churches in South Africa. During the years of apartheid, his regular visits to the nation assisted believers in uniting as one family and, thereby, the destiny of our nation was affected. His ministry was instrumental in uniting us as a nation."

–Pastor Neville McDonald
Healing Word International

"The Key to the miracle ministry of my dear friend Dr. Christian Harfouche, is that for 25 years He has always pointed people to the healer - our precious savior Jesus. In a day and age when many draw people to themselves and lift up and exalt themselves. God uses Dr. Harfouche to teach practically and with a special anointing to see Jesus and raise up miracle workers for the 21st century. "

–Dr. Rodney Howard-Browne
Revival Ministries International

"Dr. Harfouche is a proof producer, of the highest caliber. Always on the cutting edge, he is training a generation to perform signs and wonders for the Kingdom of God. Dr. Harfouche doesn't practice miracles... he sees them everyday of his life."

–Dr. John Avanzini
John Avanzini Ministries

"Rarely does intensity and joy exist happily together but when I think of Dr. Christian and Robin Harfouche their effervescent joy always comes together. I celebrate with them 25 years of miracles and ministry. May the next 25 years be just as intense and just a joyful."

–Tommy Tenney
GodChasers.Network

"In an age of **"I'll believe it when I see it"**, Dr. Harfouche challenges every believer with his inspirational teaching on miracles backed with powerful demonstration of the Word. I encourage every one who wants to be used by God in a mighty way in these last days to pick up this book and apply its principles to your life."

–Dr. R.W. Schambach
Schambach Ministries

"Dr. Harfouche is an able minister of the Gospel of Jesus Christ, uniquely qualified to minister on the subject of miracles and healing. Keep going Doc... we need you".

–Pastor Randy Gilbert
Faith Landmark Ministries

We dedicate this book to our father in the faith, Dr. Lester Sumrall.

We thank God for the day when he laid his precious hands upon us… and prophesied that God would give us the Spirit of wisdom and understanding that He gave to Joshua… to lead the Children of Israel into the Promised Land.

I'll never forget when Dr. Lester Sumrall prayed that the Lord would impart to my wife and I… the same Spirit of faith that God had given him through the lineage of other great Generals of Faith.

Dr. Christian Harfouche

Drs. Christian and Robin Harfouche were ordained personally by Dr. Lester Sumrall

DEDICATION

*This book is dedicated
to the 400,000 Miracle Workers
and the Final Harvest of Souls.*

Contents

Chapter 1
    Delegated Authority   *1*

Chapter 2
    Declaring Your Covenant   *29*

Chapter 3
    Tending to the Promise   *55*

Chapter 4
    Possessing Authority and Power   *79*

Chapter 5
    Exercising Dominion   *97*

Chapter 6
    The Power of Connection   *117*

Chapter 7
    Power in the Name   *137*

Chapter 8
    Obtaining a More Excellent Name   *157*

Chapter 9
    WORKING THE POWER WITHIN   *177*

Chapter 10
    AWAKENING TO GREATNESS   *199*

Chapter 11
    ADVANCING IN VICTORY   *221*

Chapter 12
    MANIFEST WISDOM   *239*

Chapter 13
    PURSUE AND RECOVER ALL   *259*

Chapter 14
    INSTRUCTIONS FOR BUILDING   *283*

Chapter 15
    WALKING IN AGREEMENT   *297*

Chapter 16
    THE WAY OF A CHAMPION   *319*

CHAPTER 1

DELEGATED AUTHORITY

*God deals with truth and His Word is the Truth.
The devil deals with lies, and his word is Lies.*

Your Battle Plan for Victory

We serve a God of integrity and truth. His Word is His bond. It's a binding agreement. It's a firm assurance, a written obligation. God's Word is a contract that cannot be broken or dismantled or nullified. It is a Word of surety, for God will never say one thing and then do another. He cannot contradict His own nature, for His Word is consistent with His being. He is Truth. His Word is Truth.

The Word of God says, *"Surely the Lord God will do nothing, but He revealeth His secret unto His servants the prophets"* (Amos 3:7). When God says it, God does it. If He says He's going to help you, then you can count on Him to follow through with His promise. He is a God of integrity. He will backup His promise with performance.

You are different from the average person. People read books for many reasons, but you have picked up this book because you have a desire to serve God outside of the parameters of human limitation. Not everyone can claim this desire, but within you, there is a spiritual tenacity and a willingness to go the extra mile. It's a stirring. It's a hunger. It's a fervency. There is something in you that wants to go all the way with God.

If this is your desire, as I know it is, then you must build your life upon the revelation of God's integrity. This revelation is your key to consistent victory and continual success. As a child of God, you have to know *who* God is and *what* He has called you to do. You have to know what He has promised to perform in your life. Remember, His Word is His *contractual agreement* with you. If you don't know what God has promised you, then you can't fight for it and you cannot contend for it. Therefore, you must take up His Word and fight the good fight of faith. This is your battle plan for victory. *Take up the Word and fight.*

> **Fight the good fight of faith, lay hold on eternal life, whereunto thou art also called, and hast professed a good profession before many witnesses.**
>
> **1 Timothy 6:12**

His Word must be so real to you that you can immediately detect and reject a word that does not come from God. The Bible calls this the good fight of faith and we are commanded to fight it. If you know the Word of God, then you must fight the good fight to see the Word of God manifested in your life.

God deals with truth and His Word is the TRUTH. The devil deals with lies, and his word is LIES.

Fight the GOOD FIGHT.

If the devil cannot talk you out of desiring Jesus, then he will attempt to dilute the power of God in your life. He will do everything he can to present Jesus in a religious light, to reduce His presence to a man-made concept or ideology. The devil would like to neutralize the power of God in your life. He would like to rob you of the benefits that Jesus came to give you.

> **The thief cometh not, but for to steal, and to kill, and to destroy: I am come that they might have life, and that they might have it more abundantly.**
>
> **John 10:10**

The devil comes to steal, kill and destroy. This is his very nature. Therefore, it is imperative that you have a working knowledge on how to prevent the thief from stealing, the destroyer from destroying, and the murderer from murdering. Your *working knowledge* is the good fight of faith in your life.

How do you fight the good fight of faith?

You must know that God is a God of integrity. You must know that His Word is His bond. Through the Scriptures, allow the Holy Ghost to give you a biblical revelation of the mindset and heartbeat of God. Once you *know* the will of God, no one will be able talk you out of it. Your confidence will be firmly established in the security of His integrity.

When this becomes your confidence, then there is nothing the devil can do to rob you. Your position is secured and you become a force to contend with in God. No longer are you tossed here and there by an opinion or what you read in the headlines. You *know* God and you *know* His Word. This unshakeable knowledge is your platform for victory.

He sent His Word, and healed them, and delivered them from their destructions.

Psalm 107:20

He sent His Word and that Word both healed them and delivered them. When God wants to get a job done, He sends His Word. The integrity of God is the integrity of the Word. Jesus said, *"Heaven and Earth will pass away but My Word will not pass away"* (Matthew 24:35). The Word of God will outlast the test of time. The Word of God is God and He will never become irrelevant or obsolete. He will see you through to victory!

Contending for Results

There is a way which seemeth right unto a man, but the end thereof are the ways of death.

Proverbs 14:12

This Scripture may be very familiar to you. Oftentimes, we look at it in terms of losing a soul. We say there is a way that seems right unto men, but they end up in Hell. There is, however, also a way that seems right to a Christian. This *way* can destroy their vision, ruin their marriage and cripple their finances. It can snuff out their dreams and abort both their call and their ministry. *What way is that?* It is the way of the enemy; it is the way of anything other than the Word of God. It may seem right to a man but it will end up destroying him. The devil will take advantage of anyone who does not KNOW and CONTEND for the integrity of the Word of God 24 hours a day.

I want you to say this out loud:

I have authority over the thief. I have authority over the murderer. It is delegated authority and it is resident in the integrity of God's Word.

Your authority will only work when you have both a *revelation* of the integrity of the Word of God and you are in *obedience* to that Word. For instance, the Bible refers to *"our heart condemning us"* (1 John 3:20). If a believer doesn't walk in love with another person, their heart will condemn them. When their own heart condemns them, it robs them of confidence towards God. Without this vital confidence, their faith cannot work and they cannot have the petitions that they ask of Him. Authority will not work in the absence of faith. Without faith's confidence, an individual may *try* to perform the revelation that they claim to have, but their effort will not bear fruit. Faith fuels authority. Without faith, authority fails to produce results.

Jesus is calling the Church. He is calling *you*. He is calling you to rise up and to allow Him to bring you to a different place. It is a call to go to a place where you have never gone before. *Can you hear the call?* He wants you to rise up financially. He wants you to rise up spiritually. He wants you to rise up in your character and in your integrity. He does not want you to be disappointed. He does not want you to become a calamity to the Kingdom of God. He wants you to allow the Holy Ghost to do the will of God in your life. *This is God's call to you.*

To rise up in this great call, you have to *mean business* with God. You have to *mean business* with the Word of God. Remember, God's integrity rides on His Word. As a child of God, you *can* be dogmatic to claim what God promises. You do not have to waver. You do not have to wonder. If God didn't mean to do it, He would never have promised it. He is a God of integrity, strategy and purpose. His Word was not carelessly spoken or thoughtlessly uttered into the expanse of eternity. Rather, His Word is grounded in the immutability of His nature. What He speaks, He will do. What He says, He will perform. He will not contradict what He has spoken, for His nature is not like that of fallen man. In fact, it is written, *"God is not a man, that He should lie; neither the son of man, that He should repent: hath He said, and shall He not do it? Or hath He spoken, and shall he not make it good"* (Numbers 23:19).

If He said it, will He not do it?
If He promised it, shall He not make it good?

If God has promised it, you can be sure that He means it and that He will do it. How many preachers, however, have failed because they didn't think God would do what He said He would do? How many people have stumbled at the promises of God? Some would say, *"We're all sinners."* God's Word, however, says were saved. It says we are the righteousness of God in Christ Jesus! Who are *you* going to believe? Your answer to this question will dictate the level of victory you experience on this side of eternity. *Consider your answer well.*

The Word of God says we are holy. It says we are foreknown. It says we are predestined. It says we are being called. It also says we have been justified and glorified.

What are you going to believe?

A child of God that believes they are a sinner will walk in their convictions. The Bible says, *"For as a man thinketh in his heart, so is he"* (Proverbs 23:7a). In other words, you will become what you meditate on! A person that thinks on sin and believes that they are a sinner will end up embracing the very things they profess to abhor. Somewhere down the line, a person like this may find himself or herself entangled in adultery or homosexuality.

God isn't the author of their decisions! They can't blame Him for allowing these things to come to pass! Rather, they have chosen through their own admissions to violate the integrity of the Word. They believed a word that wasn't the Word of God. Instead of the truth, they chose a lie and that lie bore fruit in their life.

The Word says you are a winner. The Word says that you can do all things through Christ which strengthens you (Philippians 4:13). He says you are more than a conqueror (Romans 8:37)! Yet, Christians want to believe they *can't* do it. Someone may say, *"I need God to help. Do something for me God."* No! You need the Holy Ghost to get your attention. You need to yield to His influence so that He can drive that point home. Allow the Holy Ghost to convince you that you can do all things through the Word. If you will allow Him to do this, He will remove the *"I can't"* from your vocabulary.

Submitting to Spiritual Hierarchy

> **And when Jesus was entered into Capernaum, there came unto Him a centurion, beseeching him, and saying, "Lord, my servant lieth at home sick of the palsy, grievously tormented." And Jesus saith unto him, "I will come and heal him." The centurion answered and said,**

"Lord, I am not worthy that Thou shouldest come under my roof: but speak the Word only, and my servant shall be healed. For I am a man under authority, having soldiers under me: and I say to this man, 'Go,' and he goeth; and to another, 'Come,' and he cometh; and to my servant, 'Do this,' and he doeth it." When Jesus heard it, He marvelled, and said to them that followed, "Verily I say unto you, I have not found so great faith, no, not in Israel. And I say unto you, that many shall come from the East and West, and shall sit down with Abraham, and Isaac, and Jacob, in the Kingdom of Heaven. But the children of the Kingdom shall be cast out into outer darkness: there shall be weeping and gnashing of teeth." And Jesus said unto the centurion, "Go thy way; and as thou hast believed, so be it done unto thee." And his servant was healed in the selfsame hour.

Matthew 8:5-13

Jesus is walking to Capernaum. On His way, He is met by a centurion. This centurion tells Jesus that his servant is at home sick, so sick that he may die at any time. The centurion explains that his servant is grievously tormented. Jesus says, *"I'll come and heal him."*

Jesus *always* had time to heal. In fact, you will not find an instance in God's Word where it claims otherwise. There is not one account where Jesus turned somebody away. He never said, *"Healing is not for you today."* On the contrary, the Word of God is very clear on this subject. There are people, however, who believe that it is not God's will to heal everybody. They are steeped in religious indoctrination and a way of thinking that is not based on the never changing, never failing Word of God. Some will preach it and some will just silently think it. They say, *"Well, you know it's all in the Lord's time. We're suffering for Jesus."*

Jesus said to the centurion, *"I will come and heal him."* Jesus offered to come to this man's house! The centurion, however, was not selfish. Instead, he replied, *"You don't have to come to my house. This is what I know. This is the process I am familiar with. I have a hundred men under me and if I say to this one, 'Go,' he will go. If I tell another 'Come,' he will come and if I say to another 'Do this,' he will do it."*

Centurions don't play games. When Paul and Silas were miraculously released from prison after singing praises to God, the prison guard was ready to kill himself. He would rather die at his own hands than face the centurion with the news of their escape! These high-ranking soldiers knew authority and the consequences of disobedience.

As a child of God and a soldier of Christ, you are commanded to carry out orders according to God's divine blueprint. If you submit to the hierarchy, you will rise up to become a hierarchy yourself. God will promote you.

The centurion that stood before Jesus had a hundred men under his command. Stop for a moment and consider how many were above him. What would happen if he didn't obey the authority that was over him? How would this affect the ranks under him?

The centurion's authority would stop working the moment he refused to obey the authority over him. The moment he said *"No"* to the guy above him, the guy under him would say *"No"* to him as well. Your authority will stop in the same way when you deviate from God's commands. When you say *"No"* to the Word of God in any area of your life, you give place for your enemy to strike. It may be a little headache demon or it may be something else. You will say, *"Do this in the name of Jesus,"* and he will say, *"No."*

Authority will only operate when a person is under authority. *When does the child of God begin to lose the anointing?* The anointing will wane when the believer violates the Word of God. They may not realize it consciously, but subconsciously they will know. The moment they step out of synch with the plan and hierarchy of God, their heart will condemn them. They will feel *condemnation*.

> **There is therefore now no condemnation to them which are in Christ Jesus, who walk not after the flesh, but after the Spirit.**
>
> **Romans 8:1**

The Bible is clear that there is no condemnation to the child of God who is walking in the Spirit. There is, however, condemnation to those who are walking after the flesh. *What should you do with condemnation?* Simply repent for walking after the flesh and then walk in the Spirit. The Word of God offers great assurance, for God knows all things, even the deep things of your heart.

> **For if our heart condemn us, God is greater than our heart, and knoweth all things.**
>
> **1 John 3:20**

When a man of God or a woman of God violates the Word, their heart will immediately begin to operate with fear and doubt regarding God. They may not even consciously recognize the offense, but they will instantly draw back in fear. When they go to use their faith to claim something, their faith will not work. Neutralized by fear, it will remain inoperative until they repent.

Troubleshooting Mountain Moving Faith

> **And Jesus answering saith unto them, "Have faith in God. For verily I say unto you, that whosoever shall say unto this mountain, 'Be thou removed, and be thou cast into the sea;' and shall not doubt in his heart, but shall believe that those things which he saith shall**

> come to pass; he shall have whatsoever he saith. Therefore I say unto you, what things soever ye desire, when ye pray, believe that ye receive them, and ye shall have them. And when ye stand praying, forgive, if ye have ought against any: that your Father also which is in Heaven may forgive you your trespasses. But if ye do not forgive, neither will your Father which is in Heaven forgive your trespasses."
>
> **Mark 11:22-26**

Jesus instructed His disciples on how to talk to a mountain and get results. He also said, *"When you stand praying...forgive."* Why did He include *forgiveness* in His mountain-moving instructions?

Some people fail to receive from God because they have not forgiven. If a person is walking in unforgiveness, they will not see their prayers answered. It won't matter how loud they shout or how much they use the name of Jesus. If there is a short in their connection and communication with God, they will not be able to receive. They will not see results. The mountain will not be moved. Jesus says, *"And when ye stand praying, forgive, if ye have ought against any..."*

When a Christian violates the law of God, there is a break in the anointing or the communication with God. Instead of yielding in obedience to the Word of God, that person may instead resort to manipulation to achieve their desired results. They may turn to soulish means to produce what they had asked for in prayer.

Why do some ministers push people down in a prayer line? They push people down because the anointing is not there. *Why is the anointing failing to work in their ministry?* There is a connection problem! Something has been short-circuited and instead of correcting the problem, they resort to manipulation.

The anointing brings liberty and the Word brings freedom. However, if someone has stepped outside of the will of God or has violated the authority that was set in place over them, their connection with God will be damaged. It will not function properly. A person in this situation has two choices. They can either repent and step back into the obedience of the Word of God or they can further deviate into spiritual manipulation.

Riding on God's Authority

The centurion said, *"I'm a man under authority. I know why I have authority—it's because I'm submitted to the person in authority over me. Now, I can tell a hundred people to do this or do that, and they'll do it."* Jesus marveled. He said, *"I have not found such great faith."*

That's Jesus! Jesus is the Word that became flesh. The Word said, *"I'll come to your house and heal your servant."* The centurion said, *"Oh, You don't have to do that. Just speak the Word only."* Astonished, the Word replied, *"I have not found such great faith."* Jesus is looking for faith! In fact, two things astonished Jesus in this account. The centurion's faith astonished Him and Israel's doubt astonished Him.

What made Jesus marvel? The centurion asked Jesus to just speak the Word. This military leader had a revelation of how authority works. He understood military commands. He understood divine decree. He said, *"If I tell one of my soldiers to do something, they'll do exactly what I say. In the same way, I know that You have authority, Jesus. So speak the Word! I know demons listen to You. Speak the Word!"*

The centurion wasn't even saved! Calvary hadn't made that provision available yet. If this man wasn't even saved, yet received from God, how much more should a child of God who is filled with the Holy Ghost receive from God through the authority of the Word?

The integrity of God's Word will always perform when He sees faith at your end.

The centurion said, *"Lord, I am not worthy that thou shouldest come under my roof: but speak the Word only, and my servant shall be healed."*

> **When Jesus heard it, He marveled, and said to them that followed, "Verily I say unto you, I have not found so great faith, no, not in Israel. And I say unto you, that many shall come from the East and West, and shall sit down with Abraham, and Isaac, and Jacob, in the Kingdom of Heaven. But the children of the Kingdom shall be cast out into outer darkness: there shall be weeping and gnashing of teeth." And Jesus said unto the centurion, "Go thy way; and as thou hast believed, so be it done unto thee." And his servant was healed in the selfsame hour.**
>
> **Matthew 8:10-13**

Jesus spoke of a people that would come from the East and the West. They would pass up the people that God had chosen. Those people would sit with Abraham, Isaac, and Jacob and the children of the Kingdom. The ones that were called to believe the promise, however, will wail, weep and gnash their teeth.

What in the world would prompt Jesus to talk about such things?

Quite simply, it was the centurion's faith. When the centurion said, *"Speak the Word,"* he forever delivered a testimony against anyone who had been given the privilege of the Kingdom of God, but had failed to believe the integrity of the Word of God.

Jesus said, *"Now, this right here is a testimony to the world that God does not discriminate. Look at those in the East and get a good look at those in the West, because everyone that understands the chain of command and the operation of divine authority will see God results."* They will be able to say, *"The Word of God is going to speak into my life and God will cause me to prosper in this life and in the life to come."* They will be able to sit with Abraham, Isaac and Jacob.

Faith… the Foundation of Your Success

Your foundation must be built upon the integrity of the Word of God in order to withstand the attacks of the enemy. That foundation cannot be built upon your bank account, your youth or any other natural thing. The things of the world will fall short. Their foundations will fail with time and with wear. Your bank account can be exhausted and your youth left behind, however, the Word of the Living God is never changing and never failing.

Two thousand years ago Jesus was looking for faith in the Earth. He said, *"I haven't found that kind of faith in all of Israel."*

Do you think Jesus is still looking for faith today?

It is not what you believe that helps you; it is *what you do* with *what you know* that will help you. Faith acts. A library full of knowledge is worthless unless that knowledge is engaged and acted upon. It is, therefore, better *not to know*, than *to know* and *do nothing* with what you know.

Israel *knew*. They had scrolls. They read the Scriptures. They attended synagogue. They observed the Sabbath. They had been around and they knew some things about the plans and purposes of God. Psalm 107 had even been read in their midst! Their ears heard the Word. They heard the promises. They heard, *"He sent His Word and healed them."* Despite all of these things, Israel failed to grasp the simplicity of that revelation. It took a centurion to say, *"Send Your Word."*

"And his servant was healed in the selfsame hour."

At the end of the day, it's not *what you know*. It's what you act upon that *proves* what you know.

If you act on God's Word, it will never fail in your life. When you believe the Word, it will produce exactly what it is promising. Jesus said, *"Go your way and as you have believed, so be it unto you."* The integrity of the Word will never fail to perform.

The moment you see it in the Word, you should immediately believe it. When you really believe it, everybody will *see* that you believe it. Your faith will tell off on you. When the storm comes, everyone will see your faith. They will see the fruit of your convictions in God. What you believe will rise to the surface and manifest itself. When a certain storm rocked the disciple's boat on the Lake of Galilee, every one of them was convinced of impending doom! They thought they were going to drown! Jesus, however, believed different. He believed that He had authority over the storm.

What do YOU do when you come face to face with the challenges of life?

If you messed up, go back to the drawing board! Don't quit and don't confess that the Word of God didn't work for you! The truth is that you didn't work on behalf of the Word. You didn't act on what you knew. Somehow, you didn't follow through. There was a short at your end because the Word of God has too much integrity to fail. It is consistent and never changing. It is the nature of God and God cannot lie.

"Faith" the Antidote to "Try"

He sent His Word, and healed them, and delivered them from their destructions.

Psalm 107:20

He did not *try* to heal them.
He did not *try* to deliver them.
Jesus did not *try* to defeat the devil.
The cross did not *try* to provide redemption.
The blood did not *try* to cleanse you.
God does not *try* to win your battles for you.

The Word of God never fails. If you feel that you have fallen short in an area, go back to the drawing board and find out where you missed it. The drawing board is the Word of God. Rely on His integrity. Allow the Word to answer your situation.

Find out where you missed the mark and set your course in line with the Word. *Sooner* or *later,* you will see where you missed it. The timetable on that revelation, however, depends entirely on you. There are those who will learn it *later* because they will insist on their own methods. They will listen to the devil and make excuses. However, once they have reached the end of human effort, they will have to repent and be healed from their hurts and delivered from disappointments. You do not have to chart the route of fruitlessness. You do not have to be the kind of person that learns it *later.* You can take God at His Word *now.*

Jesus said, *"Go thy way; and as thou has believed, so be it done unto thee."* This is how God responds to His people! Offended, some will say, *"You're saying that I don't have enough faith!"* Turn it around and understand that the Word of God will bring you the faith you need if you let it. Hook onto the Word. The Word will establish you in victory. It will bring the ingredients of success into your life.

You can walk in victory 24 hours a day.

To maintain this position of victory, you must guard your heart. You cannot walk in victory if your heart is not guarded. Therefore, guard it with all diligence, for out of it flows the issues of life (Proverbs 4:23). If you do not guard your heart, you will always be a roller coaster Christian. You will ride the waves of circumstance and get caught in the undertow of defeat. The devil will go after your heart.

Different people have different dispositions. Some are thicker skinned than others. You can hint at something to one person and it will sail right over their head. Others are highly sensitive and pick up on every innuendo, down to the smallest detail. A person like this needs to develop an extra ability to guard their heart against hurts and wounds. If they don't, their heart will be wounded.

A spiritually sensitive Christian can hear God. They can be edified by Him. They can receive from Him. The Christian, however, must be thick-skinned with the enemy, yet maintain their sensitivity to the Lord. They have to know the difference between the voice of God and that of the devil. They have to *yield* to one while resisting the other.

Faith Articulated

> **And when Jesus was come into Peter's house, He saw his wife's mother laid, and sick of a fever. And He touched her hand, and the fever left her: and she arose, and ministered unto them. When the even was come, they brought unto Him many that were possessed with devils; and He cast out the spirits with His Word, and healed all that were sick: That it might be fulfilled which was spoken by Esaias the prophet, saying, "Himself took our infirmities, and bare our sicknesses."**
>
> **Matthew 8:14-17**

Jesus is the living Word of God. He is the Word of God that lives and abides forever. When the Word of God walked into Peter's home, He touched his mother-in-law's hand and she was instantly set free of the fever. The Word of God can *touch*. Jesus does not need to appear in your home *physically* to bring deliverance. Just as the centurion discovered, the Word of God can touch you anywhere.

From this day forward, make the decision to hook into the realm of the Spirit and to allow the Word to touch you. In the same way that you allowed the cares of the world to come upon you, let those same cares roll off of you. Allow the Word of God to touch you where you are. Give Him free access in your life and rely on His wisdom rather than earthly wisdom.

When you allow the Word of God to touch you, *things* leave you. It will bring transformation and change to your life. The Word will not only deliver you physically, but it will touch you spirit, soul and body. Worries leave when the Word touches you. Fears leave when the Word touches you. Disappointments leave you when the Word touches you. Hurts leave you when the Word touches you.

You might be thinking, *"Oh, you don't understand. I've got real hurts that need to be healed."* Let the Word touch you. Get healed and stop talking about it. Be delivered from that thing! Another might respond, *"You don't understand. It is my upbringing."* Let the Word of God touch you and even your upbringing will leave you! You do not have to become the product of your environment. The Word of God will *change* your environment. Jesus is interested in touching every part of your life. The Word will touch you, if you let Him.

And He touched her hand, and the fever left her: and she arose...

Matthew 8:15a

The Word of God touched her and produced an immediate result.

The Bible goes on to say that they brought to Him all that were possessed with devils and He cast the spirits out with His Word.

How do you think Jesus articulated that?
What kind of words do you think the Lord used?

Maybe He said, *"If it be thy will, Satan,"* or perhaps He said, *"If it be Thy will, Father?"* The Word of God is not mysterious. It doesn't vacillate in a gray area. The bottom line is that you either know the Word or you do not know the Word. God's Word is definitive. It's decisive. It's direct. God says *"yes"* and God says *"no."* He never says *"maybe"* and He never says, *"I don't know."*

What does that have to do with your life?

God's will *is* God's Word. If you know His Word, you will know how to cast a devil out with that Word. If you know His Word, you will know how to utilize that Word in conjunction with His will. The Word of God will produce results. The Word will deliver the demoniac. There are certain *words,* however, that will not deliver a demon-possessed person. A *"let us pray"* word will not eject a devil. God never said to *pray* that a devil would leave.

The Word of God is alive and powerful. When faith is mixed with the Word in your mouth, it will be released through you in an affirmative declaration of internal conviction. Its sound will be clear, pure, uninhibited, untainted and untarnished. That clear sound will be God's voice in unison with your voice. In turn, the power of Heaven will be released through your spoken convictions. There is power in your words!

It is imperative that you understand what God has promised. For instance, when you are dealing with a demon-possessed person, an individual who is sick or a situation in your life, you cannot afford to have doubts about the will of God! You must know who your God is and what He has called you to do. When you know these things, you will have boldness. You will move in faith. Your faith will, in turn, move mountains. You will achieve the impossible. However, if you do not know the will of God in a situation, you can't believe for His will to take place.

God has given you power. He has given you the power to paralyze the devil and to deliver people from their destructions. That power is in your mouth. Its source is packaged in the very words that you speak! God's Word *in* your words will enable and enforce the will of God. It will produce results.

God sent His Word for a purpose. As you grow in an understanding of this purpose, you will not take His Word lightly. You will receive the Word for what it is and for what it stands for. You will embrace it with an unshakeable conviction in His integrity. When somebody says, *"You don't understand. It's impossible,"* you will say, *"Yeah, but the Word of God is more powerful than that impossibility."* If you have the

Word of God, it does not matter what kind of situation rises up against you. The Word of God in you will move the mountain. In turn, you will rise up in fearlessness and God-inspired confidence. You will stand sure in your convictions because you know your God and you know what He has promised to do. This is faith.

You are a danger to the devil when you know these two things:

1. You know the will of God.
2. You know that you are *in* the perfect will of God.

A person like this is fearless. When you know the will of God and walk in it, the enemy will not be able to rob you of what God has for you. You're authoritative. You're full of the Word of God. You cast the devil out with your word. You cast the situation out with your word. You're a force to be reckoned with.

When your word is the Word of God, you can change the circumstances with the fruit of your lips. You can open your mouth and release the force of Heaven. You can speak the mind of Christ and participate in His results. There is power in your mouth.

Exercising Your Divine Rights

God has given you delegated authority. This authority originates from God, but has been delegated to you to use on His behalf. It is your divine privilege, ability and right. He has given you the ability to exercise dominion and to take authority over all the power of the demonic realm. When Jesus rose from the dead, two dimensions became entirely subject to His influence. The Bible says, *"All power is given unto Me in Heaven and Earth"* (Matthew 28:18). Jesus was given power in two realms.

Why did Jesus have to come DOWN to get power?

During the fall of mankind, Adam traded in his God-ordained authority. He handed his divine rights over to the demonic realm.

The enemy then took what belonged to the creation of God and perverted it. The Bible calls the devil the "god of this world." To redeem mankind, God had to send someone. He had to send *Someone* to reverse the curse and to take back what the devil stole. That *Someone* was His Son.

Jesus was sent to redeem mankind from destruction. To do this, He had to overcome death, Hell and the grave. He had to take back the authority that Adam had given over to the "god of this world."

Jesus is the divine antidote to a world poisoned by sin and its consequences. The Bible says, *"He sent His Word, and healed them, and delivered them from their destructions."* Jesus is the Word become flesh.

The devil *was* your destruction.
Jesus is not *going* to deliver you from the devil.
Jesus *has* delivered you from the devil.
It is finished.

And having spoiled principalities and powers, He made a shew of them openly, triumphing over them in it.

Colossians 2:15

The Word did not stay in Heaven. The Word left Heaven and came to Earth where rebel spirit beings were trying to exercise dominion over mankind. Having settled the matter once and for all, Jesus rose from the dead and said, *"Now, I have the keys of death, Hell and the grave. I have done it. I have paid the price in full on Earth."*

The Word became a man in order to redeem man. Jesus said, *"I've paid the price and now all power in Heaven and in Earth are given to Me."* In turn, He took that power and handed delegated authority over to the child of God. He gave us *His power* so that we can demonstrate *His resurrection life* in our lives.

How do we demonstrate this in our lives? Allow the Word to have

His way.

You're born of the Word. When you allow the Word to have His way in your life, the power in you will rapidly transform you. A great acceleration will take place in your life.

As you administer the Word and rest in His integrity, the results of the Word will manifest around you. Your life will demonstrate the triumph of Heaven. The Word of God in you will prosper you on every level. Yield, therefore, to the Word. Allow Him to produce His results in your life.

Avoiding Defeat by Default

How did Jesus cast the devil out? He must have said, *"Devil, come out!"* He gave a command! He knew that the devil was subservient to the authority He had in God.

The devil is no match for the authority that Jesus has given you! It doesn't matter what tactic or what angle he is using. His methods are not new. The devil may try to get at you through sickness, disease, poverty or circumstance. None of these demonic strategies, however, can stop you. You are bigger than these things. You are a child of God, born of the Word. You are not subject to the fleeting whims of the demonic realm.

You are a force to be reckoned with. However, as a child of God, you have to *know* that you can cast the devil out with your word. If you don't, then by default, you will allow the devil to stay with your word. Imagine if Jesus had turned to the demon-possessed person and said, *"I know that you would like to be set free, but I believe it is all in the Lord's time. I believe there is a lesson to learn in all of this."* What do you think would have happened? What would the devil have done? I will tell you exactly what the devil would have done! He wouldn't have budged. He would have stayed in that person.

You must know your authority.

Do you sneeze in the morning and say, *"Man, I knew I was going to catch that flu."* If this is your practice, then you are not casting the devil out! You are not casting the sickness out. You are receiving that thing into your body. With your words, you are embracing and validating that lying symptom. Your words are the welcome mat that gives place to everything that knocks upon the threshold of your life.

Do you sit up at night worrying or do you cast worry out with your word? You can't worry and praise God at the same time. You can't toss and turn at night and prophesy at the same time. *Whose influence will you yield to?* There is always a choice involved.

Put the Word of God in your mouth. It does not matter what the devil is saying.

When he tells you that you are weak, say, *"I am strong."*
When he tells you that you are sick, say, *"I am healed."*
When he tells you that you are poor, say, *"I am rich."*
When he tells you that you are the tail, say, *"I am the head."*
When he tells you that you are out, say, *"I am in."*

Always speak the Word of God in your life. Remember, with your words you will either disallow the devil or allow his nonsense in your life. The choice is yours. Someone might think in their heart, *"I am going to try that."* Don't *try* it! Before you speak, you must know the Word and the integrity of that Word. Your convictions must rest surely in His integrity. If you *know that you know*, then there will be no need to *try*. It won't even be a part of the equation.

Give Voice to His Voice

Some would say, *"But saying that 'I'm healed' when I'm sick is a lie."* That's right, so don't lie about yourself! *You are not sick.* You are healed.

What about a headache?
Is a symptom indicative of sickness?

People say, *"Well, brother, you are way out there because when I have a headache, I am sick."* Baffled, they ask incredulously, *"But when you have a headache you are not sick?"* That's right! I am not sick because the Word of God says I am not sick. If I were to ask that same person why they were sick, they would confidently reply, *"I am sick because I have a headache."* A person like this believes in the integrity of the headache. Their convictions are based on a symptom rather than on the never failing Word of God.

Some will say, *"You are blessed. I hope to be blessed too."* Others say, *"Well, you know one day the Lord is going to bless me like So-and-So."* What makes you think that *"So-and-So"* is more blessed than you? Is it because they have *"this, that and the other?"* If this is the case, it means that you believe in the integrity of the *"this, that, and the other!"*

> You are *not* blessed when you *get* it.
> **You are blessed when you *believe* it.**
>
> You are *not* healed when you *get* it.
> **You are healed when you *believe* it.**
>
> You are *not* saved when you *get* there.
> **You are saved when you *believe* it.**

The moment a saint chooses to believe the Word of God, they will instantly receive the ability to hold onto that Word. When a person does this, Hell itself will mobilize to launch an attack against their life. The enemy will try to steal from them. He will *not* attempt to steal the power, the job, or the blessing, but rather, he will try to steal the Word of God from their life. He will go straight to the SOURCE of the saint's power. He will hit them where their strength is.

The devil knows that if he leaves the Word alone in your life, it will continue to prosper within you. It will produce a harvest in and through your life. That harvest will give praise and honor to the integrity of God's will. Therefore, know that when you stand on the Word, you stand on the undefeatable security and stability of God. These things can never be plundered or overcome by the works of the enemy.

He cast the devil out with His Word. God has placed authority and power in the SPOKEN WORD. That spoken Word had the ability to enforce the will of God. It is alive. It is full of divine energy, and when launched, it will do in your life what it has been sent to do. The Word of God will perform on your behalf. Put the Word in your mouth. Give voice to the inspiration of Heaven. Speak God's thoughts. Yield to His Word.

De·fin·ing (adj.) Faith

> **Neither is there any creature that is not manifest in His sight: but all things are naked and opened unto the eyes of Him with whom we have to do.**
>
> **Hebrews 4:13**

The Word of God will teach you how to respond to life's problems. A person can look into the Word of God and say, *"Oh yeah. That's my problem. I see where I have been missing it."* They will see it in the Word as if their very situation was in bold text. It's supernatural. The Bible says that, *"The Word of God is a discerner of the thoughts and the intents of the heart."*

The Word will show you where you are in error so that you can correct the problem. The more you respond to the Word, the faster you will grow. As you adjust and yield to its influence, you will be changed from glory to glory. This is how God coaches champions. True champions are made through training in the Word of God. This is what gives faith its *defining force.*

There are some things, however, that can stop the Word of God. One of those things is *tradition.*

> **Making the Word of God of none effect through your tradition, which ye have delivered: and many such like things do ye.**
>
> **Mark 7:13**

Some have said, *"Well, I do not want to get traditional. I am going to quit going to church."* That is not what the Word of God is speaking of. This Scripture is making reference to traditions that are inconsistent with the Word of God.

Here is a good example: *"We will anoint you with oil and HOPE you get healed."* A tradition like this makes the Word of God of non-effect because it is non-producing. It sounds nice, but you will not find it in the Bible!

Furthermore, the Word of God does not teach that the effectual fervent prayer of a righteous man availeth little. It did not say, *"Let him pray over him and anoint him with oil and the prayer of faith MIGHT save the sick and the Lord COULD raise him up."* No, it says, *"shall."* It says, *"And the prayer of faith SHALL SAVE the sick, and the Lord SHALL RAISE him up; and if he have committed sins, they SHALL BE forgiven him"* (James 5:15). There is no room for any other outcome, but God-sanctioned results.

Someone might be tempted to think, *"Oh, but you don't want to get too extreme in that stuff."* If a person doesn't want to get extreme, they might as well rip the offending pages out of the Bible! After they rip out that which doesn't mesh with their traditions, they will find little more than the maps and index.

Every page of the Word of God is filled with God-given promises that can never fail when applied with faith. Tradition, however, will short-circuit your growth and progress. It will make the Word of God irrelevant and obsolete.

"Well, brother, I just believe that the Lord is going to get it done."

The Bible also said that they heard the same Gospel that was preached to them but the Word did not profit them, not being mixed with faith in them that heard it (Hebrews 4:2).

"Well, brother, we just don't do it like that, but we have faith."

Most people think they have faith. Sinners have even professed faith! Both the world and the Church have been duped to believe that faith is nothing more than believing in *something*. They say, *"As long as you believe something, you have faith."* That couldn't be further from the truth!

If you believe what God says and what God says alone, *then you have faith*. It's not "faith" to believe that God is the healer as well as the One that makes you sick. It is not "faith" if you believe that God "can" or "might" do something that He has already promised in His Word. These things are not faith.

Faith takes God at His Word. Faith holds on to what God has said. It believes *exactly* what God has promised. This is DEFINING FAITH. This is what sets a *champion* apart from a *contender*.

Chapter 2

Declaring Your Covenant

---

*Anybody can stake their claim to the blessing of God,
but to contend for it on a daily basis requires a spiritual tenacity
and an inner conviction that defies mediocrity.*

The Word in Action

Then was brought unto Him one possessed with a devil, blind, and dumb: and He healed him, insomuch that the blind and dumb both spake and saw. And all the people were amazed, and said, "Is not this the son of David?" But when the Pharisees heard it, they said, "This fellow doth not cast out devils, but by Beelzebub the prince of the devils." And Jesus knew their thoughts, and said unto them, "Every kingdom divided against itself is brought to desolation; and every city or house divided against itself shall not stand: And if Satan cast out Satan, he is divided against himself; how shall then his kingdom stand? And if I by Beelzebub cast out devils, by whom do your children cast them out? therefore they shall be your judges. But if I cast out devils by the Spirit of God, then the kingdom of God is come unto you. Or else how can one enter into a strong man's house, and spoil his goods, except he first bind the strong man? and then he will spoil his house. He that is not with me is against me; and he that gathereth not with me scattereth abroad. Wherefore I say unto you, All manner of sin and

> blasphemy shall be forgiven unto men: but the blasphemy against the Holy Ghost shall not be forgiven unto men. And whosoever speaketh a word against the Son of man, it shall be forgiven him: but whosoever speaketh against the Holy Ghost, it shall not be forgiven him, neither in this world, neither in the world to come."
>
> **Matthew 12:22-32**

They brought to Him a person that was possessed with a devil and Jesus healed him. Jesus cast the devil out of the demoniac and set him free from his physical infirmity. The Bible says that Jesus healed him so that the man could both speak and see.

Jesus is the Word in action. He is the living Word of God. When Jesus first walked the planet, He was the only one that could provide that kind of help for humanity. He alone had authority over demon spirits. However, the living Word had a divine mission. He had a mandate to give that same anointing, that Word, that call and that ministry to His disciples. His disciples, in turn, would herald that call to the Church and to multiplied generations of believers.

Today, we can take that same mandate and reach people through the power of the Word of God. We can open the blind eyes so that they can see both naturally and spiritually. We have the authority to loose the lips of the dumb so that they can speak of this world and of the next. This is the Great Commission.

Jesus came as the Word of God. He came in human form to reveal and to demonstrate the plan of God. He came to delegate His authority to the child of God in order that they might have the ability to exercise the strength of God's will against the demonic realm.

Straddling the Place of Decision

The Bible is God's Word. Within His Word, you can find

commandments and statutes. In fact, when God says "statute" or "commandment," you can easily substitute "the Word." All of these things are the will of God. The will of God is the Word of God and vice versa. It is His statutes. It is His commandments. It is His wisdom. It is His plan for all mankind.

> **But when the Pharisees heard it, they said, "This fellow doth not cast out devils, but by Beelzebub the prince of the devils."**
>
> **Matthew 12:24**

The miraculous deliverance of the demoniac produced a religious response from the religious leadership. When the religious leaders heard about it, they dismissed the miracle and attributed it to Satan. The common people, however, saw it and called Jesus the son of David! If a person has a heart after God and is sincere about the Word of God, they will have an innate ability to bear witness to the working of the Word. However, there is another group that handles the Word of God deceitfully. When God moves, they can't see it. They are spiritually blind and dull to God's Word.

Why would someone handle the Word of God deceitfully?

A person who handles the Word of God deceitfully is one who cannot see that the Word is profitable. For instance, the Pharisees *knew* that Jesus was sent from God. *How did they know this?* They knew because it is recorded that Nicodemus approached Jesus by night and said, *"Master, we know Thou art a teacher come from God"* (John 3:2). They knew the truth, but the truth was not advantageous for them. To acknowledge Jesus in front of the people would have meant losing control over the people. It would have meant the downfall of their traditions. In turn, their religion would have gone out of style, out of time and forever out of influence. It was a sacrifice they were not willing to pay. They were not willing to change. Consequently, they handled the Word of God deceitfully.

In order to see changes in your life, there is a price that needs to be paid. You will have to *pay* for the Word of God. Yes, it comes freely; however, there is a price to pay to do it. Some people will lose their friends because of the Word. If you want to keep those friends, you will have to make a decision to violate the Word. Others will lose their jobs. The strip dancer that gets saved will have to pay the price of losing the tips. At first, a person may not have a problem with a little compromise, but there will come a time when the Word Himself will speak to them. It's not the job description of a fellow believer to condemn another. The Word is alive and He will speak to them. God knows how to speak to His own and when He does, they will see it for themselves. They will see the truth and they will change. However, if they see the truth and keep on doing what they're doing, they are then *handling the Word of God deceitfully.*

There are preachers that don't believe in healing. That may be acceptable for a time. However, when the Word of God shows them that healing is a truth for today and they still refuse to preach it for fear of losing their ordination, then they are handling the Word of God deceitfully. Eventually the devil will push them to the point of blasphemy.

The Pharisees knew *Whom* Jesus was ministering by. *"Rabbi, we know that Thou art a teacher come from God: for no man can do these miracles that Thou doest, except God be with him"* (John 3:2).

When Jesus began to rise in popularity, *they knew.* They knew that if they left Him alone, everyone would follow Him. They knew that the only way to silence Him would be to kill Him. Jesus had become such a threat to them that the enemy drove them to a place of decision.

What would make someone run out on God?

They run because they thought they had it all under control. They thought, *"I'm doing what I do for the Lord. I'm doing what I want to do for me."* The devil will stop a person with this kind of motivation. He will put pressure on them until they break. He will hassle them until they make a decision to either go all the way out of the plan of God *or* to repent and get right.

To the Pharisees, the Word said, *"I will have no other gods before Me."* Their god, however, was their position. It was their prominence and the pomp and circumstance that surrounded it. Impressed with their position and the traditions of men, they feared Jesus' rise in popularity. When the crowds sought after Jesus and the blind saw and the dumb spoke, they accused Him of operating under demonic power. They didn't say this ignorantly. These words were spoken with understanding, and in turn, they blasphemed the Holy Ghost.

Testifying to Your Convictions

A lot of people are afraid of blaspheming the Holy Ghost. Blaspheming the Holy Ghost, however, is an intentional act of premeditated disregard for the things of God. It's a place of knowing the truth, weighing it against the consequences and then intentionally violating it. It's a place of resolution and contempt where someone not only walks against the Word, but also makes a conscious decision to *talk* against the Word.

What you allow in your life will eventually force you to take sides. Your own confession will testify to the things that have been resident in your heart. Some people wonder why we are so intolerant with regard to error. They wonder why we're so extreme. This is why: *You will eventually testify to the thing that you tolerate.* Your mouth will narrate your convictions.

The Pharisees tolerated religion. They had tolerated hypocrisy. In fact, they had tolerated error for so long, that their hearts had become calloused towards the move of God. Slowly but surely, they turned against the truth. Meanwhile, the demonic realm continued to pressure them, moving them further away from the Word, and ultimately, *to a point of decision.* Blaspheming the Holy Ghost was the next step, the natural progression in their pre-meditated defiance against the Word. They were pushed to the point of verbalizing a word of accusation and rejection.

When you fail to do what the Bible says, you will eventually throw down the Bible. This can happen in any area of your life: in healing, in prosperity or in simply living as a victorious Christian. The thing that you fail to obtain from God will become the thing that you don't want to hear about. People say, *"I'm sick of preachers talking about healing. I've had it up to here with healing."* Why is that? Did you fail to get it? If you did, go back to the Word and find out where you missed it. *Did they fail to deliver it to you right?* Go to the Word and find out where they failed. Forgive them, forgive yourself and move on with God.

God never lies. His Word is always true. If a person allows an unbiblical pattern to continue in their life, they will eventually be driven to the point of dealing with it. Peter, for instance, allowed certain things in his life. One day, Jesus turned to Peter and said, *"Satan has desired you. He wants to sift you as wheat, but I have prayed that your faith will not fail"* (Luke 22:31-32).

Where did Peter get his faith?
How does faith come?

Peter received faith from hearing Jesus preach. Faith comes by hearing and hearing by the Word of God. Jesus told him, *"Now, I have prayed for you that your faith would not fail."*

Jesus why are you praying this?

"Satan is strategizing against you try to steal your faith from you. He wants to cause your faith to fail. Therefore, I want you to watch with Me. Watch and pray."

It's not enough to have faith. It's not enough to hear the Word. Life can overcome you if you're not prayed up.

Watch and pray. Peter, however, went to sleep.

"Peter," Jesus said, *"You're going to deny Me."* With great confidence, Peter emphatically assured the Lord, *"Oh no, You're all wrong. If everybody is offended, I will not be offended. If everybody leaves You, I will*

not leave You. I will die with You!" Peter is sounding a bit cocky.

Jesus said, *"Stay up and pray."* Instead, Peter went to sleep.

All of a sudden, the soldiers came with their lanterns and their swords. There are hostile voices, angry footsteps, flickering torches, and the sound of metal on metal—a great, even surreal, commotion in the night. Peter gets up and tries to solve the situation using his methods. His best is his sword. Slicing off the ear of a servant, Peter is then rebuked by the Lord and commanded to put his sword away. The arm of the flesh didn't work, so the Bible records that Peter followed Jesus from afar off.

Jesus was taken to be tried before the counsel. Outside, Peter warmed his hands over a fire. Jesus was inside. Peter nervously waited.

The devil eyed him and said, *"I'm not going to let you off that easy. You chop off one person's ear? No, you're going to testify to your convictions!"*

Noticing Peter on the sidelines, someone asks, *"You claim you believe in the integrity of the Word. Aren't YOU the one following the Word?"*

The devil knows that you are snared by the words of your mouth. He can't snare you until he sets you up. Peter denied the Lord, and then he thought, *"Man I blew it that time."* The devil retorted, *"Oh, but I'm not letting you off that easy! You're going to do it THREE times!"*

Casting Out Devils

The Pharisees opened themselves up to demonic influences. Through the decisions that they made, they granted access to the enemy. They gave him room to work. Each of them knew that Jesus was a teacher come from God, but they refused to publicly acknowledge it. Beating around the bush, they skirted their real issue. When they realized that they were powerless to stop His influence, they resorted to spreading rumors and talking against Him.

People still do that today.

People walk up to me and say, *"You know what 'So-and-So' said about you? Did you hear what 'Preacher-So-and-So' said?"* I don't care what they've said! The bottom line is that they know I'm preaching the Word. They know I'm anointed by God. They know I'm preaching the truth. If they want to handle the Word of God deceitful, go right ahead. As for me and my house, we will serve the Lord!

These are the strategies the devil uses to pull people down and to stop them from doing what God has called them to do. Talking about Jesus, they said, *"He is casting out devils by the prince of the devil."* Upon hearing this, Jesus replied, *"Now wait a minute, every kingdom divided against itself will not stand. If Satan is casting out Satan, his kingdom will not stand…but if I'm casting out devils by the power of God, then the Kingdom of God is come upon you."*

Same devils, same strategies. What he did then, he will do today.

> **Now there was a man in their synagogue with an unclean spirit. And he cried out, saying, "Let us alone! What have we have we to do with You, Jesus of Nazareth? Did you come to destroy us? I know who You are – the Holy One of God!" But Jesus rebuked him, saying, "Be quiet and come out of him!"… and he came out of him. Then they were all amazed, so that they questioned among themselves saying, "What is this? What new doctrine is this? For with authority He commands even the unclean spirits, and they obey Him."**
>
> **Mark 1:23-25,27 NKJV**

Jesus cast out devils with His *Word*. They were subject to the dictates of His authority. The Bible records that the seventy came to

Jesus and said, *"Even the devils are subject to us in Your name"* (Luke 10:17). The spoken Word has the ability to drive out devils.

You cannot speak a word that you don't believe. A spoken word that isn't backed with faith is powerless to perform. It's void of power. The seventy, however, believed the Word. In fact, they were so convinced of the Word's integrity, that they acted upon the Word. Having put action to their faith, the Word produced results that were detrimental to the work of the enemy. *Devils left.*

Jesus said, *"If I by the kingdom of God cast out devils, the kingdom of God is come upon you."* Jesus cast out devils with His Word or with the power of God. The power of God is in the Word of God.

A Word spoken with faith is backed with power.

As a believer, if you will allow the Word to come *into you*, then the power of that Word will come *upon you*. There is a place in God where the power of the living Word will be so strong in you, that the things of the natural will supernaturally organize themselves to accommodate the outward manifestation of Gods' glory.

Staking Your Claim

There is a saying, which goes like this, *"I am the king of my own castle."* Normally, the statement which follows has something to do with *"what I say rules."*

How do you know the king is the king? The king is the one whose word is supreme law. He has ultimate rulership and ultimate influence. What he says, rules and the entire kingdom is subject to that law. When he declares a word, it swiftly comes to pass. The king's authority is revealed in his rule.

Jesus said, *"If I with the power of God or the Word of God cast out devils, then the Kingdom of God has come upon you."*

How do you know if a Christian is submitted to the Word of God? The evidence is in the rulership of God in their life. When the rule of God is present, the Christian will rise up and decree judgment: *There shall no plague come nigh our dwelling* (Psalm 91:10). If the enemy trespasses, they will swiftly declare: *"I don't know what kingdom you are from, but where I live THE KING IS KING. We will accept no other rule!"* A Christian that is submitted to the Word will stake their claim to the Word. They will not settle for a contradiction, but rather, they will enforce victory through delegated authority.

What happens when the law of the King is challenged? Soldiers and guards are dispatched to execute, eject, reject and apprehend the intruder. There are rules in the land. Every king knows that his kingdom's influence will be challenged. Enemies and subversive forces will try to take over territory. Opposing forces will try to gain influence through rebellion, guile and deceit.

In the life of a Christian, there will be voices of contradiction. The devil, however, has already been defeated. He is a conquered foe. The Kingdom is in our possession and we have been made kings and priests unto God (Revelation 1:6). Speak your authority. Stake your claim.

> **No weapon that is formed against thee shall prosper; and every tongue that shall rise against thee in judgment thou shalt condemn. This is the heritage of the servants of the LORD, and their righteousness is of me, saith the LORD.**
>
> **Isaiah 54:17**

Contending Daily

How does a child of God position himself or herself for greatness?

It starts way back in the day when they could have compromised. There was a choice involved. They could have handled the Word of God deceitfully. It was as simple as letting something slide. In the beginning, it was as easy as not saying anything! Perhaps they got mad and instead of saying, *"Lord, I'm mad and I'm sorry and I forgive them,"* they said, *"Why, I just won't say anything."* Then they went to sleep and the sun set on their wrath. The next day, they woke up and still didn't say anything. It's that easy. *"It's no big deal. I'm not backsliding. I love the Lord. I went to church and I'm really anointed,"* they say. Three years down the road, that thing has developed into a root of bitterness!

The devil will push a person like this to the point of confession. He did it to Peter. He's done it for centuries and he continues to do it today. His strategies are not new. The devil will pressure a believer to speak words that will literally snare them. They will give expression to the thing that has consumed them. What was in their heart will come out of their mouth. Once they use their mouth to give voice to it, they give it power. That thing will then move into their lives to bring swift destruction. If they do not repent and allow the Word of God to deal with them, they will find themselves in a downward spiral propelled by words spoken in error. That root of bitterness will grow, sprout leaves and bear fruit for all to see.

We think we can get away with our attitudes. We think we can get away with compromise. The truth, however, is that we cannot get away with *anything* in the Kingdom of God.

The enemy is after your victory! He is in the business of creating casualties and you are on his hit list! The enemy of your soul is trying to neutralize the power of the Kingdom in your life. He can't overthrow God, so he has settled for the next best thing: YOU! His strategy is to move into your life and convince you to put something else on the throne of your heart, the throne of your mind, and the throne of your mouth.

God won't force you to speak the Word. *It's your daily decision.*

A Generation of Disciples

> **And if I by Beelzebub cast out devils, by whom do your children cast *them* out?**
>
> **Matthew 12:27**

Jesus was saying, *"Not only do I cast out devils, but your children AND MY FOLLOWERS will do the same. I will be succeeded by a generation of disciples that will use My name to perform exploits. The very works that they do will testify against you."*

The *WORKS* that we do testify against those who use the Word of God deceitfully. Those works include: casting out devils, healing the sick, saving the lost and preaching the uncompromised Gospel of the Kingdom. These are the things that testify against all those who know the truth, but blatantly disregard it.

For this reason, the religious hate us. They hate the truth. Meanwhile, the devil cannot sit still. He knows that we mean business. He knows that we are not playing games. He knows that we are *the generation of disciples* that Jesus spoke about.

We are not going to change. We are not going to back down. We are not going to alter our course. We will not diminish, dilute or decrease. Rather, we are going to increase exponentially. We are going to preach the Word of God fearlessly and without regard to the traditions of men.

Jesus said, *"If I'm casting out devils by Beelzebub, then by whom do your children cast them out?"*

"They will be your judges," He continued.

When Sin Has Conceived

Everyone, at one point or another, has had the horrifying thought that they blasphemed the Holy Ghost. I once saw a statistic that 90% of all patients in mental institutions believe that they are guilty of the unpardonable sin.

> **And whosoever speaketh a word against the Son of man, it shall be forgiven him: but whosoever speaketh against the Holy Ghost, it shall not be forgiven him, neither in this world, neither in the world to come.**
>
> **Matthew 12:32**

What is the difference between blaspheming the Holy Ghost and the Son of Man?

A person who blasphemes the Son of Man doesn't *know* the Son of Man. They have not been introduced to Him. He has not come into their heart. However, when that same person receives Jesus as Lord, they receive the ability to discern truth and to know when the Word of God is at work.

Through the Scriptures, we understand that the Word of God works through the power of the Spirit. The Word provides the authority and the Spirit backs that authority up with power. Jesus said to His disciples, *"You shall receive POWER after that the Holy Ghost will come upon you"* (Acts 1:8).

What is the purpose of this power? The power gives you the ability to do what the Lord has called you to do! It is written, *"The Lord WORKING WITH THEM confirming the Word with signs following"* (Mark 16:20).

How was the Lord working with them? The Bible says, *"He went up and He was received out of their sight"* (Acts 1:9). Therefore, the Lord was working with them *through* the person of the Holy Ghost.

What kind of person would blaspheme the Holy Ghost? A person who blasphemes the Holy Ghost is someone who has known the Holy Ghost.

It may start small. Perhaps, it's just a little compromise. Maybe it's a tiny area of disobedience, but like all sin, it will grow if not dealt with. One day, what was once a little disobedience, may sound something like this, *"I know this is the truth, but I won't preach it because they will vote me out."* It begins in a person who rides the fence saying, *"I know I shouldn't do that, but if I stop and tell everybody my real convictions, they won't be my friends anymore."* Meanwhile, the bondages in their lives keep on increasing. The more they disobey God, the harder their hearts become.

Everyone that serves sin is a slave to sin. Everyone that serves compromise is a slave to compromise. Eventually, they will get to a place where they're so overwhelmed by their compromise, that they will accuse what is holy. Just like the Pharisees, they will recognize the work of God, but outright reject it. Through much compromise, a person like this becomes accustomed to handling the Word of God deceitfully. If that pattern continues unchecked, sin will fully conceive and that individual will move on to discredit God and the work of God.

The Bible says that when such a person makes this choice willfully, they are impossible to restore. *Why is this so?* They have tasted of the Lord, the Blood has washed them and they have seen the glory of the Kingdom. If they have partaken of all these things, yet allowed compromise to dominate them to the point of blasphemy, then they are not operating out of ignorance. They have acknowledged the truth, understood it, and yet elected to disobey it. Remember, Paul persecuted the Church, but he did it ignorantly. He had not been exposed to the ministry of Jesus. He had not received Him as Lord. He acted out of ignorance.

Committing to Your Harvest

> **Either make the tree good, and his fruit good; or else make the tree corrupt, and his fruit corrupt: for the tree is known by his fruit. O generation of vipers, how can ye, being evil, speak good things? For out of the abundance of the heart the mouth speaketh. A good man out of the good treasure of the heart bringeth forth good things: and an evil man out of the evil treasure bringeth forth evil things. But I say unto you, That every idle word that men shall speak, they shall give account thereof in the day of judgment. For by thy words thou shalt be justified, and by thy words thou shalt be condemned.**
>
> **Matthew 12:33-37**

Jesus is once again talking to the Pharisees. He is telling them to make a decision and to go all the way with it. Choose *one way* or *the other* and then commit yourself to it. Make the tree good and its fruit good or the make the tree evil and its fruit evil. Make a decision, but don't ride the line!

Do you think that God is extreme? Jesus said, *"I would you were cold or hot."* What some call "balance" is what the Lord calls "lukewarm." Jesus said, *"I will spew you out of my mouth if you are lukewarm"* (Revelation 3:15,16). God is extreme.

If a person is neither cold nor lukewarm, then it must mean they are hot. Hot is the other extreme. *Hot* is being on fire for the things of God. It's an ardent desire and a passionate conviction. It is the relentless pursuit of the Kingdom of God.

Why are we called to be like this? We are called because Jesus called us. He called us to be like Him.

A person who is cold, *knows* they're cold. If you were to tell them so, they would say, *"I know."* A person who is hot, *knows* they're hot. If you were to tell them so, they would say, *"I know I'm hot, but I'm not satisfied."* A lukewarm person, however, vacillates in the middle. They say, *"I'm not really cold. I love the Lord. I go to church."* Lukewarm is satisfied. Lukewarm is halfway.

Jesus said, *"Either make the tree good and his fruit good or make the tree evil and his fruit evil."* Don't just go halfway, but go all the way. Make a decision. Give yourself completely over to God so that the abundance of the good treasure in your heart will bring forth good things.

> **A good man out of the good treasure of the heart bringeth forth good things: and an evil man out of the evil treasure bringeth forth evil things.**
>
> **Matthew 12:35**

What is the good treasure? The good treasure is the Word of God.

What is that good treasure going to bring forth from your mouth? Good things! It will bring forth good fruit. You will speak fruitfulness. You will speak good fruit.

What is good fruit? Good fruit are those things that God has promised in His Word.

If it's a good thing, you can rest assured that it has been promised. In fact, you cannot find one good thing in life that is godly that has not been promised in the Word of God. Likewise, there is not a thing in life that is evil that has not been warned against in the Word of God. When Jesus says, *"The good treasure of your heart brings forth good things,"* He is saying, *"Let the Word of God have abundance in you."* What is in abundance within you, will come forth through you. You will produce those things that have resided in your heart.

Have you ever caught yourself thinking, *"Shoot, I have been slipping lately."* It's not rocket science and there is no mystery in it. The reason you have been slipping is because you haven't been reading the Word. You probably haven't been praying either. You may have even started to slide on going to church. Other things got into your heart and now your treasure is out of whack. Spiritually, you are out of balance. You are teetering on the edge of complacency. You are lukewarm and the abundance that is in your heart is fear and darkness.

Jesus says, *"Make a decision. Choose your path, but don't wallow in the middle."*

The Pharisees walked the middle. Steeped in religion and seared by sin, they were lukewarm to the ways of God. Instead of making a decision, they straddled their lives over mediocrity. They loaded people with burdens that even they didn't intend to carry. Jesus said that the Pharisees were like those who would strain at a gnat and swallow a camel.

Have you ever met a person like that? They get mad and cuss you out, but at church, they are the personification of holiness. They balk at a woman speaking in church, but in their daily life, they don't have problem swallowing a camel.

Jesus called the Pharisees an "offspring of vipers." Jesus doesn't mince words. The Bible says that the devil masquerades as an angel of light. He is a religious spirit and a copycat. Void of creativity, he can only mimic what he sees God do. He cannot create anything new. Satan saw God get praise in Heaven and he desired that for himself. He saw God's throne in Heaven and wanted one as well. He saw Jesus build a Church and decided that he would like one too. The church of Satan is a copycat.

Examining Your Treasure

The Pharisees had a form of godliness. They cleansed the outside of the cup, but ignored the inside (Matthew 23:25). Of course, they did it ignorantly for a time, but then God sent a sign. A star shown and the wise men from the East followed it. Angels sang in the night and the shepherds voiced their message across the land. John the Baptist donned camel skins and prepared the way. God had anointed him as a prophet and forerunner. Then, in the fullness of time, Jesus came. He raised the dead and healed the sick.

The Pharisees knew that no man could do these miracles except God be with Him. They had an opportunity to cleanse the inside of the cup, but they had a dilemma. *"If I confess that what I know is not the truth, then I will have to change and lose the position I have."* Pushed over the edge of compromise, they eventually blasphemed God. Jesus said, *"You might as well either confess you're the son of a viper or make the decision to get all the way right with God. Either make it good or make it bad."*

Jesus said to the Pharisees, *"How can you being evil speak good things?"* Out of the abundance of the heart the mouth speaks (Matthew 12:34).

How can you tell what someone stands for? Watch their mouth. They will preach it. They will testify to it. They will talk it. A person's words will reveal their convictions.

Jesus said, *"Now, you can make the tree good or you can make the tree evil."* God wants you to make the tree good because a good tree will bear good fruit. A bad tree will bear bad fruit. Out of the heart or the core of that tree is the life flow that causes fruit to come. A bad life flow or an abundance of error and negativity will bring forth evil fruit. However, a good life flow of godliness, faith, confidence, holiness, forgiveness, love and compassion will bring forth good fruit. That fruit will come out of your mouth. It will come out of your heart and the world will see it.

What you put *in* will come *out*. If the Word of God is in you, the Word of God will come out of you. When you invest in the eternal treasure within, the Spirit of God will flow out of your heart and through your lips.

Practicing Spiritual Responsibility

> My brethren, be not many masters, knowing that we shall receive the greater condemnation. For in many things we offend all. If any man offend not in word, the same is a perfect man, and able also to bridle the whole body.
>
> **James 3:1-2**

You are reading this book because you have a desire to grow in God. You want to be everything that God wants you to be. This desire should be the sentiment of every believer. Every child of God should crave the Word and press in after it. That intensity, however, cannot be worked up or given by another. It is only generated by studying and meditating on the Word of God. In fact, the more you rehearse the Word, the more you will desire it and press in after it.

It doesn't take a great commitment to say, *"I want to be everything that God wants me to be."* Many have said it, but their lives have lacked the passion and conviction to back it up. Anybody can stake their claim to the blessing of God, but to contend for it on a daily basis requires a spiritual tenacity and an inner conviction that defies mediocrity.

The Bible says, *"Don't be many masters. Don't be many teachers."* Don't be too quick to jump on the teacher bandwagon. It is wise to consider the cost because there is a great responsibility that comes with taking a *position* in the Kingdom of God. For instance, if I don't know something, I don't attempt to teach it. I cannot try to teach mechanics because I have never worked on a car. Some people believe in faking it. They read a couple of books and hope no one can diagnose their lack of revelation. They try to pull it off, but before God, they are accountable for their actions.

If a teacher doesn't have a revelation of the Word of God, they will inevitably speak something that is out of line with the Word. They will teach what is contrary. When they do, they will be held accountable by

God for the words that they spoke and the damage that was done. As a result, the devil will take opportunity in their lives and condemnation will result.

Of course, when a word is spoken that is in line with the Word of God, the devil will bring *confrontation*. He will do what he can to stop that Word or to render it ineffective.

"If any man offend not in Word, the same is a perfect man" (James 3:2).

Harnessing the Tongue

Recall for a moment, the story of John the Baptist. John was stuck in prison and Jesus was rising in popularity. Questioning his deepest convictions, John the Baptist sent his disciples to Jesus. They came to the Lord with one question, *"Are you the One or do seek we another?"* Jesus answered, *"Go show John again the things you hear and see. Tell him the blind are seeing, the deaf are hearing, the poor are having the Gospel preached to them and blessed is he whosoever is not offended in Me"* (Matthew 11:4-6).

In simpler terms, Jesus said this to John: *"Do not be offended at the Word you heard. Do not be offended at the lesson you learned. You saw it. You saw the works of God. Do not let your current situation—the jail cell —change your mind about the Word that you believe in."* When a person is offended at the Word, it becomes an offense to them. It causes them to stumble through unbelief. They become double-minded and ineffective.

How does one become double-minded? First, they become offended at the Word. For whatever reason, they fail to embrace the promise. They start by saying, *"maybe that's not it,"* or *"perhaps there is another."* John's disciples asked Jesus, *"Are you the one or do we seek another?"*

"Do not be offended at the Word you heard..."

A person who is offended at the Word is one that stumbles at the promises in the Word. As this pattern of offense continues, their words will become increasingly out of line with God's Word. They will deviate further and further from the truth of the Word.

The Bible says that if any man *offends not in words*, the same is a *perfect* man (James 3:2). Likewise, it is reasonable to conclude that if any man *offends with words*, the same is an *imperfect* man. If a person is not able to control the tongue, his or her efforts to bridle the body will prove fruitless. In other words, if you cannot control your tongue, you cannot control your body.

Something that is meditated on long enough will inevitably surface. If it is allowed to grow in the heart, it will develop and produce fruit. It will push past the meditations, and it will surface in a manifestation. Once the person begins to speak their convictions, their body will begin to line up with the very thing they have confessed. As time progresses, they will become increasingly unable to bridle their body. Eventually, it will go to do the very thing they had spoken.

> **But those things which proceed out of the mouth come forth from the heart; and they defile the man.**
>
> **Matthew 15:18**

Both life and death are in the power of the tongue. This is not a physical tongue, but rather, it is the life flow that proceeds from the tongue. Life and death are in the power that proceeds from your mouth. This life flow, however, stems from the treasure within. It finds its source in the fertile ground of meditations. In other words, *a person's treasure is defined by their thought life.* That treasure will grow and eventually surface and produce fruit in the form of words. Whether this fruit is poison or divine blessing, depends entirely on what an individual has sown in their heart.

Oftentimes, people think their words are simply hurting other people. However, the Bible says that a person defiles his or her own body. When someone steps out of synch with the Word, they will inevitably allow the wrong thoughts to speak through their mouths. Giving up the throne of their authority, they will begin to speak words that are laced with poison. They will say, *"You do not understand. I am afraid. I am terrified. I am depressed. I am angry. I hate you."*

People have walked up to me and said, *"For the past six weeks I've been mad at you."* I wanted to tell them, *"Yes, that was very apparent. You have been wearing the suit of defilement to church for the past six weeks."*

Sometimes a person will walk up to me after I have ministered and say, *"The last time you came to my city you said 'this and that' and I was so upset that it took me six months to forgive you."* I want to shake them and ask, *"My God, why would you do that to yourself?"* You see, I was having a good time! Their offense didn't hurt me. I wasn't even touched by it. However, they allowed the enemy to rob them of their authority. They gave place to the wrong thing and that *wrong thing* produced the fruit of defilement in their lives.

Drawing Near to God

God resists the proud, but give grace to the humble. Therefore submit to God...

James 4:6b-7a

Why does God resist the proud? God resists the proud because of the *words* of their mouth. Sometimes Christians have this religious concept of God dispatching his angels to stop the proud. God, however, doesn't have to use angels to resist the proud.

How does God resist the proud? He just stands back.

What does the proud person do? The proud person does not humble himself or herself to the Word. They do no submit to God's Word, but rather, pay tribute to their own opinion. *"I know the Word says forgive him, but I don't feel like it,"* they say.

This is called pride.

When a person walks in pride, demon spirits say, *"Aha! The Word of God is not settled in their life."* Having based their existence on feelings, evil spirits take opportunity and create havoc. Things start going haywire and everything seems to go wrong. Confused, they feel anger towards God. Like a ship without bearing, they are tossed to and fro on their own emotional sea.

What happened? Instead of fighting the good fight of faith, they succumbed to the circumstance. They didn't know how to fight the good fight to keep him out. This is why the Bible says, *"Take heed, brethren, lest there be in any of you an evil heart of unbelief, in departing from the living God"* (Hebrews 3:12).

How does a person depart from God? First, they depart in their thought life. Second, they depart in their words. After their words bear fruit, they will become unable or unwilling to bridle their body. Having defiled their body with words, a root of bitterness will lodge itself within their heart. If left intact, it will grow from that place of defilement and then defile *many*.

A person that has strayed this far out in bitterness and disappointment usually stops going to church. Mad at God and reeking with their own poison, they then contaminate others. They isolate themselves and build a sHell around their life. Other Christians may try to speak goodness and blessing over them, but having been so seared by sin, they are unresponsive.

How did this ugly scenario begin?

Renegade thoughts, left unchecked, led to *words*.
Those *words* produced *fruit*.

The integrity of the Word of God cannot be violated without

consequences.

> **Therefore submit to God. Resist the devil and he will flee from you. Draw near to God and He will draw near to you.**
>
> **James 4:7-8a**

Say this out loud:

> *If I draw near to God with my thoughts, my lips and my words, He will draw near to me. He will be right there, close to me and I will be able to resist the devil. The Bible promises that the devil will flee from me. Therefore, as I draw near to God and submit to His Word, I will be able to resist the devil every time.*

Draw near to God. Declare His Word!

In order to resist the enemy effectively, you have to speak. Sometimes you have to speak out loud. The famous revivalist, John G. Lake, would look in the mirror and say, *"God lives in that person!"*

You need to speak out loud! Speak to yourself. Confess the Word of God out loud. If you're concerned about pride, then give someone else just as much attention! Tell them, *"You are anointed by God! God lives in you. Greater is He that is in you than he who is in the world"* (1 John 4:4). You cannot talk like that about someone else and grow in pride.

God has given each of us the ability to put His Word in our mouth. As you do this, the power and the integrity of His Word, will go to work in your life. God will personally see to it that everything falls into place. One by one, things will line up to accommodate His will. As you declare His covenant with you, the power of God will move in to fulfill His promises toward you.

CHAPTER 3

TENDING TO THE PROMISE

*If the devil can get your eyes on the cares of life,
he can distract you from purpose.*

Seeds of Greatness

Therefore hear the parable of the sower: When anyone hears the Word of the Kingdom, and does not understand it, then the wicked one comes and snatches away what was sown in his heart. This is he who received seed by the wayside. But he who received the seed on stony places, this is he who hears the Word and immediately receives it with joy; yet he has no root in himself, but endures only for a while. For when tribulation or persecution arises because of the Word, immediately he stumbles. Now he who received seed among the thorns is he who hears the Word, and the cares of this world and the deceitfulness of riches choke the Word, and he becomes unfruitful. But he who received seed on the good ground is he who hears the Word and understands it, who indeed bears fruit and produces: some a hundredfold, some sixty, some thirty.

Matthew 13:18-23 NKJV

In the Kingdom of God, a great emphasis is placed on sowing and reaping. In fact, God likens His Kingdom to a very small seed that has tremendous potential. Although small and easily overlooked, when properly nourished, this seed has the capability of growing into a tree that shades other trees. It will grow to be a tree so large that the birds of the air will come and find lodging and shelter within its many branches.

> **It is like a grain of mustard seed, which a man took, and cast into his garden; and it grew, and waxed a great tree; and the fowls of the air lodged in the branches of it.**
>
> **Luke 13:19**

The Word of God is the seed. Just as the mustard seed, although small, contains the genetic infrastructure for greatness, so does the seed of the Word. The Word of God is filled with divine potential and the ingredients for unlimited success and exponential increase. It is filled with the life and the nature of God. This is why the Bible teaches that exceeding great and precious promises have been given to us through the Word (2 Peter 1:4). These promises, although sometimes mistaken for mere words, are filled with divine ability and supernatural initiative. They are the substance of God. They are the framework for the divine. They are alive and when nurtured properly, will produce a great harvest within the life of the believer. They will enable the believer to become a partaker of God's divine nature.

God's Word is at work in your life. The reason your transformation in Jesus is not overwhelming is because this process is like that of a tree. What starts as a seed, germinates and grows into greatness.

The Key to Your Harvest

> **Take heed unto thyself, and unto the doctrine; continue in them: for in doing this thou shalt**

both save thyself, and them that hear thee.

1 Timothy 4:16

Not every tree seed becomes a tree. While the seed does contain the genetic composition to grow strong and tall, nutrients aren't always available to grow that seed. Some wither, some are eaten, and some are trampled underfoot. However, if the soil has been prepared and the seed receives those things that are vital to its growth, it will grow and it will produce a harvest. In the same way, the Word of God in your life contains great potential. Only you, however, can yield to its growth. The climate of your heart will either nourish the seed or allow it to remain dormant and unresponsive. You determine the vitality of the seed of the Word in your life. It will only work if you let it.

As you give yourself wholly to the seed of the Word, the Word of God will begin to work in your life. It will grow and bring your life under its influence and inspiration. The blessings and the goodness of God will cover your life and promote you.

Jesus said that the parable of the sower contained the key to understanding all parables. The sower sows the seed and that seed is the Word of God. When the seed is sown, it falls into the soil of a person's heart. What happens after that depends entirely upon the *decisions of the recipient.* The sower can only sow the seed. It is the atmosphere of the recipient's heart that determines the harvest. Only you can nurture the seed of the Word of God in your life. You possess the seed and its innate potential. You hold the key to your harvest.

Watering Wayside Promises

Just because you are saved does not mean that you are mature. Just because you are Spirit filled does not mean you are Spirit led. Spiritual growth is dependent upon the priorities that are applied in our lives. You cannot prioritize the wrong things and still grow. For instance, if my priority was *not* preaching the Word of God, there would be no diligence in my life to continue. If I was *not* fully persuaded on what God has called me to do, then inconsistencies would appear in my daily walk. Someone like this will say one thing and then when contrary winds blow, do another. They will say, *"The Lord told me to do this,"* and then three weeks later the Lord has changed His mind!

We have to know how the Kingdom of God works. We have to understand the power of the seed and how to harvest that power. Simply knowing that there is a promise is not enough. It must be embraced by faith. It must be nurtured with FAITH DECISIONS and FAITH ACTIONS that are conducive to growth. The parable of the sower is the methodology of the Kingdom of God.

> **Therefore hear the parable of the sower: When anyone hears the Word of the kingdom, and does not understand it, then the wicked one comes and snatches away what was sown in his heart. This is he who received seed by the wayside.**
>
> **Matthew 13:18-19 NKJV**

Jesus described four different types of soil. The first kind of soil or *heart* received the seed, but the person lacked understanding and the wicked one was able to snatch that which was sown. Jesus called this the seed that was sown by the wayside. The Bible says that when one receives the Word, but doesn't understand it, the enemy is able to snatch what was sown but not embraced. In other words, when you hear the Word, but do not understand it, the devil immediately goes to work to steal the seed of the Word out of your life.

None of the soils referenced in this parable were predisposed to barrenness. Each could have produced a harvest for God. That means it does not matter what any of our excuses have to say. There is a potential for the one hundred-fold return in each of our lives.

The devil will tamper with the Word of God in your life. He will attempt to steal the Word that has been sown. Even the devil knows that a Word, although dormant, has great potential if harnessed.

Revelation will harness and energize a dormant Word.

Go to the place where the Word is preached. Faith comes by hearing. When faith comes you will understand. Through faith we understand the deep mysteries of how God created the world. Through faith, we understand the Word of God. When a person doesn't understand, it is because they have not yet received faith. Lack of faith is proportional to lack of understanding. True understanding can only come through the Word of God.

Do not tire of hearing the Word of God. Don't say, *"Oh, well I've heard that before."* Rather, open up your spirit and keep on hearing. Faith comes by hearing and that Word—THAT SEED—is alive. Within it is the potential for the full measure of the promise of God. Therefore, do not give up on yourself. Do not become weary in well doing. Don't say, *"What's wrong with me?"* Don't say, *"Oh, it doesn't work for me."* Hang around that Word. Give that seed *time* to be watered and *time* to grow strong.

The Word is alive and it will prosper. It will break through and succeed in bringing faith into your heart. When faith comes, you will understand. When you understand, you will step into the wisdom of God.

The Bible says that the wisdom of God is the Word of God (1 Corinthians 1:24).

What is the beginning of wisdom?

It is the fear of the Lord (Psalm 111:10).

How do you fear the Lord?

You reverence His will (Hebrews 12:28).

When you reverence His will, you respect His Word. Where respect is, wisdom begins to prosper. *What does reverence look like?* It's not a fearful reverence, like one would fear a rattlesnake or a robber.

It's a reverence that stems from the expression of love, for faith works by love.

Exposing Enemy Propaganda

This is Hell's strategy:

> **Make the heart of this people fat, and make their ears heavy, and shut their eyes; lest they see with their eyes, and hear with their ears, and understand with their heart, and convert, and be healed.**
>
> **Isaiah 6:10**

Who is making the heart of this people fat? The Bible says that the god of this world has blinded the minds of them that believe not, lest the light of the glorious Gospel of Christ, should shine unto them (2 Corinthians 4:4). The devil blinds them so that the light does not shine in the form of understanding or revelation.

What does the Bible say about someone who does not understand? When a person does not understand the Word, the wicked one comes and steals the Word.

However, through *faith* we understand. Through faith we procure the promises. It is only through *unbelief* that a person fails to receive faith.

"Make their heart fat. Make their eyes heavy."

It's a demonic strategy that is as old as the devil himself. When a believer taps into a source other than the Word of God, they tap into information from a lower realm. This lower frequency will dull their ears and weigh their spirits. Their spiritual ears will become heavy with the report of the world. Weighed down and overburdened, they become unreceptive to the voice of the Spirit.

"Shut their eyes... lest they should see."

The god of this world works through unbelief and through doubt, to shut the eyes of people. He does not want them to see or hear. If they do, understanding will surely come. However, if he can prevent a person from seeing through the eyes of faith, he can stunt their growth and diminish their effectiveness. Without sight, a person will *never* understand.

Jesus said, *"He that has an ear, let him hear."*

Would God Almighty create one person with an ear to hear and then indiscriminately deny another? In eternity, would He then blame that person for not using the ear He never gave them? *Of course not!*

What did Jesus mean when He said, *"He that has an ear let him hear?"*

It means your priorities will determine the degree to which your ears hear and your eyes see. That prioritizing takes place in giving preference or first place to the hearing of the Word. When a person tunes their ear into the Word, they will hear and they will see. Understanding will come into their heart and the light of God will bring revelation to their soul.

Who is it that does not understand the Word of God? The person that does not understand the Word is the one who has heard, but has put it on the shelf. They heard the good news, but they didn't give it preeminence. They gave it the same consideration as they would to any report in the world. They put what God said right next to the latest headlines. They put it side by side with the six o'clock news. It didn't outweigh what Uncle Albert said or even Aunt Bertha's take on life. They stacked the Word of God right up against every other opinion. When they failed to prioritize the Word, it gave place to confusion. Taking opportunity, the devil stole the sown Word.

Silencing Contrary Voices

Thy Word have I hid in mine heart, that I might not sin against thee.

Psalm 19:11

How does one hide the Word? They understand it. When a person understands the Word, the devil cannot steal it. He cannot steal what is understood. He cannot convince you to deny that which you know to be true. A Word that is heard, seen and understood is *undefeatable*. It must produce a harvest.

"lest they see with their eyes, hear with their ears, understand with their heart and convert…"

What does "convert" mean? "Convert" is synonymous with "change." When a person hears and sees, they convert. They repent and change their ways. This isn't a one-time packaged process. Rather, every time an individual looks into the Word of God, they should see an area that they can improve on. They should look into the Word, repent and *walk out the decision* they made in God.

And be not conformed to this world: but be ye transformed by the renewing of your mind, that ye may prove what is that good, and acceptable, and perfect, will of God.

Romans 12:2

SEE the Word. HEAR the Word. UNDERSTAND the Word. When you understand, you convert. This decision transforms you by the renewing of your mind. Rather than settling for the status quo, you contend for the promises of God.

What is the devil's job description? The devil takes a personal interest in cluttering your life with "stuff." He wants to make sure that your receptivity to God is clouded with contrary "voices." He knows that confusion will make a heart fat.

"Make their heart fat. Make their eyes heavy. Shut their eyes...."

The devil doesn't want you to hear the Word. He doesn't want you to get a hold of it. He knows, all too well, that it cannot fail to produce a harvest. The Word is a threat to him, so he desperately works to cloud the understanding of God's people. He reasons, *"If I leave them alone, they are going to see it. So, instead, I am going to steal the Word."*

Indicting the Seed Bearer

In the case of Jesus, the devil sought to discredit Him. Jesus was perfect in all His ways, yet all sorts of fraudulent accusations were launched against Him. The Bible calls the devil *"the accuser of the brethren."*

If Jesus wore a suit and walked into your church next Sunday, there would be some people who would find something wrong with Him! Not every believer is ready to see and to understand all that Jesus is. Everyone is growing. All are being converted. All are being transformed. We are walking out of every *tradition*, every *lie* and every *ideology* that is not the byproduct of the Living Word.

The devil is the accuser of the brethren. He doesn't wait until a person has done something wrong, rather he pits people against people. He tells a person that they have the gift of discerning of spirits. In actuality, it is only the operation of suspicion. They will use what they perceive to be a gift to discredit and defame another.

The devil will try to discredit your godly figure. He will move in to slander the carrier of the seed in your life. That carrier could be a person, a ministry, a pastor, a church, a school, a spouse or anything else that serves as a platform for the Word of God. The devil cannot kill the seed, but he can kill the reputation of the seed bearer. Through deceit, he will *always* try to cut you off from the influence of the seed carrier in your life.

If they called Jesus the head of Beelzebub, what are they going to call you?

You must guard your mind. If you don't, the devil will move in and make suggestions. If you claim them as your own, you will believe the lie and repeat the lie. You will say, *"They don't love me. They don't care."* It may start small. It may seem trivial at first, but the devil *will* work to erode your confidence in the integrity of the seed carrier.

The devil knows that the power of the seed cannot fail. He knows that in the presence of the seed you will see, hear, understand, and convert. If he cannot steal the seed or defame the seed carrier, you will be transformed.

You are just like Jesus in the Spirit. Perhaps your life doesn't quite measure up yet, but you're growing in God. You are going to continue to grow up by allowing the Word of God to change you.

Impaled Power of Darkness

"...lest they see... hear... understand ... convert, and be healed."

CONVERT and BE HEALED.

Jesus said, *"If I be lifted up as Moses lifted up the serpent in the wilderness, so shall the Son of Man be lifted up. That whosoever believeth in Him should not perish but have everlasting life"* (John 12:32).

The people grumbled. The people complained. They were tired of desert life and wilderness living and they murmured amongst themselves. Their collective disobedience unleashed fiery serpents that bit the people. Moses, having received instruction from the Lord, lifted up a brazen serpent on a pole for all to see. All who looked upon the brazen serpent lived.

The serpents bit the people because they murmured against the integrity of the Word. Instead of putting the Word of God in their mouth, they spoke words that were laced with venom.

There is integrity in the Word of God.

God told His people, *"I am going to take you to a land flowing with milk and honey."* That was the Word of God. It was their *prophetic* Word. However, instead of believing in the integrity of that Word, they believed the report of the desert. With their mouth, they made confession of that report...*and fiery serpents came.*

He that diggeth a pit shall fall into it; and whoso breaketh an hedge, a serpent shall bite him.

Ecclesiastes 10:8

People say of Job, *"Well, the Lord took the hedge away from Job."* No, this couldn't be further from the truth. Job broke the hedge with his *own* mouth. Remember, it was Job that said, *"The thing that I greatly feared has come upon me."* He was talking about his fears. He complained, he murmured and spoke his worries and doubts. So all-consuming was this fear that he didn't even sleep at night! Job broke his hedge of protection and the serpent bit him. He testified to the wrong report and gave access to the enemy. The good news, however, is that God still came through. In the end, the Lord gave Job twice as much as he ever had.

"I am going to take you to a land flowing with milk and honey."

So, the people murmured and the people complained. God had given them a Word, but they gave voice to grumbling and discontentment. They broke the hedge with their own mouths. Fiery serpents came. They were stung and they were poisoned.

God said to Moses, *"Build a brazen serpent on a pole, lift it up and it will come to pass that everybody that will look at it will be healed"* (Numbers 21:8).

Some two thousand years ago, Jesus was lifted up on a cross. He took the curse upon His own body. Many years before this time, a wayward people in the wilderness looked upon a brazen serpent for deliverance. If they could have fast-forwarded to Calvary, they would have known they were witnessing a type of the *impaled power of darkness*.

When your eyes see that your enemy has been thrust through, you will understand that the devil is dead is your life. When his defeat is held high, you will realize and receive the health of God. When you see that the head of his power, his sting and his bite, have been impaled and made a public spectacle, you will not tolerate anything less than the victory that has been won for you.

If you don't understand, keep reading. Keep meditating on this chapter and the light of revelation will come. If you prioritize it, the devil will not be able to steal it.

Attention: Word-At-Work

Do not let the devil steal the seed. *Guard the seed.* Honor the seed bearer. As you give the voice of God preeminence in your life, your ear will hear, your eye will see and you will convert and be healed.

Humanity may have inherited the nature of Adam. His lineage may have been infected with venom from the snake in the Garden. The antidote, however, is found in the Word of God. His poison is rendered powerless when you see, hear and convert. In the presence of understanding, healing comes and his influence is destroyed in the life of the one who has received the Word.

The Word of God must be mixed with faith. Faith is the activator of the promises of God. It is the primary ingredient in *divine results*. Faith in the promise will produce *performance*.

If you don't understand yet, don't settle into frustration, but continue in the Word. Saturate yourself with the Word. Read and reread this book. Immerse yourself in the Word of God. As you prioritize, *faith will come*. It will rise up in your heart from a place of supernatural understanding. Remember, the Word of God is Spirit and life.

Jesus is the Word. The Word created Adam. The second person of the Trinity had always been ready to become flesh. It was with anticipation that all of Heaven looked forward to the day when Jesus would redeem the offspring of Adam to His image. The Bible says that God foreknew us and predestined us (Romans 8:29).

The Word is alive and active. Even if the sower doesn't deliver the Word clearly, that Word is alive, and once released, it has an inherent ability. Performance is packaged within the Word of God. If the hearer is willing to keep the Word, the Holy Ghost will work through that Word to bring the promise to pass.

A Word that is kept and guarded within the heart cannot be stolen. Even if it is not yet fully understood, that Word will remain and work. Sooner or later, the light will dawn and faith will rise within the heart of the hearer. When the light of revelation has come, the hearer will see, know and participate in the promise. One day they will rise up and say, *"Wait a minute—I AM BLESSED."* Understanding will come and they will declare, *"I AM HEALED!"* The lame will walk. The blind will see. The manifestation of the promise will come because the Word is alive. It packs the power to do what God has sent it to do.

Rooted and Grounded

> **But he who received the seed on stony places, this is he who hears the Word and immediately receives it with joy; yet he has no root in himself, but endures only for a while. For when tribulation or persecution arises because of the Word, immediately he stumbles.**
>
> **Matthew 13:20-21 NKJV**

In the first kind of soil, the person didn't understand the Word and the enemy took opportunity to steal the seed. Perhaps the person stopped coming to where the Word was preached or perhaps they listened to a contrary voice. Whatever the case, the Word was stolen for lack of understanding. They didn't guard the seed and it was whisked away.

In the second soil, however, the person receives the Word with joy, yet they are without root. When faced with tribulation or persecution on account of the promise, they are offended. Without a root, the seed cannot endure.

They shouted, danced, jumped up and down and fell out under the power. The person received the Word with great joy, but the deceitfulness of riches choked the Word. After the shout, they became unfruitful. They didn't develop roots. They were not rooted and grounded in the Word. Sure, they received the Word with gladness, but a root system takes time to establish itself. An oak tree doesn't become established overnight. Only through careful watering and much attention is a tree of such stature established in the soil.

Why wasn't this soil conducive to growth? The answer lies in the fact that they had not established themselves in the Word. When persecutions came, they failed to endure because they were not rooted in the substance of their hope. The Bible says that they only endured a short while. However, if they had kept the Word, they would have developed root in the Word. Perhaps, in their heart they said, *"Am I not a spiritual giant yet?"* They became frustrated and could not endure.

When you stay plugged into the promises of the Word of God, you will not become overwhelmed by the cares of life. The Word will provide for all of your needs. However, if a person pulls away from thinking and talking the Word, then that tender root will wither. They will become weary and faint in their minds.

Yet he has no root in himself, but endures only for a while. For when tribulation or persecution arises because of the Word, immediately he

stumbles.

Matthew 13:21 NKJV

A person gets saved. They get filled with the Holy Ghost. With great enthusiasm they tell their friends, *"I'm going to the bar to witness."* Before you know it, despite their good intentions, their mind is in the gutter. Alongside, is the person they're witnessing to.

What happened? They didn't have enough root. They weren't strong enough to walk in there, get everybody saved and then walk back out.

If you haven't been rooted and grounded in God, stay home. Go to church. Study the Word. Develop roots. Yes, if you're strong, lead your friends to the Lord. If you're not, your friends will lead you back into the world.

The enemy is a thief. If you understand his methods, you will recognize his works.

Answering the Wind

Grace to you and peace from God our Father and the Lord Jesus Christ. We are bound to thank God always for you, brethren, as it is fitting, because your faith grows exceedingly, and the love of every one of you all abounds toward each other, so that we ourselves boast of you among the churches of God for your patience and faith in all your persecutions and tribulations that you endure, which is manifest evidence of the righteous judgment of God, that you may be counted worthy of the kingdom of God, for which you also suffer.

2 Thessalonians 1:2-5 NKJV

The Bible says that persecution and tribulation arise for the Word's sake. The person with no root is overcome easily. The winds blow, things happen and they wilt at the first sign of opposition.

The moment the Word goes to work in your life, you change. The moment you change, people fuss. Your friends would have been fine with your old self, but the change rubbed them the wrong way. It is all right to have a powerless religion. It's okay to be going nowhere and doing nothing, but the moment you move on, people get riled up. They don't like it and they go to persecute the one that has had the breakthrough.

These are the strategies the devil uses to catapult people right back to the place where God has taken them from.

First, through lack of understanding, he tries to steal the Word. If he can't steal the Word, he may try to wear the person's endurance down through contrary winds. He brings persecutions and tribulations. Eventually, the person may tire of holding onto the promise.

"…for your patience and faith in all your persecutions and tribulations that ye endure …"

Why does a person endure only a short while? That person didn't mix their faith with patience. The Word came with joy and they received it. They understood it and had the faith to receive the promise, however, they didn't have patience. Without patience, a person can only endure a short while.

The devil knows your *buttons*. He knows how to solicit a reaction. He says, *"They are understanding the Word so I can't steal the Word! So onto Plan B… I will cause persecutions to arise. I will wear them down."*

Persecution comes. Contrary winds blow. If the person hasn't developed root, they will become frustrated and throw in the towel. Instead of holding their position of victory, they grow weary and faint in the face of opposition. They haven't been established. An established root is one that has been watered and well grounded in the soil in which it was planted. It's not a shallow root, rather, it's a root that runs deep below the surface.

This is a good illustration:

A person receives a revelation from the Lord. A light goes on within them. With great excitement they tell their friends:

> *"God is going to bless me. I'm training under the International Miracle Institute. I have been learning about my authority, my heavenly identity, miracles and I know God will prosper me. I am going to be blessed. In fact, God wants everybody blessed!"*

Upon speaking their revelation, they are challenged by someone *without* a revelation.

> *"Well, God is going to make some people blessed, but you never know."*

The one with the revelation responds:

> *"No! You don't understand. I got a revelation from the Word of God. God wants to bless everybody."*

The other counters:

> *"No, no, you're just stupid and they are teaching you false hope and hyper-faith. I hate to see you hurt."*

The Christian who received the Word of God with joy goes home and says:

> *"God, you know I trust You. I believe in You. Now, bless me so that I can prove to everybody that you are telling the truth."*

One month goes by, two months pass, three months pass. As each day passes, they grow in their frustration. Unable to endure the winds of persecution, they give up.

This person became offended at the Word. They became frustrated with the promise. Remember, the Bible says that persecution will come for the Word's sake. The enemy fought their revelation. He challenged their ENDURANCE. In the end, they failed to procure the manifestation of the promise because they did not mix PATIENCE with their faith.

John the Baptist said, *"Are you the One or should we seek another?"*

Jesus said, *"Listen, John, you are on the verge of being offended in Me. Don't quit now. Don't let the jail talk you out of your convictions. I'm going to show you again. I'm going to give you the same sermon."*

> **Jesus answered and said unto them, Go and shew John again those things which ye do hear and see: The blind receive their sight, and the lame walk, the lepers are cleansed, and the deaf hear, the dead are raised up, and the poor have the Gospel preached to them. And blessed is he, whosoever shall not be offended in Me.**
>
> **Matthew 11:4-6**

Clipping the Thorns

The first type of soil did not understand the Word. Rather than contending for revelation, the person dismissed the Word. The devil, taking opportunity, stole the seed that had been cast on the wayside. The second type of soil was the one who received the Word with joy, but failed to endure the climate. They received the revelation, but persecutions came and they gave up on the promise because they were not rooted in that Word.

Don't ever change your mind about the Word. If you don't

understand it, stay around the Word. Meditate on it. Rehearse it. Continue to hear, continue to receive teaching. Don't give up on the promises of God. Don't allow the enemy to steal the Word, but harness it with faith and patience. *Water your revelation.* Tend to your promises.

> **Now he who received seed among the thorns is he who hears the Word, and the cares of this world and the deceitfulness of riches choke the Word, and he becomes unfruitful.**
>
> **Matthew 13:22 NKJV**

The third type of soil succumbed to a land of thorns. Those thorns choked the Word. In other words, the cares of life strangled the Word and it became unfruitful. It was stifled by what seemed to be an unyielding environment.

This person heard the Word, but the cares of life were so all-consuming that they choked its influence. The deceitfulness of riches became the foremost element in their life. Rather than giving the Word preeminence, this person allowed a secondary influence to override the promise.

You go to work. You drive through rush hour, eat dinner, deal with people, pay bills, handle a household and live life. It's impossible to live on Earth without being exposed to cares and contradiction. While you are on this planet, you will encounter these things.

What is the secret to living above life's distractions?

Pray. Get in the Word. Fellowship with godly people. If you spend time with cold people, they will wear on your tenacity in God. Their tepid influence will rub off. Therefore, spend time with God and enjoy the company of godly people. Make friends with those who challenge, encourage and sharpen you. Don't allow lapses of time to go by where you have neglected to stir up the gift of God on the inside of you. Catch yourself. If you find yourself thinking and worrying about cares, stop yourself! *Pray.* Go back to the Word. Rehearse your revelation. Like Jesus said, *"Go show John again."*

The cares of life will pressure you. The devil will utilize them to push you over the edge. If the devil can get your eyes on the cares of life, he can distract you from purpose. A person like this will say, *"Leave me alone. I have my own problems."* This is one that has become heavy laden. Care has become their all-consuming burden. A mind that is wrapped in anxiety cannot hold onto the promise, but becomes offended in it.

When one becomes offended in the Word, whatever the cause, they become unfruitful. The Word is in them and the tree is good, but the tree is not producing fruit.

What is the cause of their barrenness?

THEIR PRIORITIES are the cause of their unfruitfulness. They have been so mindful of the cares of life and the deceitfulness of riches that the life of God was cut off from the seed. Their minds were full of things that were not profitable to the seed. Instead of meditating on the Word and considering the promise, they meditated on the care.

You must fight for your revelation.

Say this out loud:

> *If I do not understand the Word, I am going to continue to meditate on it. I will not let the Word go. If I get persecuted because I believe the Word, I will not be offended at God or at anybody else. Let it be known, I will not allow my mind to be dominated by cares and worries. I will not allow the deceitfulness of riches or life's concerns to rob me of fruitfulness.*

Tending to the Garden of God

> **But he who received seed on the good ground is he who hears the Word and understands it, who indeed bears fruit and produces: some a hundredfold, some sixty, some thirty.**
>
> **Matthew 13:23 NKJV**

Notice that the thorns, stones and rocks have been removed from this ground. The soil has been made ready. It has been prepared for the seed.

"Is this not a garden for God?" says the good soil. *"Let us make this ground bloom. Even if it's a desert soil, this ground will bloom like a garden oasis."*

This soil was prepared by *someone* who meant business with God.

If a person plants God's Word next to the seeds of care and worry, thorns will creep up and choke that Word. Although they have received the Word, its seed will become unprofitable. It's not that they didn't have the Word, but that they allowed renegade weeds to choke their garden.

If you heard the Word but didn't understand it, *guard it*. Meditate on it. Tend to the promise! Do not let the devil steal it, but rather, receive the seed into the earth of your heart.

Do not allow persecution and tribulation to offend. When a person is offended in the Word, that Word cannot produce a harvest in their life. Prepare the soil of your heart. Say to yourself, *"Whatever the Lord tells me, I'm going to do it. Whatever I hear out of the Word, I'm going to be. Whatever I learn, I am going to put into motion."*

If something goes a little haywire, don't deviate from your course! Pray in tongues. Listen to the Word. Call someone and pray together and go to church whenever the doors are open. *Do what you know to do in God, and as you do, faith and patience will work.* Together, they will produce a harvest: some thirty, some sixty and some one hundredfold.

> **But if ye have bitter envying and strife in your hearts, glory not, and lie not against the truth. This wisdom descendeth not from above, but is earthly, sensual, devilish. For where envying and strife is, there is confusion and every evil work.**
>
> **James 3:14-16**

Bitter envying and strife always lead to confusion and evil works. If every evil work is present, the Word will be unable to produce a harvest. Strife is like discord. It is a lack of agreement with the Word of God. It is out of synch with the voice of God.

Envying and strife does not necessarily have to take place between people. Strife can be something that the enemy has been harassing you with. It can be an area of *contention* that is keeping you out of agreement with the wisdom of God.

Is there an absence of PEACE in your life?

If your answer is *"Yes,"* it is because cares have taken predominance. They have taken center stage and interfered with your connectivity in God. That interference is strife. It is discord and it is at odds with the Word. For a harvest to take place, strife and discord must be uprooted. Only then, when the soil has been made ready, can a person come into full agreement with the Word.

If strife leads to every evil work, then the absence of strife must mean the presence of every good thing from above.

CHAPTER 4

POSSESSING AUTHORITY AND POWER

*Revelation demands obedience.
If God has revealed something to you, it is your
responsibility to act on His Word.*

Word Enforcement

Within the world, there are authority figures. These authority figures hold jurisdiction or rulership over certain areas of influence. The police officer, the judge, the governmental figure, the captain and the boss all walk in a realm of authority. For this reason, many in authority positions carry a symbol of their authority, such as a badge or perhaps a uniform. The badge or uniform is a representation of the power they hold.

In the same way, Jesus Christ has granted you authority. He gave you the badge of His power to stand against all the wiles of the devil. He also saw fit to place authority figures within His Church to build it. The Bible says, *"He gave gifts unto men… and He gave apostles, prophets, evangelists, pastors, and teachers"* (Ephesians 4:8-11). Within the army of God, there is both rank and position. Every part has been fitly framed together so that all may contend as one.

God has called every saint to have *dominion* over the works of the adversary. Each one has been given a realm of authority, position and influence. Just as the police officer has been given a precinct to watch over, the saint has been given a realm of jurisdiction. In the same way that a military unit has been given jurisdiction over occupied territory, the believer has been given jurisdiction over the planet. They have been given the right, the power, and the authority to administer justice. This is their realm of "Word Enforcement." It's where the Word of God is commanded and enforced.

The place of your jurisdiction is where your authority is implemented. It is where you exercise the rights you've been given. If a person is faithful in their area of jurisdiction, God will promote them and increase their level of responsibility. The Bible says, *"He who is faithful in what is least is faithful also in much; and he who is unjust in what is least is unjust also in much"* (Luke 16:10).

The dictionary defines authority as the right to COMMAND and to ENFORCE obedience. It is the power to determine justice, issue dictates and punish violations. Authority settles the issue.

What gives the police officer the right to command? It is the position. It is the office. It is the badge that they wear and the authorization that they have received. The badge tells everyone that he or she is authorized to command justice in a given jurisdiction. That jurisdiction may be a precinct, a city, a department, a country or a territory. If they step outside of this realm of influence, their authority will cease to function. Authority will fail if it violates its boundaries or undermines the law.

The captain of a ship has authority over that vessel. Authority has been conferred upon that individual in order that they might rule over their realm. They have been given *governing power* and *enforcing power*. This responsibility was delegated to them by a higher authority.

Likewise, the centurion was a man with authority. His commanding officer had delegated a realm of jurisdiction to him. He said, *"I tell this man 'Go,' this man 'Come' and he comes and I tell my servant 'Do this' and he does it"* (Mathew 8:9). He had the right to both command and enforce.

The BADGE gives you the right to COMMAND.
The GUN gives you the power to ENFORCE.

If there were nothing to back the badge, some people would resist the authority it represents. If the law had no power to enforce, the criminal would violate its dictates without fear of reprisal. The good citizen may willingly obey, but the criminal has to see consequence. *Authority necessitates enforcement.*

Likewise, as a believer, you have been given a realm of authority. You have been given jurisdiction. If your call and your position did not have any ENFORCING POWER behind it, the renegade forces of darkness would challenge it without fear of consequence.

Jesus did not only give you the right to command, but He gave you the power to enforce the commands that you give. He didn't just give you the ability to stand, but He gave you the power to overcome the forces that stand against you.

Jesus has conferred on you the right and the divine privilege to exercise His dominion and power. He has given you the right to enforce His Word and to command obedience. There is power behind your authority. Spiritually speaking, your gun is not only cocked, but it is loaded.

Ruling Your Realm

Jesus has given you the right to implement, and if necessary, *force* your authority. He gave you the *right* or *title* to act, but you can live your life without *acting*. You have been given the right to govern, but you can live your life without *governing*.

> **And hath made us kings and priests unto God and His Father; to Him be glory and dominion for ever and ever. Amen.**
>
> **Revelation 1:6**

Jesus is the King of *kings* and the Lord of *lords*. The Word of God says that you have been made a king and a priest unto God. As a king, you possess the *authority* and the *artillery* to back up the command.

Jesus has given you these two elements so that you may partake of all that He has promised. He has granted you the authority and the power to procure health, prosperity, victory, happiness, wisdom and every other divine promise. How you utilize your *title* (i.e. Saint,

Believer, Christian, Child of God) will determine the measure that you walk in. In other words, it takes both the badge *and* the gun to cash in on your benefits. Your authority must be enforced. This is a responsibility that *only you* can exercise.

In the Greek language, authority is translated *EXOUSIA*.

Exousia is defined as:

- Privilege
- Capacity
- Competency
- Delegated Influence
- Authority
- Jurisdiction
- Liberty
- Strength

Jesus has given His Church the PRIVILEGE
to see the Word of God manifested.

He has given us the CAPACITY
to enforce the Word of God when challenged.

He has given us COMPETENCY
in His DELEGATED INFLUENCE.

He has given us LIBERTY
to exercise His dominion.

Jesus has given you a place of influence in the affairs of life. You are an influential person on account of your authority. As a believer, you are called to influence your jurisdiction with the Word of God.

The wisdom of God said, *"You're going to need My authority. You're going to need a badge and a position. As a member of My body, I am giving you this authority so that you can enforce My Word."*

This authority is in *complete agreement* with the Word of God. Jesus has given you a delegated responsibility to carry out and enforce His Word. When a person steps outside of the Word of God, their authority will cease to operate. A police officer, for instance, that beats a person without cause, will be prosecuted. He or she has misused their authority. The abuse of power brings consequence.

In the same way, a Christian that violates the Word of God, steps outside the parameters of their God-given authority. The person who misuses liberty will find himself or herself in danger of bondage. It is the enemy who takes advantage of disobedience.

God has given you the final say, but your results in life are determined by your obedience to the Word of God. This revelation will only benefit you if you put it to work in your life. I can teach you to take the limits off God in your life. I can impart to you and train you, but in the end, *your daily decisions will determine your level of victory in God.* Remember, as the keeper of your own garden, you determine whether your soil will yield a return of 30-fold, 60-fold or 100-fold.

The Power in the Promise

Jesus said, *"I give you POWER over all the POWER of the enemy"* (Luke 10:19). The translators of the King James Version used the word "power" to define two different categories of power. As you already learned, one of those categories is "Exousia" or authority. Exousia is the jurisdiction, right, liberty, influence, ability and privilege to do what God has called you to do. The other category is "Dunamis." Dunamis is miracle-working power. It is the kind of power that God has and that God exerts.

If exousia is the badge, then dunamis is the gun. If exousia is the office, then dunamis is the power that backs up that office. When an ambassador is sent from one nation to conduct business with another, they come as a delegate, representing the power, authority and interests of their nation. Although they are one person, they represent a government, an administration and a military force. There is a power that backs up their delegated authority.

Likewise, you have received delegated authority through the Word of God. Heaven is backing up your mission on Earth. When Jesus said, *"Go ye,"* He did not say, *"You're going alone."* He said, *"I'm going to be with you. I'll never leave you nor forsake you. When you face the enemy, don't allow him to lie to you. Not only have I given you a badge, but I have given you the power to back up the badge."*

Your mission is not just a position.
It is *reinforced* by the miracle-working power of God.

There are many, however, that have been given authority, but have failed to cash in on the power behind that authority. You may have even seen this in the pulpit. The minister has jurisdiction. They have influence and liberty in their sphere, but there is no real power to bring it to pass.

If Jesus has delegated *rights, privileges, authority, ability, jurisdiction, influence,* and *competency* to the believer, it would be a shame to go without the things He has promised.

What if a KING acted like a pauper,
because the king didn't know?

What if a MILLIONAIRE lived broke,
because the millionaire didn't know?

What if an HEIR lived without their inheritance,
because the heir didn't know?

What if a SAINT lived sick,
because they didn't know divine health was available?

People say, *"Well, you know, the flu is going around."*

Authority will only operate when you know *who* you are and *what* you have been given. If an ambassador does not know their authority, they cannot appropriate their power. Authority is a title and that title is only as good as the power behind it. Authority, therefore, will only work if it is *understood* and *exercised* in agreement with what it represents.

As a believer, Jesus has bestowed on you a certain *position* in the Kingdom. He has given you a title and an office. He has given you the delegated ability to enforce His will. The scepter of your authority is yours to pick up and to rule with. It is your divine right. As an ambassador of the Kingdom, you have been granted the ability to succeed, to represent Him, and to overcome on His behalf.

The Authoritative Message

> **But He passing through the midst of them went His way, and came down to Capernaum, a city of Galilee, and taught them on the sabbath days. And they were astonished at His doctrine: for His Word was with power.**
>
> **Luke 4:30-32**

In the Scripture above, the Word "power" literally means "exousia" or "authority." They were astonished because His Word was with authority. Nothing will astonish the religious crowd quicker than an authoritative Word. A Word that proclaims the absolutes of God will upset religious tradition. It will challenge the theology of those who claim a *"whatever will be, will be"* doctrine.

An authoritative message is one founded upon an absolute assurance and knowledge of the Word of God. This message of authority can only come through an instrument that has *received authority* into their lives. When you receive authority, you operate in authority. When the police officer says, *"Stop in the name of the law!"* he or she is issuing a decree that commands obedience. If somebody was to question that authoritative command, artillery power is present to enforce.

Jesus wasn't teaching in the manner of the Pharisees or the Sadducees. There are people that can talk for an hour, but never convey or impart the reality of a revelation. Authority speaks with confidence of delivery. Authority declares a clear answer from God.

Authority says, *"God will heal you."*
Authority says, *"God will bless you."*
Authority says, *"God will prosper and promote you."*
Authority says, *"God will bruise the enemy under your feet."*

The authority Jesus preached with, carried a visible manifestation of the promise. The people were astonished because His Word carried authoritative power. It was not an *empty Word* with *empty promises*, but it was an authoritative message filled with dunamis.

Shut Up and Come Out!

And in the synagogue there was a man, which had a spirit of an unclean devil, and cried out with a loud voice...

Luke 4:33

The man with the unclean devil didn't cry out, *"Hallelujah!"* He cried out in torment, anger, and fear. He cried out because the demons in him encountered a message of authority and enforcing power.

Perhaps, Jesus preached on deliverance. Whatever His message, it is certain that He didn't say, *"My Father might work,"* or *"My Father sometimes works."* No, He came with a certain message. He knew *what* God said, *who* He was, and *what* God had called Him to do.

You are called to walk in the same confidence.

When you know the Word of God and submit to its authority, devils tremble. Their greatest fear is the believer that knows WHO they are, WHAT they are called to do and HOW to do it.

> **"Let us alone; what have we to do with Thee, Thou Jesus of Nazareth? Art Thou come to destroy us? I know thee who Thou art; the Holy One of God." And Jesus rebuked him, saying, "Hold thy peace, and come out of him." And when the devil had thrown him in the midst, he came out of him, and hurt him not. And they were all amazed, and spake among themselves, saying, "What a word is this! For with authority and power He commandeth the unclean spirits, and they come out."**
>
> Luke 4:34-36

Jesus is preaching the Word of God with exousia, with privilege, with right and with jurisdiction. He is occupying His realm of influence with the Good News of the Kingdom. He is declaring to all present, *"I am a messenger from Almighty God. I come with a clear message. Let him that hath an ear hear it."* Suddenly, a person with an unclean spirit cries out.

"Let us alone! Stop preaching now… Go away!"

This is the religious response to a Word preached with authority. All over the world, people either love the message or hate it. Some want to hear more and others don't want to hear it ever again. This is because the message of authority does not validate complacency or inactivity. It's not a casual chicken dinner type message. Rather, authority carries the fire of challenge. It inspires people to answer the call of God and to commit to greatness. Those who are unwilling to respond with such fervency wish to silence the message.

"Well, that really doesn't have anything to do with the devil."

It most certainly does. People who do not want to obey God's Word have taken the first step toward becoming overcome with an unclean spirit. If a person does not yield to what God has to say, they will eventually yield to what the devil has to say.

"Leave us alone. What have we to do with you?"

Jesus commanded, *"Hold your peace!"* A good biblical translation for this is, *"Muzzle up!"* or *"Shut up!"* Authority will always tell the devil to shut up. It will not give the enemy equal time.

"Shut up and come out of him!"

Breaking Enemy Lines

If Jesus rebuked the devil in *His* ministry, do you think that you will have to do the same in *your* life? There are certain things that you have to *speak to* or *rebuke* with authority. However, before you can rebuke with authority, you have to walk and talk with authority.

Jesus did two things before He confronted the devil.

1. He WALKED with authority.
2. He TALKED with authority.

People said, *"That man…HIS WORDS are astonishing!"* He did not talk like the scribes; rather, he spoke with a clear-cut authoritative message.

> **But Jesus rebuked him, saying, "Be quiet, and come out of him!" And when the demon had thrown him in their midst, it came out of him and did not hurt him. Then they were all amazed …**
>
> **Luke 4:35-36**

Jesus was in the synagogue. The man with the unclean spirit was also there. Chances are the man had been in that synagogue many times before. In fact, he may have come daily and listened to the scribes, but up until today, the message had never commanded a response.

When you operate in the delegated authority that Jesus gave, the anointing on your authority will cause the opposition to surface. The power behind your very words will force a manifestation and demand immediate deliverance.

Have you ever come to church feeling down and left free?
Have you ever come to church sick and left healed?

The authoritative message carries enforcing power. That Word has the power to deliver the hearer from bondage.

"And when the devil had thrown him in the midst..."

The man wasn't thrown down *before* Jesus spoke. He was only thrown *after* Jesus said, *"Hold your peace and come out."* When the Lord released that authoritative command, it carried something more than authority. It carried the dunamis power to enforce.

> **And they were all amazed, and spake among themselves, saying, "What a word is this! For with authority (exousia) and power (dunamis) He commandeth the unclean spirits, and they come out."**
>
> **Luke 4:36**

As Jesus taught, He utilized exousia and the congregation experienced the authority of the Word. However, when the authority of the Word forced a manifestation, it necessitated something more than the badge. He needed something more than the position or the uniform to take dominion. He needed *the gun of dunamis power* to back up the authoritative Word.

When the devil started talking, a *rhema* Word, fueled with the dunamis of God, rose within Jesus. The moment He released that Word, the devil had to obey. All of a sudden, the man fell down on the ground and was set free from his bondage. When this happened, all who were present knew that Jesus spoke with authority (exousia) and power (dunamis). They saw it and they were amazed.

The integrity of the Word of God will never fail.

While authority will speak to the mountain, dunamis will cause the mountain to move. Notice that having and exercising exousia is not enough. We must employ dunamis.

Authority + Power = Performance

> **Behold, I give unto you power (authority) to tread on serpents and scorpions, and over all the power (dunamis) of the enemy: and nothing shall by any means hurt you.**
>
> **Luke 10:19**

You have the right to win and the right to prevail over your enemy. You have been given the right to overcome the works of darkness. You have been given the privilege to exercise jurisdiction over all the powers of Hell. Jesus gave you this right, but it is up to you to walk in it. Just because a person has been given authority does not mean they are enforcing it.

How many Christians have been hurt by the devil?
How many have been killed before they fulfilled their destiny?
How many families have fallen apart?

Did Jesus lie when He said, *"…and nothing shall by any means hurt you."* Was He confused? Perhaps He meant to say, *"and nothing that I can think of at this very moment will hurt you."* No, Jesus did not lie and He was not confused!

The individual who falls short of the promise is the one who has neglected or misunderstood their divine rights. Remember, authority *receives* and *exercises* the promise while dunamis *enforces* it. A promise not harnessed will simply remain a promise. It takes exousia (authority) and dunamis (power) to participate in it.

According to the Word of God, you have been given authority over all the power of the devil. This authority gives you the right to receive all the dunamis power you need to overcome the power that he exerts. God has given you the ability to prevail. What you do with that ability is proportional to your level of victory.

God didn't just give you the badge, He gave you the gun. The Bible says, *"The Lord also working with them confirming the Word with signs following"* (Mark 16:20). In other words, He gave them the badge, the uniform, the position *and the gun*. Equipped with both authority and power, they went everywhere preaching the Word with power demonstrations following. Dunamis power accompanied the exousia Word. There is *power* in the *integrity* of the Word of God.

The Place of Power

The devil has a certain level of dunamis. For instance, he may perform superhuman feats like breaking chains or cutting himself with stones and not feeling pain. When the enemy gains access over a situation or a life, he brings his own kind of power into it. It is not a creative power like God, but a lower counterfeit power.

Jesus has instructed us to remain unmoved by the devil. The power of the enemy is no match against the dunamis power of God. We are stronger and greater in every way, for the Church has been given the greatest power in the universe. Miracle-working power backs the authority of the believer. In other words, when the word you speak is THE WORD, the power of Heaven will enforce the authority you stand on. That's a good place to be in God!

You are an ambassador of Heaven. You have been granted delegated authority to conduct business on behalf of the Kingdom of God. This ambassadorship, this commission, is not just a position. It is not just a title or a badge. There is power that backs your authority. Jesus says, *"The power is right behind you. Go ahead and preach My Word and right behind My Word, there is the power you need to overcome the feats of darkness. Behind My authority there is enforcing power, and nothing shall hurt you."*

Why do people get hurt?

People get hurt when they step outside of the Spirit. The dunamis of God or the anointing only operates when the believer is walking in the Spirit. It does not function when the child of God is walking in the flesh. Fear, doubt and unbelief will short-circuit your connection with God. You can't worry, fight, argue *and* walk according to the Spirit. When you step out of the Spirit, you step out of your place of power. Those who wander beyond the fortress of God's Word, make themselves available to the enemy.

Smith Wigglesworth once said, *"If you have to wait until you need the power to pray, then it is already too late."* While you live on this planet you will encounter situations that demand an immediate anointing. If you're not walking in the Spirit, then you will not be equipped to deal with the situation effectively. This is why it is wise to remain in a place of power. Your place of power is your place of prayer. It is a realm of communion with the Word and fellowship with the Spirit of God. Don't wait for the circumstance or the challenge to blow your way, but fortify yourself with the Word of God.

There is a place in God where the anointing always abides. It is a place of continuous prayer and ever-present fellowship. If you maintain this connection in your walk with God, you will always be prepared to respond to life with authority and power. Christians only get hurt when they walk outside of the Spirit. Therefore, the key to not getting hurt is to walk in the Spirit.

People always ask, *"What about the disciples? They were martyred.*

Didn't they have authority?" The disciples walked in great authority. They had authority to exercise jurisdiction over everything in their life. In fact, some of them *chose* to exercise their authority in giving their life. These said, *"I'm going to be martyred and lay down my life."* It was their decision.

Rights and Responsibilities

God has given us an endowment. Without this endowment, the life of a person is like a ship without a rudder or a boat without a sail. Without authority, there cannot be a confession or a declaration of assurance. Just as the ship requires the rudder, your walk with God necessitates the authority of the Word of God. This authoritative assurance from the Word is the source of all stability and direction. In its absence, there is instability, weakness and confusion. There is strength in the Word of God.

This is why the devil seeks to bring confusion. He knows that confusion brings distraction and that distraction has the power to steer you off course. If he can move you from your course in God, he can move you *outside* of your jurisdiction. God has called you to walk in the Sprit. When you step outside of the Spirit, you step outside of your jurisdiction.

When a person does not use authority in their jurisdiction, they will deviate from their course in God. God cannot promote a person that is not employing what He has given them. *Revelation demands obedience.* If God has revealed something to you, it is your responsibility to act on His Word.

The believer not only has rights, but responsibilities.
It is your responsibility to use your authority.

You don't have to miss the mark in God. You can sail straight into the fullness of all that God has called you to. If you will keep your mind and your mouth in line with God's Word, He will see you through to victory. Those that walk, talk and think on the Word will not stray from their course. They will navigate turbulent seas and silence the violence of the storm. Success is inevitable to the one who does not relinquish their power.

Representing God's Interests

The purpose of authority is to make GOD'S WILL and RESOURCES accessible to the believer. The Bible says, *"Let us come boldly to the throne of grace"* (Hebrews 4:16). This is a person that approaches the throne with great plainness of speech. They come not only knowing the divine will, but also knowing their rights to that will. It's not a place of wavering, insecurity or timidity. It's a place of boldness, confidence and plain speech. When you know your rights, you don't mince words.

What produces great boldness? The person heard the Word, believed the Word, and faith came. That faith gave them an unshakeable conviction in the promise. The Bible says that without faith it is impossible to please God (Hebrews 11:6). Faith pleases God. Half-stepping doesn't move mountains.

If a corporation hired an employee and said, *"We're hiring you as the representative of this firm. Go to Taiwan and make an offer for this product. Tell them we are willing to go as far as necessary. Tell them that we're prepared to pay all the way up to one hundred million dollars."*

Imagine if that employee landed in Taiwan, sat down in the boardroom and then hemmed and hawed. What if that person nervously fidgeted and said, *"Ah...well I think that...I...ah, I mean we... could possibly maybe come up with twenty-five million."*

What if that company responded, *"No deal!"* and the employee, resigned to failure, flew back to their firm with the unhappy news. When the firm is advised on the failed venture, they will confront the employee that didn't represent their interests. They will say, *"What did we tell you to tell them? Didn't you believe what we said? What kind of representative are you? Who are you working for? We told you that we were prepared to do whatever was necessary all the way up to one hundred million dollars!"*

It's the same when you walk into the presence of God. God says, *"Who are you believing? Who are you working for? Why is it that you are hesitant to believe exactly what I have told you? Don't you believe that you have jurisdiction to lay claim to the promises that I have given?"*

Investing in Diligence

The Bible says, *"He is a rewarder to those who diligently seek Him"* (Hebrews 11:6). A person like this will *seek diligently* in order that they might *find*. Someone who does not seek diligently is someone who is not sure that their diligence will produce a result. Therefore, a person that does not *seek* diligently, does not *find* either.

When you seek, you will find.
God rewards those who diligently seek Him.

A person who diligently speaks the Word is operating in delegated authority. They are using their exousia to assert their jurisdiction. Exousia says, *"Devil, take your hands off my money! I will not fear. I will not back down. I believe every bill is paid. I believe every need is taken care of."*

The platform of exousia will net a dunamis miracle. When exousia is combined with His dunamis, your diligent confession will produce a manifestation of the promise. The end of your exousia-authority is always His dunamis-power.

Ask, and it shall be given you; seek, and ye shall find; knock, and it shall be opened unto you.

Matthew 7:7

You have authority to find, therefore, ***seek.***
You have authority to receive from God, therefore, ***ask.***

CHAPTER 5

EXERCISING DOMINION

You do not have to be on a mountain peak in God to deal with the devil. You don't have to swing from spiritual clouds!

Understanding Your Divine Rights

You have the right to *believe* what God has promised.
You have the right to *forbid* the enemy from stealing.
You have the right to *prevail* in everything that you do.

These are your divine rights. They are your God-given privileges. If you fail to receive in any of these areas, God is not to blame. He has freely given you everything that you need to enforce His will in your life.

Authority enforces God's will and procures Kingdom resources. It is the *vehicle* that harnesses your divine rights. If you're failing to cash in on this promise, God's sovereignty is *not* to blame. He is both willing and able to supply for your situation. The problem, rather, is *your* slackness concerning the promise. God has given you authority to see results. Only through the *diligent seeking of faith* and *steadfast confession* can one participate in these benefits.

Authority will enable you to reach your goals and to fulfill your dreams. You have the right to finish the course. You have the right to rise up and live the high call. You have the right to participate in the triumph of Heaven. These are your rights. God has delegated them to you. If you will enforce what is yours, the authority inherent in His Word will bring every facet of your life into alignment.

When you rise up in your realm of jurisdiction and decree your destiny, the power of God will accompany your words. Even the circumstances in and around your life will line up with your authoritative decree. All things will move to accommodate the authority of the Word of God.

When you rise up in authority,
you will never think of yourself as a failure.

When you stand on the authority of the Word,
you will never think of yourself as poor.

When you speak the Word at all times,
you will never be dominated by the devil's words.

You have jurisdiction over your mind. You have jurisdiction over your finances. You have jurisdiction over your body. Your authority governs your realm of influence.

Kingdom Casualties

Authority is a command. If a police officer pulls over a carload of criminals, he has the right to call for backup. However, if he gets shot after wandering down a dark alley without a gun, he cannot blame anybody but himself for his carelessness. He had the authority to access the backup power, but he didn't utilize it.

Likewise, within the Church, back-up power is available but often remains unused. Distractions cause many to reprioritize things other than the dunamis power of God. Instead of reaching for the power that God extends, many believers tend to grope at the natural realm. Having become dulled to the Spirit, these become Kingdom casualties. Their slackness concerning the promise is the fatal flaw that brings their downfall.

It is not an accessibility problem. The backup power is easily accessible and readily available. The Church, however, has allowed *distractions* to override the dunamis of God. Instead of reaching for the power of God, many have become accustomed to turning to the natural realm for soulish answers. These become entangled by the very affairs that they were given dominion over.

The power of God is available to the one who acts on the Word of God. There's no great hidden mystery or secret key. The believer must only receive the Word into the soil of their heart and act on it. Authority can never fail because it is based on a Word that will never return void. Exousia will reach its goal.

Go Ye and Duplicate Thyself

> All power (exousia) is given unto Me in Heaven and in Earth.
>
> Matthew 28:18b-20

Once again, "power" is the word "exousia" or "authority." All authority in Heaven and Earth has been given to Jesus. All *right* and *privilege* has been granted to Him. He has been given *jurisdiction*. Jesus said, *"All jurisdiction in Heaven and in Earth is given to Me."* In other words, He is saying, *"You won't find any nook or cranny anywhere that I have not been given authority over."*

> Go ye therefore, and make disciples of all nations, baptizing them in the name of the Father, the Son and the Holy Ghost. Teaching them to observe all things whatsoever I have commanded you (not suggested, not hoping to see fit to do, not might be led) and lo I am with you always, even unto the end of the world.
>
> Matthew 28:19-20

Jesus rose from the dead and declared, *"I've got Good News for you. It is a different hour. It has never been like this before."* All privilege, authority, and jurisdiction was given to Him. Having received these things, He immediately turned to His own and said, *"Go and make disciples of all nations."*

Jesus took what was His and gave it to the Church. He said, *"I am done with my Earthly mission. Therefore, I am now giving you the delegated right and authority to go into every corner of the Earth and make followers of Me. Baptize them in the name of the Father, and of the Son, and of the Holy Ghost."* Jesus carried revival. At the end of His Earthly mission, He commissioned His disciples to carry out His work.

God has given the Church the authority to go to every corner of the Earth and make disciples, yet many are waiting on God. They are waiting on God to sovereignly do something about the world situation. They are waiting on a "someday revival" instead of acting on what has been delegated. Jesus has delegated His mission to the Church. It's called, of course, the *Great Commission*.

The Church has been commissioned to carry revival. Just as the early Church "turned the world upside-down," we too have been given the authority to herald the Gospel of the Kingdom. Jesus said to make disciples of all nations. Much of the Church world, however, is praying for revival to come. They are praying for God "to do something."

The problem is not that Jesus doesn't have the authority to convert the nation, and it isn't that the Church lacks the authority to preach the Gospel. Look closely at what Jesus said: *"Teach them to observe the things that I commanded you."* The only problem lies in the fact that before you can make disciples and teach them to observe, you have to *remember* the things that Jesus commanded!

Jesus has commanded us to be doers of His Word. More simply put, before we can make a disciple, we have to become a disciple.

Sometimes God's Word is regarded as a compilation of suggestions. Perhaps God just suggested that we should praise Him in everything. Perhaps it's just a recommendation that we should live holy as He is holy. Despite the consensus of popular opinion, God's Word is not a suggestion, a recommendation or a saying. His Word is His command. It is an authoritative order.

This is what Jesus is saying to you:

> *"All exousia is given to Me and I'm giving it to you. Now go and make disciples. Go teach them. Go baptize them and I will be with you. I will be with you through the person of the Holy Ghost. So don't worry… the badge you are wearing will be backed up by the gun that I provide. The mission you are on will be backed up by the dunamis that I provide. Go, therefore, without fear. You will not be harmed. Preach it like it is. Go without fear, for the authority I give you will be backed up by the power that I provide. I am with you always. I am with you 24 hours a day. They might shoot at you, but the bullet doesn't have to hit you. It doesn't have to hit you because it is within your jurisdiction. Speak the authority I have given to you. With confidence, declare, 'No weapon formed against me shall prosper and every tongue that rises against me in judgment will I condemn.' All of this is within your jurisdiction."*

Commanding Your Mission

The Church has distanced itself from the Great Commission. Having received a great promise, we have moved away from the reality of it. We have not utilized the endowment. This disassociation from the promise has not changed the fact that Jesus rose from the dead and gave the Church jurisdiction over the planet.

Many have said, *"Well, we will just praise the Lord and He will go out and do battle for us."* That's not how it works! The dunamis never goes out and does anything unless an obedient servant has spoken with exousia. It won't operate until the saint says, *"I heard Him say 'Go ye,' so I went and now I'm operating on exousia. I'm witnessing and I'm declaring the exousia authority of the Word of God."*

When a person acts upon the exousia of the Word of God, dunamis power will back it up. Those that act upon the exousia of the *"Go ye,"* will witness the miracle-working power of God in operation. That dunamis will get people saved, healed and delivered. As they continue to operate in their authority, the dunamis will continue to validate the Word.

"Go ye…"

Not only do you have the authority to *"Go,"* but you have the right to expect the Lord to be with you wherever you go. You have authority to speak the Word and the right to expect Him to bear witness with signs following. These are promises that God has given you. There is integrity in the Word of God.

The end of your authority, therefore, is the expectation that the anointing will break every yoke. Faith's confession sees the power of the promise in manifestation. Paul said, *"I'm not ashamed of the Gospel of Christ for it is the power (dunamis) of God unto salvation"* (Romans 1:16).

Do not be ashamed of the authority of the Word of God. Preach the Good News. Live the Good News. Stand on the Good News. When people inquire about your confidence, tell them the truth. Tell them, *"I'm not ashamed, I'm blessed!"*

Inevitably, they will ask, *"Why are you so blessed? Did you get a check in the mail? Did you receive a raise on the job? Do you have a million in the bank?"*

They may not like your answer.

"Well, it's simple," you reply, *"I'm blessed because God said it and I'm not ashamed of it."* All of a sudden, the inquisitive smiles turn to blatant accusations. *"You are a nut,"* they say, *"You know what is going to happen to you? You're going to fail. It's false hope. What are you going to do when you 'believe God' and He doesn't do it?"*

There is no such thing as disappointment when you are operating on exousia, for the Word of God cannot fail. Those who receive the Word and make it their own will see the expectation of their faith. Before long, that exousia, that diligent seeking, that unashamed believing of the Word, will hook up to the dunamis and a miracle will manifest. It will manifest in the life of the one who has believed the promise.

There is integrity in the Word of God.

Connecting to Your Power Provider

> Behold, I send the promise of My Father upon you: but tarry ye in the city of Jerusalem, until ye be endued with power (dunamis) from on high.
>
> Luke 24:49

There is wisdom in the Word of God. Notice Jesus' strategy. He gave His disciples authority, but He followed it up with this instruction: *"Don't act on that authority until you receive the back-up power to enforce it."*

This is an important truth: Your authority is dependent on the anointing behind it. The manifestation of the promise is dependent upon the power behind the promise.

The power available to you is potentially infinite. There is no measure to its potential. There are, however, definite restrictions to it in our individual lives. For instance, someone who does not walk close to the Lord will have a lower level of the presence of God manifested in their life. Someone who does not practice the presence of God will have very little anointing. The person who walks in strife will see very little dunamis in manifestation.

However, the person who walks closely with God will *maintain* a strong anointing on their life. They are connected to the power source. That "live" connection will manifest the promise. It will activate the expectation of their faith. It will "turn on" performance. When they need the power, it is there to perform. They don't need to "work up" anything because they are already dwelling in the place of power.

In terms of receptivity, *connection is everything.*

Putting the Promise into Perspective

"Tarry in Jerusalem, wait until you are endued with power" (Luke 24:49).

"Ye shall receive power after the Holy Ghost is come upon you" (Acts 2:8).

"…and He shall baptize you with the Holy Ghost and power" (Matthew 3:11).

All of these power-words refer to *dunamis*, the miracle-working power of God. The power of God is essential for daily victory. Without it, the promise stays a promise. It never materializes into "the expected end." It never becomes that which was hoped for.

The purpose of the anointing is to enforce and manifest the will of God. It is the anointing that makes the promise of salvation a reality. A person cannot even be born again without the anointing of the Holy Ghost. The Bible says, *"That which is born of flesh is flesh and that which is born of Spirit is spirit"* (John 3:6). The anointing gets the job done. It is for action. It is the force that brings the will of God into manifestation.

(It's) not by might, nor by power, but by My spirit, saith the LORD of hosts.

Zechariah 4:6b

Despite the vastness of the promise, many only participate in a very small measure of the anointing. Without a strong revelation of authority, the anointing is limited in expression. It's available and operating to a degree, but its function is almost irrelevant. A person's understanding of the Word of God can hinder the work of God.

For instance, when the Holy Ghost fell at the turn of the 20th century, most people didn't really have an understanding of the Word of God. They didn't know all that is known *today* because it hadn't been previously "discovered" in the Word. Remember, revelation that is based out of the Word of God is progressive. It's progressively revealed. If you aren't entirely convinced, recall for a moment the revelation of a German Catholic monk in the Middle Ages.

In the early 16th century, a man named Martin Luther received a revelation that *"The just shall live by faith."* His revelation challenged and rocked the world. No one had ever heard of such a thing and many called him a heretic. Today, however, every Protestant can trace their roots back to this man's revelation from the Word.

The entire Protestant Reformation is attributed to the revelation and subsequent actions of this one person. From that point forward, people took an interest in the Word of God. They started to learn about the things of God and to grow in revelation.

By the turn of the 20th century, people understood that the Holy Ghost was available. That revelation generated a hunger for the Baptism of the Holy Ghost. Their revelation, however, was that the believer had to "tarry" for the power. They had to wait until God came. In those days, they called it "praying the power down." When the power came, they would experience the tangible presence of God.

Many received the Baptism, but they didn't know what to do with the power. History records that they shouted, danced and rolled in the aisles. They had the power, but they didn't know what it was for.

Today, the opposite is true. People know authority and can break it down in the Hebrew and the Greek. They can give you a seven-point sermon on the subject, but they don't know how to exercise it. They use big words, big promises, but in the end, there is no power.

God never intended for us to choose *between* authority and power. It was not His intention for the Church to know the Word, but not the Spirit. Likewise, He doesn't want His children to know the Spirit without the Word. Authority without power is irrelevant. It doesn't help anybody. It only sounds good.

Walk Like a Son

Jesus said, *"You shall receive dunamis power,"* but the world does not lack for powerless people. How many Christians are baptized with the Holy Ghost, yet the only evidence of power in their life is the ability to speak in tongues? I have been in churches where the only sign of power was in tongues and interpretations. *Where did the power go?*

Likewise, the Bible says, *"The love of God has been shed in our hearts by the Holy Ghost"* (Romans 5:5). If this is true, then why do some fail in this area? Is the love of God not available to them in the Holy Ghost?

It's not that the Word of God didn't work. It's simply that the recipient had not fully yielded their lives to the Spirit of God. The power is there. The Holy Ghost is present, but they have yet to tap into that power source.

> **But the Comforter, which is the Holy Ghost, whom the Father will send in My name, He shall teach you all things, and bring all things to your remembrance, whatsoever I have said unto you.**
>
> **John 14:26**

The Holy Ghost is committed to reminding the Church of what Jesus said. He will lead us into power and show us things to come.

That leading takes place through the avenue of exousia or authority. When He shows it to us, we have the authority to receive it into the soil of our heart and to grow thereby. We can water the promise and see it into fruition. The child of God is led by the integrity of His Word.

> **But as many as received Him, to them gave He power (exousia) to become the sons of God, even to them that believe on His name.**
>
> **John 1:12**

Jesus has given the believer the right and the privilege to grow up to be sons. A son is someone who uses their authority to grow up in God. They know the promise, they obey the promise and they participate in the results. Having grown up on the Word, they are proficient in the use of both authority and power. They rule over their jurisdiction and enforce the authority of the Word. When faced with a contradiction, they know how to stand steadfast, with their feet firmly planted on the Word of truth. Like Jesus, they become strong in spirit, grow in grace and excel in wisdom (Luke 2:40).

The Bible says that when Jesus was baptized with the Holy Spirit, the Spirit came upon Him. Suddenly, a voice was heard from Heaven saying, *"This is My beloved Son in whom I am well pleased"* (Matthew 3:17). He was not a child anymore, but a full-grown son.

Immediately following, the Spirit led Him into the wilderness where He fasted and prayed. During this time, He was confronted by the devil. *"If you are the Son of God, command these stone to become bread"* (Matthew 4:3). At the moment of His temptation, He did not use dunamis, but employed exousia to overcome. He said, *"It is written. It is written. It is written."* He used the authority of the Word of God.

This is good news! You do not have to be on a mountain peak in God to deal with the devil. You don't have to swing from spiritual clouds! All that is required is for you to act upon the exousia that you've been given. Rise up and quote the written Word of God! Within that written Word, the dunamis of God will see to it that the forces of darkness are dealt with.

After Jesus had overcome temptation with His authority, the Bible records that *"He returned in the power of the Spirit"* (Luke 4:14). He returned in the dunamis of God. Walking into the synagogue, He opened a scroll and quoted Isaiah, saying, *"The Spirit of the Lord is upon Me. He has anointed Me to preach the Gospel to the poor. He has sent Me to heal the broken hearted, to deliver the captives, to open the blind eyes, to set at liberty, and to preach the acceptable year of the Lord"* (Luke 4:18-19). Jesus was testifying to the power He had received.

Jesus said to His disciples, *"Verily, verily, I say unto you, He that believeth on Me, the works that I do shall he do also; and greater works than these shall he do; because I go unto my Father"* (John 14:12).

Jesus spoke of "greater works" because of the promise of the Father. He knew that the Spirit would lead them into all truth and into the subsequent greater works of sonhood.

You have been given the right to grow and to become what God has called you to be. The knowledge of the truth will give you the authority to grow up to be a son. Those that do not use their authority, however, will remain a child. As long as that child is underage, they will be treated as such.

To grow in God, the believer must utilize the exousia that Jesus handed to them. They must allow the Holy Ghost to lead them into all truth so that they can see clearly into the Word. Your growth in God is dependent upon your dedication to the Word of God and your obedience to the Spirit.

"And ye shall know the truth, and the truth shall make you free" (John 8:32).

The Proof is in the Power

> And He said unto them, "Verily I say unto you, That there be some of them that stand here, which shall not taste of death, till they have seen the Kingdom of God come with power (dunamis)."
>
> **Mark 9:1**

Jesus heard God and spoke His faith: *"There be some of them that stand here which shall not taste of death until they have seen the Kingdom of God come with power."* He spoke the exousia of that Word and then submitted to the leading of the Holy Spirit. He knew that a Word spoken in faith would immediately place a demand on dunamis power to bring it into fulfillment.

When the Holy Ghost speaks into your spirit and gives you a revelation, no one sees the power working in you. Nobody can see the dunamis or the visitation of God. The power that is at work cannot be detected by natural means. *Spiritual things are spiritually discerned.*

When God speaks to you, let His Word be *your* word. Let the confession of your heart resound with the rhema of Heaven. When you go to speak, your words, infused with the life of God, will draw the power necessary to bring them to pass. Dunamis always accompanies exousia. There is power in a Word released.

When Jesus spoke the revelation, His disciples only heard the sound of His voice. He spoke *of* power and He spoke *with* power, but there was nothing to show for it *except* His words. When He spoke the Word, He released faith into the atmosphere. Faith always harnesses power. Perhaps some stood there thinking, *"What in the world is He talking about?"*

They didn't realize that an exousia Word places a *demand* on dunamis power.

> And after six days Jesus taketh Peter, James, and John his brother, and bringeth them up into an high mountain apart, and was transfigured before them: and His face did shine as the sun, and His raiment was white as the light.
>
> Matthew 17:1-2

A week later, the Spirit said to Him, *"Take with you Peter, James, and John."* It isn't hard to imagine that the remaining disciples more than likely put pressure on Jesus to bring them as well. Jesus, however, had to remain obedient to the direction of the Spirit. If He had not, it would have short-circuited the power at work.

You only have authority to do what God has said. When you do what God has commanded you, dunamis will back up the command. Men and women may pressure you, but realize that authority and power are only released in your explicit obedience to the Word. If God says it and you do it, you will participate in *God results*. If you compromise on the Word that you have heard, you will participate in *your results. Obedience sets the stage for the visitation of Heaven.*

"His face did shine as the sun…"

Jesus took Peter, James and John to a high mountain. While He stood with them, the anointing changed His appearance. His face and clothing radiated with resplendence. Somewhere beneath the brilliance, Peter, James and John fell down under the power. They were overcome by the magnificence and the glory of God.

"…they fell on their faces and were greatly afraid" (Matthew 17:6b).

The exousia Word that was spoken into the atmosphere released dunamis power. The Kingdom of God had indeed come with dunamis, and the evidence was in the manifestation of the promise. Peter, James and John could not deny the authority of the Word, nor the power behind it. The proof was in the power.

On another occasion, Jesus said:

> **But if I with the finger of God cast out devils, no doubt the Kingdom of God is come upon you.**
>
> **Luke 11:20**

What is the proof that the Kingdom of God is on Earth? The proof is in the power behind the authority. It's one thing to say you have authority, it's quite another when there is power to back it up.

Men and women will question authority. Religion will question authority. Your friends and relatives will question the authority in your life. However, if you have the dunamis of God working in you, all will see the blessing of God upon your life.

The Secret Place of Power

If you will believe and press in, the devil will not have a place of influence in your life. God can be your influential factor. He can be the King in your home and the King in your life. The Word gives promises to those who will obey them.

> **He that dwelleth in the secret place of the most High shall abide under the shadow of the Almighty.**
>
> **Psalm 91:1**

The secret place of the Most High is where the Word of God has ultimate authority. It is a place that is protected by the shield of faith. There is not a fiery dart that can penetrate its fortressed walls. The Bible says that this is the place where you are called to dwell. It's a promise and you have the exousia to walk in it.

Those who believe the Word operate on exousia. When authority is working, your shield is up. You are alert and armed with the Word of God. This is the secret place of the Most High. Here, under the canopy of God, the fiery darts of the enemy cannot reach their mark. The saint that abides under the shadow of authority dwells in dunamis.

If you will abide in the fortress of authority, the power will abide upon you. When dunamis overshadows you, *"You will trample under foot the lion, the adder, and the dragon"* (Psalm 91:13).

You will take up His Word and speak your faith. It will be your confidence and shield. In its presence, every fiery dart will fizzle out and lose power. *"A thousand will fall at your side, ten thousand at your right hand, it shall not come nigh you"* (Psalm 91:17).

Those that rule their jurisdiction well will say, *"No plague shall come near my dwelling"* (Psalm 91:10). These will see the delivering power of God and the enemy will know the authority of their rule.

Victory Under the Shadow

A saint that operates under authority will be covered by the Most High. The shadow of God, which is the anointing, will come upon them. Dunamis will overshadow them.

"Behold a bright cloud overshadowed them" (Matthew 17:5a).

Peter, James, and John saw the cloud come. Under its shadow, they fell under the power and had a revelation. When you operate in your authority, God will see to it that the anointing of God will come upon you.

> **I will set him on high, because he hath known My name. he shall call upon Me, and I will answer him: I will be with him in trouble; I will deliver him, and honour him. With long life will I satisfy him, and shew him my salvation.**
>
> **Psalm 91:14b-16**

Exousia gives you the right to survive when others die. It gives you the right to stay healthy when others get sick. It gives you the right to win when others fail. It gives you the right to move on when others quit, and the right to move up when others move down.

God has given you the right to decide the direction of your life. He made you a sovereign being with the ability to choose between life and death. Don't settle for anything less than God's best!

If you will dwell in the place of authority, you will abide in the place of anointing. You will walk not only in your delegated authority, but you will be overshadowed by power. The only thing that can hinder you are the fiery darts of the enemy. If your shield is lowered, he can hit you in your mind, will and emotions. Therefore, guard your heart. Raise your shield of faith. *Stand in the secret place and allow the power to come.*

The devil will try to interfere with your confidence and short-circuit your anointing. More often than not, he will use people to speak words that are laced with poison. If he can wound you, he can short the anointing on your life. If he can get at your heart, he can interfere with your connection. When a person takes in a fiery dart, they do so because they don't see the consequence. A person that has surrendered to enemy fire is no longer abiding under the shadow. They have given up the shield of their authority.

When you're in the secret place, nothing can find you. Jesus dwelled in the secret place and He could never be pinned down or located. With futility, the Pharisees tried to figure Him out. When you abide under the shadow, you are sheltered within the hidden place of power.

The devil will want to locate you. He wants to move *you* into *his* territory so that you will share common ground. He wants you on his turf so that he may hurt, disappoint, distract, accuse, reject and spread rumors. He wants to slander God's own. If he can pressure you out of the secret place, you will lay down your authority and his fiery dart will pierce your heart.

You have the right to block these things.
You have the right to live ABOVE them.

Use your authority
to keep your ears closed.

Use your authority
to keep your heart blocked.

Use your authority
to keep your eyes stayed on the Word of God.

As you use your authority,
"nothing shall by any means hurt you."

CHAPTER 6

THE POWER OF CONNECTION

*The only limits to your authority
are the limits you impose on yourself.
There is no mountain too big; there is no hill too high.*

While You Were Out

The purpose of authority is to make God's *will* and *resources* accessible to the believer. The benefit of authority is to insure that the Word reaches its goal in the life of those who claim it. Authority will put the Word into motion and power will bring it to pass. The child of God has the privilege to contend for all that God has promised.

> "Lord, have mercy on my son, for he is a lunatic, and sore vexed; for often times he falleth into the fire, and oft into the water. And I brought him to Thy disciples, and they could not cure him." Then Jesus answered and said, "O faithless and perverse generation, how long shall I be with you? How long will I suffer you? Bring him hither to me." And Jesus rebuked the devil, and he departed out of him, and the child was cured from that very hour. Then came the disciples to Jesus apart and said, "Why could not we cast him out?" And Jesus said unto them, "Because of your unbelief, for verily I say unto you, if ye have faith as a grain of mustard seed, ye shall say unto this mountain, remove hence to yonder place, and it shall remove, and nothing shall be impossible unto you. Howbeit this kind goeth

not out but by prayer and fasting."

Matthew 17:15-21

Jesus was walking down the mountain with His disciples. He had just come through a major spiritual experience. The anointing that was in Him had transformed His body. Glory permeated His pores and His face shined with the intensity of the sun. Even His clothing had taken on the brilliance and splendor of light. Peter, James and John had witnessed this visitation and the residue of that experience had left its impression on them. When the glory lifted, He cautioned His disciples to share it with no one until He had risen from the dead.

As they descended the mountain, Jesus saw that a great multitude had surrounded His other disciples. Looking further, He saw some scribes vehemently arguing with them. Immediately, when the multitude saw Jesus, they were amazed and ran to greet Him.

When Jesus had walked into the midst of the crowd, He asked the Scribes, *"What are you talking to them about?"* He wanted to know why the religious leaders were arguing with His students.

Right away, a man pushed through the multitude. Kneeling before Jesus, he desperately pleaded for help.

> **Lord, have mercy on my son: for he is lunatick, and sore vexed: for ofttimes he falleth into the fire, and oft into the water. And I brought him to thy disciples, and they could not cure him.**
>
> **Matthew 17:15-16**

The Scribes were silent. So were the disciples.

The Scribes had obviously seen the disciples fall short of a promise. All the father wanted was deliverance for his son, but the religious leaders took opportunity to cause contention. Jesus answered the situation and said, *"Bring him here to Me."*

How to Handle Pressure

> Then they brought him to Him. And when he saw Him, immediately the spirit convulsed him, and he fell on the ground and wallowed, foaming at the mouth. So He asked his father, "How long has this been happening to him?
>
> **Mark 9:20-21a NKJV**

A believer that is walking in their authority will never allow the devil to pressure them into immediate action. If you feel like you have to do it "right now, this second," there is a good chance that it is not God's leading.

On the eve of His betrayal during the Passover meal, Jesus dipped a piece of bread and handed it to Judas. As soon as he had taken the bread from Jesus' hand, Satan entered him. Jesus' last recorded words to Judas were, *"What you do, do quickly"* (John 13:26-27).

Jesus told Judas to *"do what you have to do quickly"* only because the wrong spirit was in operation. You, however, do not have to be in a hurry to respond to the devil. At times, the devil will bring a symptom into your life or hit you with a contrary circumstance. These are situations that are designed to distract you and to draw your attention away from God's authority. His goal is to captivate your senses so that you would surrender to His influence. Like a traveling circus act, these things are nothing but a passing show.

Remember: If you lose your peace, your authority will not work.

> **And the peace of God, which passeth all understanding, shall keep your hearts and minds through Christ Jesus.**
>
> **Philippians 4:7**

Commanding a Situation

The boy's father told Jesus of all that had taken place in His absence. He said, *"So I brought them to Your disciples, but they could not cure him"* (Matthew 17:16). Upon hearing the situation, Jesus turned to the demon-possessed boy and commanded the devil to come out of him.

> **Then the spirit cried out, convulsed him greatly, and came out of him. And he became as one dead, so many said, "He is dead." But Jesus took him by the hand and lifted him up, and he arose.**
>
> **Mark 9:26-27 NKJV**

It's amazing that some people would wonder if *falling down under the power* is of God. The boy *"became as one dead"* only because the power of God (or dunamis) was supernaturally addressing the situation. For possibly years, the power (or dunamis) of the devil had been working on this child. The Bible records that from childhood this individual was afflicted with seizures and convulsions. The father recounted how oftentimes the devil would throw him into fire or water to destroy him (Mark 9:22). When the child fell to the ground as dead, he was being delivered from all that the devil had tormented him with. He had fallen under the power of God because the dunamis of God was setting him free. Jesus spoke the *authoritative command* and *dunamis power* backed it up.

The power of the devil is no match against the power of God. In the presence of the power of God, the devil can only submit and concede to failure. When an ambassador or an authorized messenger speaks a command, an anointing will immediately go to work to enforce the Word spoken.

Jesus cast out devils with power and authority. Wherever He went, He utilized the power of God to enforce the Word. When He came down from the mountain, after having had a dunamis visitation, He found His disciples arguing with the religious leaders. Jesus had given them authority to cast out devils, yet the disciples had failed in this task. Immediately, Jesus addressed the situation and brought a quick resolution. The boy was instantly delivered and he lay lifeless under the peace of God. Jesus lifted him up and presented him to his father completely free.

After the crowd had cleared and the disciples had come into the house, they privately asked Jesus a question: *"Why could we not cast it out?"*

Jesus' reply was frank and to the point: *"It's because of your unbelief. If you have faith as a mustard seed, you will say to this mountain, 'Move from here to there,' and it will be done; and nothing will be impossible for you. However, this kind does not come out except by fasting and prayer"* (Matthew 17:20-21).

In other words, Jesus was saying that "even this mountain here" is within your realm of jurisdiction. If you need it to move, then you can tell it to move and it will do as you say. The only limits to your authority are the limits you impose on yourself. God is not sovereignly withholding His promises. You have the God-given authority to expect and receive the will and resources of Heaven. There is no mountain too big; there is no hill too high. All things are possible to those who believe.

As a believer, you can grow to a place in God that is more stable and steadfast than any mountain before you. With authority, you will speak and the obstacle will be removed. The answer to their failed efforts with the demon-possessed boy was that they were in unbelief. Their faith had missed the mark.

Little Prayer. Little Power.

"O unbelieving breed of men who have been morally distorted and twisted, how long shall I

be with you? How long shall I bear with you?"

Matthew 17:17 Wuest

Jesus is talking to His disciples and He is upset. He calls them an "unbelieving breed of men." His students probably wished that this rebuke was for the Scribes, but it was not the Scribes who had failed to see the promise into manifestation. The ones that were closest to Him *knew better.*

He gave them authority and then left for a short time. Upon His return, the disciples had drawn a crowd and were debating with the religious leadership. In all probability, His students were defending the delegated authority that they claimed to have. Jesus had given it to them, yet they failed to produce the proof. When Jesus walked in on the situation, He found them in a place of subservience to the religious influence. They were in the underdog position and weakly defending their claims. The quarreling had become a public spectacle and was only aggravating the situation. Jesus was not very happy.

When the devil is controlling a situation, it is only because men and women have become *morally distorted.* Religion may present itself with sobriety and reservation, but it is nothing but a distortion of the truth. In the sight of God, it is a grave immorality when the devil is allowed to do the teaching. It is twisted when the enemy is attacking and the Church is merely holding the fort. The Gospel works, and if it does not, it is because someone's authority has failed to operate. Somehow, somewhere, there was a short in their connection with God.

It is like the police officer. They patrolled a certain neighborhood and witnessed a crime. Jumping out from their car, they yelled, *"Stop! You're under arrest!"* The criminal, seeing that this person was unarmed, chased the officer down and beat him up.

What happened?
Where was the gun?

"Oh, I didn't feel like carrying it that day."

The badge is not enough. The authority is not enough. You need the gun. Always remember, your authority is not dependent upon what you feel. It is not dependent upon what you hear in the natural. God's Word remains unmoved in the face of feelings, fears and circumstances. If you will embrace your rights, you will remain unmoved as well.

THINK the Word. TALK the Word.
WALK the Word.

Dunamis is what brings results in the battlefield. The level of power in your life is directly proportionally to how you talk, what you think about, who you spend time with, and how you spend your days.

Remember:

Much prayer. Much power.
Little prayer. Little power.

Connection and Communication

Howbeit this kind goeth not out but by prayer and fasting.

Matthew 17:21

This was a different kind of devil. The disciples had cast out other devils with success, but for some reason, this one was different. It required a greater degree of power. Today, some people might say, *"Well, I just believe that the Lord didn't want the boy free yet."* They would take their *failure* and *justify it* with incorrect doctrine. This was the position the disciples were in. They had experienced success before, but didn't know how to explain the failure at hand.

The disciples took Jesus aside and asked, *"Why could we not cast it out?"* They knew that there had to be a reason, and given the "unbelieving breed of men" rebuke in front of the multitude, they were probably eager to bring resolution to the situation. Sometimes, without a rebuke, correction does not take place.

In the privacy of the house, Jesus talked to His disciples about unbelief, having "faith as a mustard seed" and the mountain that must move. When He was finished, He added, *"This one does not come out except by fasting and prayer."*

Prayer is the vehicle that draws you near to God. Within in it, is the power of *connection* and *communication*. Prayer will increase the anointing or the dunamis on a believer's life. Fasting, however, is something that is done when someone is pressing into God.

The person who pursues a life of prayer moves closer to God. Those who walk closely with the Lord are never without access to His will and resources. The soil of their heart has been made ready, their spirit is primed, and they are receptive to the voice of God. They are in synch with the wisdom of the Word and the leading of the Spirit.

Paying the Price: Bread for the Day

So then faith cometh by hearing, and hearing by the Word of God.

Romans 10:17

Faith is the hearer's response to the Word of God. When a person hears the Word, faith will arise in their heart. That faith will then lead the believer to *act* in absolute confidence of the Word heard. Faith always produces an action to its conviction.

Dunamis is the power that backs up the action of faith. It is the firepower behind the authority. The strength of dunamis is founded upon the foundation of prayer. Those who walk closely with God will have confidence in their connection with Him.

Draw near to God and He will draw near to you.

> **But He answered and said, "It is written, Man shall not live by bread alone, but by every Word that proceedeth out of the mouth of God."**
>
> **Matthew 4:4**

The saint cannot live on "yesterday's manna" today. They cannot live on *yesterday's* Word or on *yesterday's* prayers or on *yesterday's* God encounter. The yesterdays have come and gone and are now relegated to memories. What transpired *then*, should not feed you *now*.

For each day, there is a fresh Word and a fresh anointing. Don't live off of a Word from days gone by or prayers from ages past. Draw near to God *today*. Delve into His Word and feed on His promises. Drink of His rivers and delight yourself in Him. There is neither famine nor stagnancy in God.

Jesus came down from the mountain. A crowd had gathered. The disciples were arguing. A demon-possessed person was flailing about. The father of the child was distressed. The scribes were reveling in the moment. The disciples were cowering in defeat and contention was thick in the air. Jesus quickly took command of the situation, rebuked the disciples and then cast the devil out. When all had been said and done, the disciples approached Jesus privately and asked, *"Why couldn't we cast out the devil?"*

Jesus said to them, *"Listen, your faith didn't work because you are trying to live off of yesterday's Word and yesterday's anointing. Now as a result, TODAY, you were not walking in the Spirit. You did not draw near to God in prayer and fasting and because of this, you were unprepared to deal with the situation."* Jesus continued, *"The devil I dealt with today was stubborn. This kind does not bow its knees to your badge, but it needs to see a loaded gun in your life. The devil won't come out just because you served God one day, read a chapter the other day or walked in the Spirit last week. This kind will only come out by fasting and prayer. You need to walk close with God TODAY in order to be recharged with the dunamis TODAY. If you had done this and then exercised your exousia against the devil, the dunamis would have been present to enforce your command."*

Jesus utilized the anointing upon His earthly ministry in order to set the demon-possessed person free. His disciples had fallen short of enforcing deliverance because they were walking in the flesh. Having had success on previous occasions, they became lackadaisical in their walk with God. Distractions mellowed out their spiritual tenacity.

God is not impressed with our history.

TODAY is the day that the Lord has made. Yesterday is in the past, but today is in the present. The Lord does not want the believer to walk in yesterday's victory, nor does He want the believer to live off of yesterday's bread. There is fresh victory and fresh bread for everyday.

Be committed **TODAY**.
Be anointed **TODAY**.
Contend for His presence **TODAY**.
Connect in prayer **TODAY**.

This kind does not come out except by fasting and prayer (Matthew 17:21). Only dunamis can force compliance into a situation like this. Although dunamis power is freely given to those who seek, it is not given haphazardly. There is a price to pay. That price comes through fellowship, prayer, fasting, praise, worship and simply drawing near to God. When you dwell within the shadow of the Almighty, you abide in the power of the anointing. In that place, the peace and the power of His presence will begin to operate in your life.

Be everything that God has called you to be. Resist the devil and what he throws your way. Do not let him disappoint you, rob you or lie to you. You are called to be a miracle worker, and the devil is nothing more than a smooth-talking liar, peddling his ungodly wares. He has been a liar from the beginning and there is no truth in him. You are growing in God, and that in itself is priceless and beyond comparison.

> Keep moving forward.
> Keep pressing in to be bigger
> and stronger in the Lord.
>
> **And let us not grow weary while doing good, for in due season we shall reap if we do not lose heart.**
>
> **Galatians 6:9 NKJV**

Command Ye Me

> **Thus saith the Lord, the Holy One of Israel and his Maker, "Ask Me of things to come concerning My sons, and concerning the work of My hands, COMMAND ye Me."**
>
> **Isaiah 45:11**

The word "command" in the Hebrew means:

- Command
- Constitute
- Enjoin
- Appoint
- Charge

In the Scripture above, the Lord is saying, *"Find out the way I really made you and then YOU command Me about it."* How does one command God? *"Enjoin to Me. Charge Me in that situation. Appoint Me in that circumstance."*

God means business. Through His Word, He has given the believer the right to command and enforce His Word. He has already given the promises, but He is seeking sons that will make those promises their own. To do so, each believer must command the Word with authority

Dr. Robin & Dr. Christian Harfouche with Dr. Lester Sumrall.

Orlando Campmeeting.

City Harvest Church in Singapore.

Dr. Robin & Dr. Christian Harfouche
with Dr. Morris Cerullo.

Dr. Harfouche returning with Dr. Morris Cerullo from an awesome series of meetings in Latin America.

Dr. Robin ministering an Altar Call in Singapore.

The deaf hear in Asia.

Dr. Robin shares her testimony.

Dr. Harfouche on the set of Miracles Today.

Altar Call in Kuala Lumpur, Malaysia.

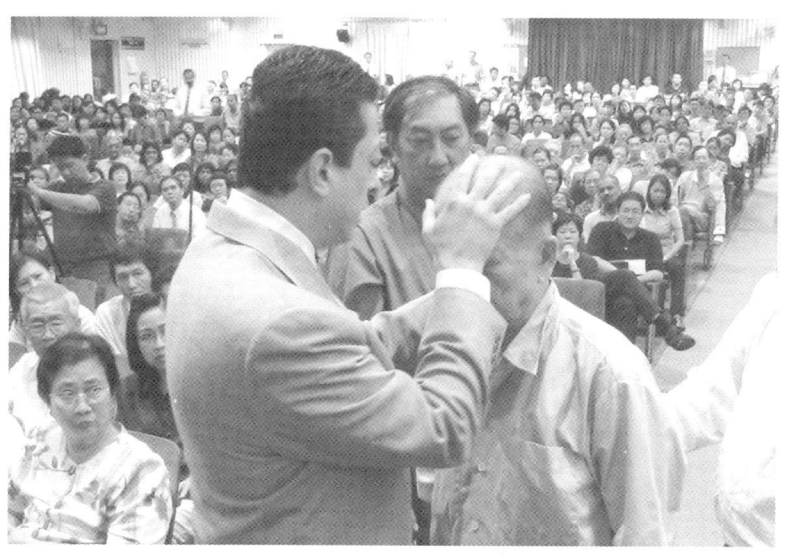

Dr. Harfouche ministering in Malaysia.

Dr. John Avanzini ministering on the set of Miracles Today.

Dr. Christian Harfouche with Dr. Norvel Hayes.

The sick are healed during New England Miracle Crusades.

More miracles in New England.

The deaf hear at a campmeeting in Tampa, Florida.

Dr. Christian & Dr. Robin Harfouche
ministering in the prophetic.

Dr. Robin asking Dr. Christian questions during the closing portion of the show.

School of Acts in Malaysia.

Dr. Christian & Dr. Robin while ministering in Africa.

School of Signs & Wonders, Italy.

Dr. Harfouche ministering during a School of Signs & Wonders in Italy.

Thousands ministered to in Indonesia.

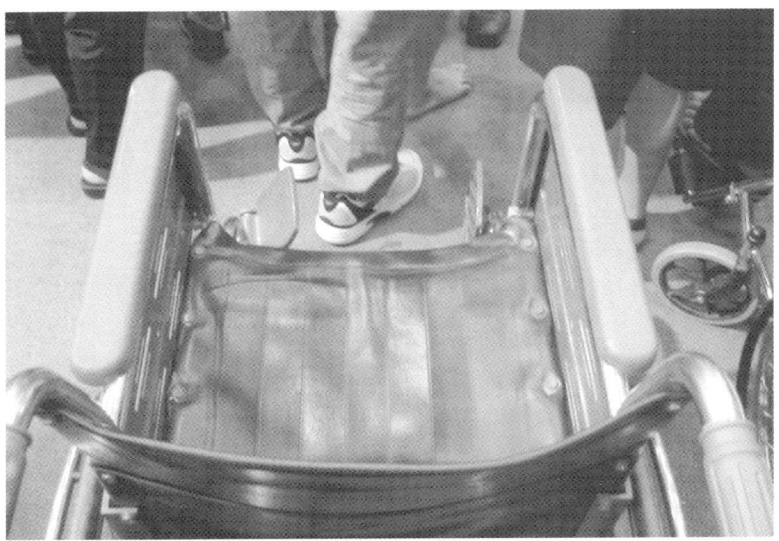

The wheelchairs were emptied in Indonesia.

Mass crusades in Latin America.

"Victory."

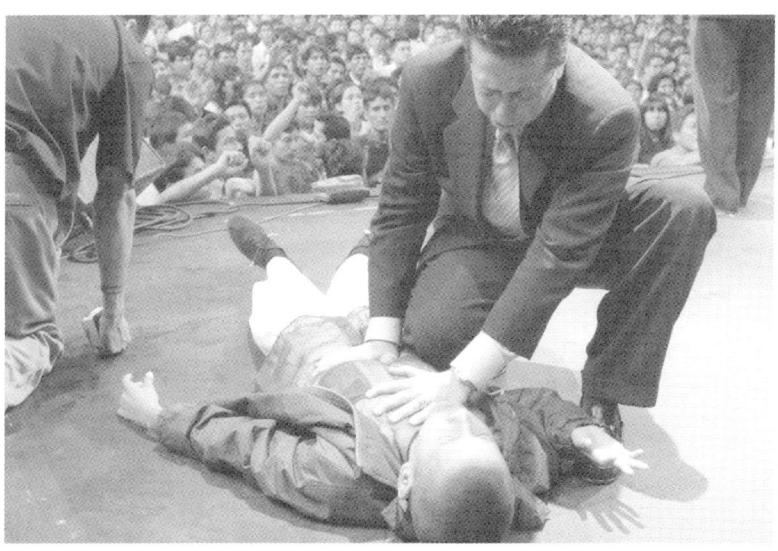

The sick are ministered to in Latin America.

Dr. Harfouche ministering in Trinidad.

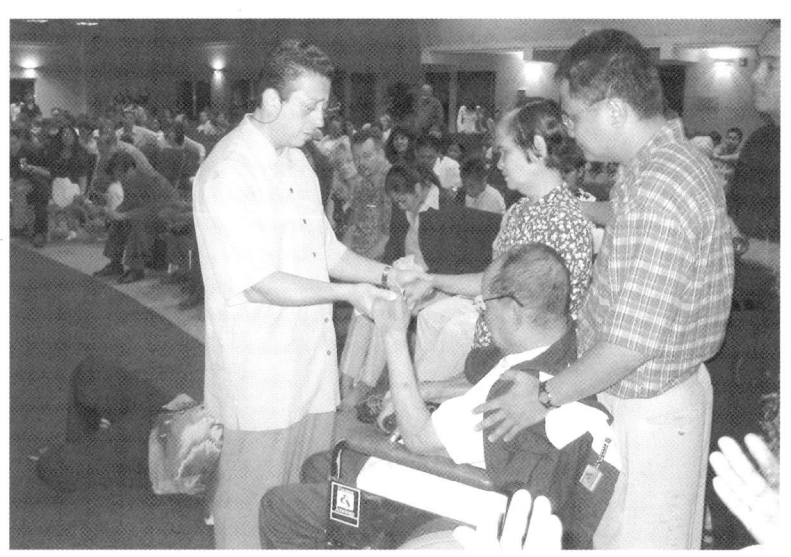

The lame walk in Guam.

Dr. Harfouche ministering with Reverend R.W. Schambach on the set of Miracles Today.

and power.

"Ask Me of things to come concerning My sons."

Sons are those who are mature. They have taken the Word of God and made it the rehearsal of their heart. They invest time in prayer and in communion with the Holy Ghost. These are those that refuse the works of darkness, uphold righteousness and rule their realm. Sons say, *"Take your hands off my children."* They say, *"Stop, you cannot have this city."* They are people of authority, obedience and power. They are men and women that know who they are in Christ Jesus and where He is taking them.

Say this out loud:

> *Power of God, I know who the sons of God are. I know that they are not immature or double-minded. Right now, I declare, I decree, I appoint and I charge the power of God to reach my life. See to it that I have the power necessary to be transformed into the image of His dear Son."*

Working the Works of God

On a certain day, Jesus and His disciples passed a blind man. Stopping in front of him, the disciples asked their Teacher, *"Who sinned, this man or his parents, that he was born blind."*

> **Jesus answered, "Neither hath this man sinned, nor his parents: but that the works of God should be made manifest in him."**
>
> **John 9:3**

What are the works of God?

The works of God are those things that Jesus had commanded the

Church to do in His stead. If He were still walking the planet, He would open blind eyes, heal the sick, deliver the oppressed and preach the Gospel of the Kingdom. Jesus, however, has delegated these works to the believer. It is the job description of the saint to *work the works of God*.

The works of God are miraculous and each requires the power of God. Although the believer has been clearly commissioned with authority, it takes more than the badge or the position to produce a miracle. Only power can open a blind eye. Only power can eject a devil. Only power can repel darkness. It takes dunamis power or the anointing of God to *work the works*.

Therefore, use your authority to come boldly before the throne of grace. Ask of God, command Him concerning His promises. Say, *"God, I am not here to beg. I am not here to wonder. I do not have a double mind. Rather, I am here because I know that the blood of Jesus has given me the right to stand here. I draw on and declare every ounce of anointing that I need to do what You have called me to do. I charge this situation with the dunamis of God."*

Act on your authority. Unless you harness the power available, it cannot benefit you. This is the difference between a prevailing Christian and one who never goes anywhere in God: The prevailing Christian took the power available and harnessed it, used it, and expected certain things from it. The other said, *"Well, whatever will be will be."*

Someone once told me that the Chinese were the first to invent gunpowder. They created it, yet they couldn't find a suitable use for it except in the form of fireworks. Later, someone came up with the idea of loading it into a projectile and firing it. The firepower was always there, but it took a revelation to employ its use in the cannon and the gun.

In the same way, the dunamis is here. It's not far off. It's not beyond your reach. It's not even on a high shelf reserved for the elite. *You are the elite.* You have been chosen and commissioned by God to bear His name and to work His works. The strength behind this mission is the dunamis of God. It is the power that will enable you to reach your goal and to enforce the integrity of the Word. Dunamis is the dynamite of Heaven.

God wants you to harness His power, channel it, and decree where it should to go. Do not say, *"If God wants to bless me, He knows my address."* Rather, act on what you have been taught! Take the power and through your authority, harness it, decree it, and enforce the promise. Use it so that it can impact your life and produce the expectation of your faith.

Pressing into the Power

> Now a certain woman had a flow of blood for twelve years and had suffered many things from many physicians. She had spent all that she had and was no better, but rather grew worse. When she heard about Jesus, she came behind Him in the crowd and touched His garment; for she said, "If only I may touch His clothes, I shall be made well." Immediately the fountain of her blood was dried up, and she felt in her body that she was healed of the affliction. And Jesus immediately knowing in Himself that power had gone out of Him, turned around in the crowd and said, "Who touched My clothes?"
>
> **Mark 5:25-30 NKJV**

For 12 years, the woman had suffered. She spent all of her money seeking a cure, but the doctors could not help her. Her condition did not get better, but rather, only grew worse. In the natural, because of the nature of her sickness, she did not have the right or the authority to go out in public and hunt Jesus down. However, she violated religious protocol and made her way to Jesus. The Bible says that great multitudes followed Jesus and thronged Him (Mark 5:24b). Pushing through the masses, she contended for her miracle. In her heart she said, *"If only I may touch His clothes, I shall be made well."* After pushing through the multitude, she came up behind Jesus and touched His garment.

"Immediately the fountain of her blood was dried up..."

Although she had broken the rules of religious tradition, it was within her spiritual jurisdiction to seek out Jesus and to receive deliverance from her affliction.

Whenever you hear the Word of God, it is within your authority to decide your response to that Word. The woman heard the Word and had a choice to make. She could have remained passive and not touched Him or she could have pressed in as she did. The hearing of the Word always necessitates a decision.

Action is a decision, but then, *so is inaction.*

The moment you hear the promise and receive it, you receive the legal right or the jurisdiction to go after it. The woman heard about Jesus and she began to move people out of the way. It was within her authority realm. It was her decision to go after the Word of God, to go after Jesus. When she touched the hem of His garment, the dunamis answered the expectation of her faith.

"And Jesus immediately knowing in Himself that POWER had gone out of Him..."

It is your legal right to decide what happens after you touch God. No one coerced the woman to touch Jesus. The hearing of faith had put the promise into her jurisdiction. When she heard of Him, faith rose in her heart and she went after the promise. She made up her mind to press into power.

The woman operated on exousia. She operated in faith on a decision she had made in her heart. When she touched Him, Jesus perceived that virtue (or dunamis) went out of Him. Authority accesses power. The woman knew how to conduct transactions with God.

Power was available because Jesus was a Man of prayer. His batteries were charged and He was primed with dunamis. When she touched Him, a transaction took place.

Jesus could have slacked in His prayer time. After all, He did have a demanding schedule and throngs were continually following Him. He could have cut down on His intensity, but He did not. He did not leave the realm of prayer.

When Jesus received the anointing at thirty, He never left it or neglected it. He lived on the Word of God and walked in the Spirit, never forsaking His connection with the Holy Ghost.

Lighting Your Lamp

> You are the light of the world. A city that is set on a hill cannot be hidden. Nor do they light a lamp and put it under a bushel, but on a lamp stand.
>
> **Matthew 5:14-15 NKJV**

In the Church, sometimes the lights go out. The person was shining. They were glowing with the glory of God, but then something happened. Weary in well doing, they tapered off on the diligence of prayer, fasting, and the Word of God. Slowly, they walked away from the Presence. Instead of walking in the Spirit, they ended up in the flesh. They got off course and their lamp went out.

The only reason virtue came out of Jesus was because virtue was in Him. The only reason the power of God comes through you is because you have been with the Lord. When you abide in the anointing, the presence and the power of God will undergird you.

In the account of the woman with the issue of blood, her exousia connected her to His dunamis. This is also a pattern for prayer. As you are obedient in exercising your authority to pray and to meditate on the Word, the Holy Ghost will pour His power into your life. Remember, authority is only as strong as the power behind it. God has given you unlimited access to the throne of grace, but only you can decide if you will walk in the Spirit or get sidetracked in the flesh.

The Word of God is faithful and trustworthy. You cannot employ your exousia and meditate on the Word long, before your obedience is rewarded with the outflow of His power. As you begin to *work your authority* in obedience to the Word, the energy, vitality and anointing of God will move on your behalf. If exousia is the switch, then dunamis is the current that activates the lamp. When your exousia and His dunamis are united, it is as if there is a live wire present. This energy will cause the affliction to go, the tumor to dissolve, the fear to leave and the flaw to be erased. The anointing that you hook into will answer your situation.

Your schedule may not permit you to pray for an hour, but you can still walk in the Spirit. If you will maintain your connection with the Holy Ghost, your authority will stay connected to the power source. When you need to draw on that power, it will be there to supply. Your gun will be loaded and you will be ever ready to pull the trigger on the enemy.

> **And Jesus, immediately knowing in Himself that power had gone out of Him, turned around in the crowd and said, "Who touched My clothes?**
>
> **Mark 5:30 NKJV**

When the woman with the issue of blood touched Jesus, He literally felt power go out from His body. He recognized in the Holy Ghost that virtue had gone out of Him and addressed a situation. Likewise, the woman knew in her body that the virtue of God had healed her. The Bible records, *"She felt in her body that she was healed of the affliction"* (Mark 5:29). The dunamis can affect your life physically.

When you are overwhelmed or tired, get in the anointing. It will quicken you. It will make your mortal body alive and will charge you with the life of God.

"Who touched My clothes?"

Throngs of people were following Jesus and pressing to get near him. At any given time, any number of them could have touched Jesus or brushed against His clothing. Yet, there was one *touch* that was different. It harnessed and drew on the anointing that was in Him. Immediately turning around, Jesus said, *"Who touched My clothes?"* Given the circumstances and the great crowd, the question seemed a bit far-flung. Peter quickly answered, *"The multitudes throng and press you and you say, 'Who touched Me?'"* In other words, Peter was saying, "What in the world are You talking about, everyone is touching you!" A person that is walking in the natural cannot relate to the one who is walking in the spirit.

> But Jesus said, "Somebody touched Me, for I perceived power going out from Me." Now when the woman saw that she was not hidden, she came trembling; and falling down before Him, she declared to Him in the presence of all the people the reason she had touched Him and how she was healed immediately. And He said to her, "Daughter, be of good cheer; your faith has made you well. Go in peace.
>
> **Luke 8:46-48 NKJV**

Jesus has given the believer the authority to have faith. He said to the woman, *"Your faith has made you well."* The woman's faith connected her to His dunamis. It was the catalyst that drew on the supply of Heaven.

Your authority will lead you to miracle-working power. If you will stay plugged in, the current of your faith will connect with the dunamis of God. Once you have received your breakthrough, use that same authority to guard your jurisdiction. Do not let the devil steal your miracle, but keep what you have received. Remember, not only are you *made whole* through exousia, but you also *stay whole* through exousia.

Chapter 7

Power in the Name

*There is no limit to your potential in God.
Glass ceilings do not exist in the Kingdom.*

Crossroads of Revelation

Those who have a strong foundation on the Word of God can never be shaken. A foundation based upon opinion, religion or tradition will surely wash away in the presence of rain. A foundation built upon the Word, however, will outlast the test of time. All authority is based upon the Word of God and is delegated through the name of Jesus. In the same way that an ambassador receives authorization through a higher power, the believer has received authorization through Jesus. His name is the signer on the privileges that every believer has been given.

> **My people are destroyed for lack of knowledge: because thou hast rejected knowledge, I will also reject thee, that thou shalt be no priest to me: seeing thou hast forgotten the law of thy God, I will also forget thy children.**
>
> **Hosea 4:6**

God has supplied His authority and power to every saint. Each one has been given the delegated ability to act on behalf of the name of Jesus. If there is a shortage or lack of performance, it is not at God's end, but at man's end. Somewhere along the line, something derailed the believer's experience. In most cases, this derailment happens just before the crossroad of revelation. God's Word is very clear that people perish for a lack of knowledge.

There is integrity in the Word of God and the good news to every believer is that the Holy Ghost *has been sent.* He has been sent to lead the child of God into the experience of all truth and triumph. Equipped with Heaven's ability, the Holy Ghost will teach and reveal the Word of God.

The child of God is not called to live in the dark. Revelation knowledge is available and accessible to those who will place a demand on it. Through the Word of God and the leading of the Spirit, each can participate in divine understanding. The Word of God is complete and there is no reason for the believer to suffer from a lack of knowledge.

Allow the name of Jesus to have its way in your life. The days ahead carry opportunity for those who will search the Word and discover their divine rights.

The Better Day

> **...for he that cometh to God must believe that He is, and that He is a rewarder of them that diligently seek Him.**
>
> **Hebrews 11:6b**

Rewards are for those who diligently seek God. A person diligently seeks through the pursuit of truth. It's a pursuit of revelation into the Word of God. Sometimes, a certain event may transpire which seems to contradict God's promises. That situation may declare, *"You see, God is not going to supply." "You are not healed." "You are not saved."*

Whatever the situation may be saying, the diligent one must remain anchored and steadfast on the Word of truth. They must believe God's promise and make a decision to reject the influence of circumstance, opinion and report. They must refuse and shut their ears to the thing that violates the integrity of the Word. Even then, the saint's patient endurance and steadfastness may not be enough if a renegade spirit is involved. Just because a believer has been versed in their rights, does not mean a devil has to leave. If the believer does not know the power of the Name, they may be pressured right out of the will of God.

As you continue in this chapter, the Holy Ghost will reveal and expand on the power of the Name. Your understanding of this principle will put the devil on the run. When you know what has been invested in you, you will never accept anything less than what is rightfully yours.

> **And in that day you will ask Me nothing. Most assuredly, I say to you, whatever you ask the Father in My name He will give you. Until now you have asked nothing in My name. Ask, and you will receive, that your joy may be full.**
>
> **John 16:23-24 NKJV**

Jesus told His disciples, *"Up until now you have been asking Me. When you had a need, you asked Me personally. You are putting My anointing to work in your life because I am physically present with you. However, the day is going to come when you won't ask Me personally. You won't ask Me to undertake. You won't ask Me to interrupt or interfere. You won't ask Me to step in, but you will ask the Father in My name."*

Up until this moment, the disciples had not asked for anything *in the name* of Jesus. His name had not been made available to them. The disciples knew, however, that when they were with Him, they did not lack for provision. When they walked within the context of Christ's authority, they had all of their needs met, yet the Lord said there was a *better* day coming.

"There is a BETTER DAY for you than that which you have experienced. You went out seventy, two by two, and you saw the demon spirits subject to you in My name. I sent you by My authority. Now you will not ask of Me, but you will ask of My Father in My stead."

Through instruction in the Word of God, you are learning how to put faith to work. As revelation dawns in the horizon of your heart, you will see and know how to take the limits off God. Your eyes will see the vastness of His provision and understanding will swell from within. Remember, the only limits in your walk with God are the ones you allow.

As a soldier in the army of the Lord, you have been appointed to prevail. You have been called to the good fight of faith. This good fight does not take place on the devil's territory or use his methods of warfare. Rather, you have been commanded to fight according to the blueprint of God's Word. That blueprint can never fail.

Receiving Power of Attorney

E.W. Kenyon was teaching one afternoon on the name of Jesus and a lawyer interrupted him, asking, *"Do you mean to say that Jesus gave us the power of attorney or the legal right to use His name?"* Intrigued, Kenyon replied, *"Brother, you are a lawyer and I am a layman. Tell me, did Jesus give the Church the power of attorney?"* The lawyer answered, *"If language means anything, then Jesus gave the Church the power of attorney."* Kenyon inquired further, *"What is the value of the power of attorney?"* The lawyer answered, *"It depends on how much there is behind the name, on how much authority and power this name represents."*

This interaction sent Kenyon on a quest to research how much authority Jesus had.

The power of attorney is a legal authorization for one to act in another's stead. It is when an individual, such as an owner of an estate, turns over the administration of the estate, their business, their wealth and all of their assets to a representative to run on their behalf. That individual represents and manages their interests.

The power of attorney is a legally binding authorization. Both individuals must go through legal channels to make the representative's signature just as valid as the estate holder's signature. In the end, the representative will have full authority over everything that belongs to the estate holder.

When Jesus gave you His name, He gave you the power of attorney over all of His will and resources. Within the Word of God, He established this authorization as if it were a legally binding document. There is integrity in the Word and God cannot, and will not, retract His Word. He has given the Church power of attorney so that the child of God might have, through faith, confidence to represent the interests of the Kingdom with unwavering conviction. Your work on behalf of Christ is endorsed by the strength and power of the Son of God.

It's as if someone signed a check and handed it to you blank. You could write any figure on that check as long as the resources behind it could support its face value. However, it wouldn't do you any good to write a check for one million if there was not one million in the checking account. The signature is only as good as the resources behind it. To have a signed check and not know the resources available would prove unprofitable.

When Jesus gave the Church the Great Commission, He did not place limits upon the children of the Kingdom. In fact, He has given the believer a blank check and access to all of His resources. The believer can go all the way in God, for the name of Jesus is backed by all the power of Heaven. His name has been made available to the Church to represent His interests on this Earth.

Embrace the Name. *Work the Name in your life.* When you do, the power that is behind it will be made available to you. If you knew what was yours, you would look to the Word and not anywhere else.

When you put the Name to work, you will see results. As an acting representative of the Kingdom, you have been entrusted with the name of the King. You bear the seal and signet of His authority.

The More You Know, The More You Grow

God has given the Church the power of attorney. While it is true that the believer holds jurisdiction over Kingdom interest, this legal right will not benefit them unless faith has come through the Word of God. Some people talk of big jurisdiction, but they do not walk the walk. Others have faith, but it never profits them because it is not released. The Bible says that faith without works is dead (James 2:26). In other words, faith is released through action. Sometimes a person will not act on the Word on account of past failures. Perhaps they tried to raise someone from the dead and failed. They heard the Word and their faith was on "headache level," but instead of acting on the faith they had, they moved into presumption and got hurt. When they saw their good intentions come to naught, they gave up on faith.

The saint must exercise the faith they have, not the faith they don't have. If they will work what they have, they will grow into greater measures of faith. Like an athlete in training, if the Christian will exercise their faith where it is, they will grow to a place where their *faith capacity* has been increased.

There is no limit to your potential in God.
Glass ceilings do not exist in the Kingdom.

As long as you are willing to hear the Word and obey, you will continue to receive further revelation. Revelation is what gives faith its confidence. It is also the active ingredient in *every* realm of greater faith. When a believer moves from *faith* to *faith*, it is only because they have moved from *revelation* to *revelation*. Revelation is the source of all growth and advancement in the Kingdom. The more you know, the more you grow, and to whom much is given, much is also required (Luke 12:48).

Prayers That Don't Bounce

There is power behind the Name. In natural law, the power is called *the balance*. It is the balance in the bank account. It is what backs up the check. In the Spirit, power backs the believer. It is the heavenly reserve that substantiates the believer's claims to authority. This is precisely why the devil has to obey. God does not only give the saint jurisdiction, but He has given the saint power to back up the jurisdiction. In other words, the saint's words are not empty. There is power behind the authority.

When a religious person prays and fails to receive an answer, their lack of revelation may force them to justify their experience with incorrect doctrine. Having failed the test of life, they walk blindly, speaking of things they don't know. Jesus' prayers, however, always reached the ears of His Father. He did not pray one prayer that bounced back into the earth realm. *Jesus got results.*

> **And in that day you will ask Me nothing. Most assuredly, I say to you, whatever you ask the Father in My name He will give you. Until now you have asked nothing in My name. Ask, and you will receive, that your joy may be full.**
>
> **John 16:23-24 NKJV**

Judas had left to betray His Teacher, leaving Jesus and the remaining disciples to enjoy one last Passover meal together. It was during these last moments on Earth that Jesus left His students with some final instructions on prayer.

The Lord said to His disciples, *"Until now you have not had the opportunity to pray this way. You have been asking Me. I have been with you and I have done miracles in your midst. Now, you have the Name. Now, you have the power of attorney. Ask and you will receive so that your joy may be full."*

Jesus was teaching the disciples to pray using His name.

The ambassador of Christ should boldly come before the throne, saying, *"I am here by the Spirit of Christ crying, 'Abba, Father.' In the Name that is above every name, I am claiming my legal rights. I am coming boldly to the throne of Grace. As I come, I will not wonder what His will is because I know His Word. The Word is living in me and I am living in the Word. My Father always hears my prayers and my joy is full."*

This kind of person is able to boldly confess, *"My prayers are always answered."* They know their rights. They know their Word and they are confident in His performance. There is no question as to His willingness.

Bearing the Name

"Whatever you ask in My name…"

It is not *"for Jesus' sake,"* but it is *"in Jesus' name."* Jesus doesn't need the healing, He is the Healer. Those who pray *"for His sake,"* do not know His Word. Nobody has taught them the Word so that they might grow in the strength of revelation and faith.

God has administered, endowed, and given the name of Jesus to the Body of Christ. If the head is called Jesus, then the body is also a part of Jesus. If the Spirit of Jesus is the one flowing in you, then as you approach God, Christ *in you* is praying *through you*. If your prayers are based upon the authority of God, you will receive that your joy might be full.

You do not *get* joy unless you *receive* joy. People lose their joy because they believe that God is sovereignly withholding the answer. Meanwhile, the devil is working overtime to keep those same people in the dark and without revelation. If a person truly understood their authority, they would do more in two years than the average person does in a lifetime.

If a person asks God in faith, He will grant them exactly what they have prayed for. If they ask for wisdom, they will get wisdom. Not only that, but those who receive wisdom will experience the fullness of joy. The person who receives from God rejoices in God. Their joy is full.

Those that know the meaning *behind* the Name, will call on the power vested *in* the Name. It's not a religious term or a play on semantics. Rather, there is a literal force behind the Name. Jesus gave you His name so that you can operate on His behalf. That means you don't have to wrestle the demon-possessed person or hope for the best when you pray. Like Jesus, you can walk in unwavering confidence and conviction. You too, will be able to say, *"My father always hears my prayers"* (John 11:42).

There is power behind the Name. When you have a revelation of the authority and jurisdiction that God has invested in the name of Jesus, you will use His name in prayer, in dealing with demons, and in ministering healing.

Using the Name in prayer does *not* involve trial and error. It's not hit and miss. It's not sporadic and it's not intermittent. Rather, the name of Jesus is what seals and secures your petition. When you approach the throne, bearing the name of Jesus, you are granted *immediate audience*. The Father Himself will hear your petition. Jesus said, *"Whatever you ask the Father in My name He will give you."* You can have confidence before the throne of God.

> **"No weapon that is formed against thee shall prosper; and every tongue that shall rise against thee in judgment thou shalt condemn. This is the heritage of the servants of the LORD, and their righteousness is of Me," saith the LORD.**
>
> **Isaiah 54:17**

The name of Jesus is the authority, the power, the security, the assurance, and the enforcement that puts demonic spirits on an inferior plane. The devil may fight the power of the Name, but his efforts will be brought to naught in the lives of those with understanding. Those that bear the Name with confidence will see their prayers prevail. They will witness the failure and catastrophic defeat of every ungodly force launched against them.

This is the heritage of the servants of the Lord.

The name of Jesus is all-powerful, however, His name will not work to enforce a petition that is unbiblical. The power that undergirds the saint's prayers finds its source in the Word of God. If the substance of a prayer doesn't carry the breath of Heaven, it cannot access the promise or the performance. *God's Word is truth.*

Bold as a Lion

> **Whereby are given unto us exceeding great and precious promises: that by these ye might be partakers of the divine nature, having escaped the corruption that is in the world through lust.**
>
> **2 Peter 1:4**

When you were born again, the Holy Ghost came into your heart and filled you with the nature of your Father. You were created in the image of Jesus Christ. As a partaker in the divine nature, *His nature* has become *your nature* and your *new nature*, *His nature*. The very fabric of your being has been woven into the heart of God. It is through this that you have been given access to every great and precious promise. There is nothing that God has *freely promised* that He will not *freely give*.

> **As newborn babes, desire the sincere milk of the Word, that ye may grow thereby.**
>
> **1 Peter 2:2**

Since the child of God has been given such great promises, it is imperative that they partake of the Word. A promise hidden cannot benefit the believer. It is only the promises known that can affect change and growth in God. The believer, therefore, must pursue the Word like a babe desiring milk. Just as milk is able to nourish the child, so will the Word of God nourish and grow up a saint. God knows how to grow a child into a son.

A son knows the Word, contends for the Word, and is fearless in the face of opposition.

> **The wicked flee when no man pursueth: but the righteous are bold as a lion.**
>
> **Proverbs 28:1**

The name of Jesus carries the authority of the Son of God. Those who use the Name, access both power and provision. The Name, however, will not endorse a petition that is unbiblical, nor will it work in the presence of unbelief or fear. In the same way that an apple orchard requires favorable conditions for harvest, the Word of God in the soil of one's heart must be nurtured. A seed that is watered by fear or frozen by unbelief will wither.

The righteous are as bold and fearless as a lion. They, through the name of Jesus, have authority to resist the devil. These walk in unfettered boldness, despising even the hint of fear. While the wicked flee, the righteous stand, upholding the name of Jesus and the integrity of the Word of God.

> **Submit yourselves therefore to God. Resist the devil, and he will flee from you.**
>
> **James 4:7**

Be persuaded by the Word. Do not allow the Word to be demoted to a place of opinion in your life. Hold the Word high as a banner and be sober and vigilant. Those that remain sober in God will be prepared to meet the challenges of life. They will not be caught off guard, but rather, in the face of opposition, they will rise up with the Word in their heart and the Word in their mouth. With understanding and fearless expectation, they will defeat every adversary.

> Be sober, be vigilant; because your adversary the devil, as a roaring lion, walketh about, seeking whom he may devour:
>
> 1 Peter 5:8

Benchmarking Dominion
The Sky is the Limit!

Through prayer, the believer can expect to receive the same results that Jesus received while walking this Earth. His results were not intended to be unique to the Son of God, but rather, they were accomplished so that the believer would have an example. Jesus set the benchmark for the believer to aspire to He set the standard and told the saint to pursue the "greater works." In other words, with the Name, the sky is the limit!

Even if you are not participating in the fullness of this promise yet, you can still walk in the 60-fold or the 30-fold. If 60% of your petitions were answered, you would be doing pretty well! If 30% of your petitions were answered, you would have fullness of joy!

In the same way that a general of a great army commands subordinates, so does the Word of God *command*. When the Word speaks, there are no other options except compliance. The Word carries authoritative power. When Jesus spoke to a situation, it had to obey. When He spoke to the fig tree and said, "*No man eat fruit of thee hereafter for ever,*" the tree had to comply (Mark 11:14). When Jesus spoke to the paraplegic and said, "*I say unto thee, arise, and take up thy bed, and go thy way unto thine house,*" the paralysis had to leave (Mark 2:11). An authoritative command in the name of Jesus necessitates obedience. There is power in the Name and those who *bear the Name*, will get Name results.

It is not you. It is Christ in you. When a situation requires the power of His name, you will say, *"I do not come to you in my name. I come to you in the name of the King of Kings and the Lord of Lords and I know I have been sent."* Those who are sent, bear the seal of His authority. This seal, *this authority*, can only come from a revelation of the Word of God.

The saint that ejects devils must do so biblically. They must do it through the authority of the Word and the power of the Name. As the saint *works their revelation* of the Word, the power of God will enforce their spoken decree and the devil will have to leave. He knows, firsthand, the power of the Name and those who bear the seal of the King.

During one of our crusades in North America, a woman suddenly began foaming at the mouth and slithering around the floor like a snake. As this display was taking place, a man, getting up from the front row, placed a Bible next to her and then sat down again.

Placing a Bible next to a demoniac will not get them delivered any faster! Neither will holy water or olive oil from Jerusalem. It is unfortunate that many Christians have not been taught effectively. Instead of feeding on the pure Word of God, they have been fed a diet of super-spirituality and dead tradition. Dead tradition does not have the power to raise a child into sonhood.

The only thing that will put the devil to run is a revelation of the name of Jesus. Those that believe, will *work His works* in the power of His authority. They will walk in the power of dominion.

Work your revelation.

Signs of the Believer

> And these signs shall follow them that believe; In My name shall they cast out devils; they shall speak with new tongues; They shall take up serpents; and if they drink any deadly thing, it shall not hurt them; they shall lay hands on the sick, and they shall recover.
>
> **Mark 16:17-18**

This is called the *Great Commission*. When Christ heralded this new dispensation, He released an army to invade the world. He released the Church to cast out devils and take dominion over every threat of the enemy. He said, *"Go into the world. Preach the Gospel. Baptize people and these signs will accompany you. Anyone who believes will be able to cast out devils in My name."*

Jesus had completed His earthly ministry. He said, *"I am finished with the earthly ministry. I did what I needed to do. Now you have the position and the right to live just as close to God as I did. You have the authority to receive just as many answers from the Father. I will give you the Name that qualifies you to have access. This Name, MY NAME, can never be denied. It will take you directly into the presence of God. I am now going to retire from ministering bodily on the Earth, but I want you to go on My behalf and do those things that I have commanded you."*

Jesus did not leave any room for failure.

"And these signs shall follow those who believe; In My name they shall..."

Believing is the byproduct of *faith*. Some people, however, seem to think that faith just means hope or agreement on a happy ending. Faith is hearing the promise, believing the promise and standing on the promise. Those who have received faith possess an unshakeable assurance in what they believe. Their convictions do not waver or grow weak in the presence of contradiction.

Jesus said to Peter, *"Follow Me"* (Mark 1:17a)! Peter, immediately receiving faith to act upon the Word, left all and followed Jesus. The Word of God has the ability to impart faith into the heart of the hearer. On another occasion, Jesus came walking to the disciples on water. Upon seeing Jesus, Peter yelled from the boat, *"If it is You, bid me to come to You on the water!"* Jesus answered, *"Come"* (Matthew 14:28,29).

> **And when Peter had come down out of the boat, he walked on the water to go to Jesus.**
>
> **Matthew 14:29b**

Peter received the Word *"Come!"* into his spirit. That Word immediately imparted faith into Peter and he was able to take dominion over a natural law. That natural law stated that it is impossible for a human being to walk on water, yet Peter's faith superseded natural law and he walked where it was not possible to walk.

> **But when he saw the wind was boisterous, he was afraid; and beginning to sink, he cried out, saying, "Lord save me!"**
>
> **Matthew 14:29b-30**

Peter lost his faith when he got his eyes off of the promise. Distracted by boisterous winds, he allowed fear to short-circuit his miracle. Immediately, the supernatural element that was in operation, stopped. Faith was replaced with fear and Peter began to sink.

Fear is a spirit. If it's not resisted, it will sink your faith.

Before a person believes a promise, they must hear it and then know it to be true. When a promise is heard, the supernatural element within it, will immediately impart *ability* to the hearer. That ability will enable the hearer to *know* it, to *agree* with it, to *believe* in it and to *act* on it.

> **And these signs shall follow those who believe...**
>
> **Mark 16:17a**

Jesus told the disciples to cast out devils, heal the sick and to not die by snakebite or poison. He gave the Church privilege and authority. In doing this, He also gave a delegated responsibility to the generations to come.

You are an ambassador of the Kingdom. As a believer, there are certain signs that should follow you. In other words, in your presence devils should be cast out, the sick should be raised and the promises of the Kingdom established in the earth realm. These are the delegated responsibilities that Jesus has conferred to you.

Agreement with the Word

> **Verily I say unto you, whatsoever ye shall bind on Earth shall be bound in Heaven: and whatsoever ye shall loose on Earth shall be loosed in Heaven. Again I say unto you, that if two of you shall agree on Earth as touching any thing that they shall ask, it shall be done for them of My Father which is in Heaven. For where two or three are gathered together in My name, there am I in the midst of them.**
>
> **Matthew 18:18-20**

The Bible says that if two agree, it shall be done. *Come into agreement with the Word of God.*

Whatever the believer disallows is disallowed. Whatever they allow is allowed. When the flu comes, you can either "catch it" or resist it. You have authority to either allow it in your life or to disallow it in your life. This is authority at work.

God is obligated to His Word and He will uphold His end of the promise. He will not sovereignly decide to overlook your faith, nor will He shut His ears to the cries of the righteous. As long as the believer comes believing, they will see results, some 30-fold, some 60-fold, and some 100-fold.

> **All power is given unto Me in Heaven and in Earth. Go ye therefore, and teach all nations, baptizing them in the name of the Father, and of the Son, and of the Holy Ghost: Teaching them to observe all things whatsoever I have commanded you: and, lo, I am with you alway, even unto the end of the world.**
>
> **Matthew 28:18b-20**

Delegated authority is like a child that went to the store and told the owner, *"My mother said give me a can of beans and put it on our account."* If the storeowner knows the mother of that child, he will hand them the can of beans and send the child on their way!

That is a very simplified representation of the authority that Jesus has given to the believer. If you know who you are, who you represent and what you've come for, you will never leave empty-handed! If your word is God's Word, signs will accompany you.

Delegated authority gets the job done.

> **And they went out and preached everywhere, the Lord working with them and confirming the Word through the accompanying signs.**
>
> **Mark 16:20 NKJV**

Some are born to a great name and others receive it through adoption or marriage. Still others acquire a great name through achievement or discovery. Whatever the case may be, their name represents greatness.

The Lord Jesus Christ was born into a great name. He both inherited a great name and received a great name by conquest.

Do you know why God spent so much time in the Old Testament giving Himself names?

This is so that the saint would have a comprehensive understanding of *who* God is and His intentions toward His children. Jesus is the embodiment of every name that God has ever given Himself. He is the full expression of the Word of God. He came to the Earth to manifest His name so that all might know the fullness of truth.

As an heir of the Kingdom, you bear the name of the King of Kings. That honor, like an ambassadorship, carries certain privileges and responsibilities. As you have already learned, God has given you both authority and power to rule over your realm of jurisdiction. You have authority over all the power of the enemy.

For this reason, God has equipped the believer with both the badge and the gun. The gun or the dunamis of God, enforces the exousia authority of the badge. The name of Jesus accredits both of these things. His name is the authorizing force that gives the believer the right to bear His authority and to exercise His power.

- **The Badge:**
  (exousia, authority)

- **The Power:**
  (dunamis, miracle working power)

- **The Jurisdiction:**
  (your realm of influence)

- **The Name**
  (Jesus, the King of Kings)

Your revelation of the *badge*, the *power*, the *jurisdiction*, and the *Name* will determine your level of dominion in life. This is why it is imperative that you give yourself fully to these truths. Faith comes by hearing and hearing comes through the Word of God. If there is an area of truth that hasn't become well established in the soil of your heart, then give yourself to diligent study and meditation. *Water the seed.* Go back and re-read earlier chapters so that the Word of God can impart the light of revelation into your spirit.

Remember, just because you have been given a promise does not automatically guarantee that you will participate in it. Just as a farmer tends his field and diligently anticipates the harvest, so must you tend the field of your heart. Allow the Word of God to mature you into a son. Spend time in prayer and in fellowship with God. Stay connected to your Holy Ghost power source and disallow distraction. As you put action to your faith and rely on the integrity of the Word, the promises of God will reach their mark in your life.

Chapter 8

Obtaining a More Excellent Name

*When the devil attacks, it is an opportunity for a testimony.
It is an opportunity to demonstrate
the preeminence of the Name.*

Declaring Your Inheritance

On two separate occasions, my radiator overheated and exploded in my face. On both occasions, I immediately addressed the situation with the Word of God. Before it could even register in my mind, I spoke out of my spirit and said, *"I don't burn in the name of Jesus!"*

Since I had been meditating on the promises of God, the power was there to instantly address the situation. When I spoke, although the water was scalding, I did not receive one burn. I had been drenched with water, but I was perfectly preserved. There was not one burn on my body.

When I said, *"I don't burn in the name of Jesus,"* I was declaring my authority and the inheritance I had received. I was saying, *"I am part of the Body. I am one with the Lord and I am here on behalf of Jesus."*

> **Fear not, for I have redeemed you; I have called you by your name; You are Mine. When you pass through the waters, I will be with you; And though the rivers, they shall not overflow you. When you walk through the fire, you shall not be burned, nor shall the flame scorch you. For I am the Lord your God, the Holy One of Israel, your Savior.**
>
> Isaiah 43:1b-3 NKJV

When you read the Word, you must decide *who* the Word is talking to. It's written to the *believer*, but you have to decide if you are the one that *believes!*

Allow the Word of God to be the foremost authority in your life. Believe its report over every other report. When a situation demands a response, let your word be *The Word*. The reason I didn't burn was because I exercised my authority in my realm of jurisdiction. The moment I spoke, the power of God went to work to protect me from the scalding liquid.

My authority was backed up by power.

There is power ready to work on your behalf. There are angelic beings on standby, ready to enforce your authoritative command. When you speak the Word, angels go to work and demons flee. Even Heaven responds to the very sound of the Word of God. As a saint, that sound is in your heart and in your mouth. When you give expression to it, the power of God is released into your realm.

There is no comparison between the devil's power and the power that has been made available to the Church. The power of darkness is weak and defeated. The power within the Church is strong, triumphant and glorious.

Greater is He that is in you, than he that is in the world.

1 John 4:4

When do you need the Name?

The saint needs the Name when a situation demands supernatural results. If a person can't make it happen in their own ability, they will need the power of the Name to bring a miracle into manifestation. The Name will answer the situation. It will remedy the problem. It will correct the flaw.

There is power in the name of Jesus, yet many believers spend their time worrying. Instead of *contemplating the miracle*, they sit in church *contemplating their fears*. All along, the answer was in the Word of God, but they became so sidetracked by distraction that they lost sight of the breakthrough.

The Word of God will answer the problem.

God has given the believer all things that pertain to life and godliness (2 Peter 1:3). He has made these divine promises available to the one who will take Him at His Word. There is *value* in the Word of God. If a person will invest themselves in it, the Word will go to work on their behalf. It will increase and expand them into greater levels of promotion, influence and success. This can only happen, however, if the believer will give themselves to diligent study and meditation.

Born into Privilege

Jesus obtained a more excellent name by *inheritance*.

God, who at sundry times and in divers manners spake in time past unto the fathers by the prophets, hath in these last days spoken unto us by His Son, whom He hath appointed heir of all things, by whom also He made the worlds; Who being the brightness of His glory, and the express image of His person, and upholding all things by the Word of His power, when He had by himself purged our sins, sat down on the right hand of the Majesty on high; Being made so much better than the angels, as He hath by inheritance obtained a more excellent name than they. For unto which of the angels said He at any time, "Thou art my Son, this day have I begotten thee?" And again, "I will be to him a Father, and He shall be to me a Son?" And again, when He bringeth in the first begotten

into the world, He saith, "And let all the angels of God worship Him."

Hebrews 1:1-6

Angels have names. Do you remember the angel Gabriel? *"I am Gabriel and I stand before the presence of God"* (Luke1:19). At one time, Satan's name was "Lucifer," meaning son of the morning or light bearer. He fell from Heaven and weakened the nations. He lost his brilliance and his position. The name "Satan" now represents the highest authority in the kingdom of darkness.

Witches, warlocks, and wizards will call upon the names of the spirit beings that equip them. As they are promoted, they have the potential to receive more names and greater power. The names of these demon spirits are *evoked* or *called on* by name.

The Christian, however, has been given a *better name*. They do not need to start at the bottom and work their way up, nor do they need to entreat the little angels, work up to Gabriel and then to Jesus. It doesn't work that way in the Kingdom! Jesus is the name that the saint is born into. He becomes their identity and the source of their inheritance. It's a name of privilege and class. It's the *better* Name that the child of God is born into.

Jesus was not born in the image of angels, nor did He take on their nature. The Father did not turn to an angelic being and say, *"You are my Son. This day have I begotten thee."* Rather, Jesus came in the likeness and in the form of man. He came as the promised seed to redeem the children of the Kingdom. Although He was God, He walked the Earth as a man anointed by the Holy Ghost. God said, *"Let all the angels worship Him."*

The saint has been born of God. They have inherited a more excellent name and a more excellent nature. His nature has become *their nature*. His substance has become *their substance*. As heirs of the Kingdom, they have been born into privilege, power and influence.

"Who being the brightness of His glory, and the express image of His person..."

Jesus is the brightness of God's glory. He is the express image of God's person. If you want to know the will of the Father, watch Jesus in action. He never turned anyone away. He never said, "No" or "Maybe." Jesus is the "Yes" and "Amen." He is the complete expression of God's will.

Jesus is the brightness of glory and yet people pray, *"In the name of Jesus, if it be Thy will."* They might as well say, *"In the name of Buddha, Hare Krishna or Mohamed."* If a person does not know the will, it is pointless to use the Name. The Name can only benefit the person who knows the power behind it. It is reserved for the ambassador who knows the will and is committed to its enforcement.

The Keys of the Kingdom

And I will give you the keys of the Kingdom of Heaven, and whatever you bind on Earth will be bound in Heaven, and whatever you loose on Earth with be loosed in Heaven.

Matthew 16:19 NKJV

Those who have the keys, have the power to open and close doors. When the plague comes, they can boldly say, *"No!"* and lock the door. If the devil counters, *"By what authority do you do this,"* those possessing the keys can say, *"by the One that told me I have authority."*

To pray, *"If it be Thy will"* is a gross misunderstanding of the will of God. The will of God *is* the Word of God. If the believer knows the Word, they will know the will. Scores of people have taken the phrase, *"If the Lord is willing"* out of context. They have used it to justify ignorance and inactivity.

The devil seeks to promote lies and misconceptions within the Kingdom. If he can make the Christian's prayer life ineffective, then he can separate them from the power of their new nature. Once again, this is why it is so vitally important for the saint to know and meditate on the will of God. Those who know the Word, know how to identify a word that is not full of the substance of God.

Jesus is the brightness of God's glory. He is the express image of His person and upholds all things by the Word of His power. The Word of God not only created the universe, but it is holding the universe together. There is power in the Word of God.

> **In the beginning was the Word, and the Word was with God, and the Word was God.**
>
> **John 1:1 NKJV**

Jesus is the Word become flesh. He is the second person of the Trinity. There is no beginning to Christ's history, for He is from everlasting to everlasting.

When God said, *"This day have I begotten you,"* He was not talking about a day when He created "God the Son." He was referencing a day that was like no other. If, through the Word of God, that day can be identified, then it can be established when Jesus inherited a more excellent name.

> **God hath fulfilled the same unto us their children, in that He hath raised up Jesus again; as it is also written in the second Psalm, "Thou art my Son, this day have I begotten Thee."**
>
> **Acts 13:33**

When did Jesus inherit a more excellent name?

Jesus went to the cross in order to gain authority in Heaven and in Earth. He was obedient to His mission. When God raised Him from the dead, He said of Jesus, *"This day I have begotten Thee."* Jesus inherited a more excellent name when He rose from the dead. Through conquest, He recovered all that the enemy had stolen.

Back to the Garden

In the Garden of Eden, God told Adam, *"Of every tree of the garden you may freely eat; but of the tree of the knowledge of good and evil you shall not eat, for in the day that you eat of it you shall surely die"* (Genesis 2:16-17). If Adam disobeyed, God said that he would die in the same day. Of course, you know that Adam and Eve did disobey and eat of the forbidden tree. They ate, and yet, they lived on the planet for many years after.

This account proves that man is more than just a body. God declared to His creation, *"for in the day that you eat of it you shall surely die,"* yet they did not die *physically* that day, they died *spiritually*. No sooner had they eaten, did the curse then come upon them.

There is a *spiritual death* and there is a *physical death*. Adam died a spiritual death the moment he put the fruit to his mouth. That spiritual death took years before it manifested in his physical body. Like all things, what happens in the spirit will eventually manifest in the natural. Through transgression, death had been introduced into the Earth. Yet, it took years for the full impact of decay to completely erode the lifespan of God's creation.

Since that day, the lifespan of humanity has decreased from approximately 900 years to 70 years. Death has been in operation for centuries. It entered the world by sin and subjected the planet to its corruption. However, before sin infected the world, it first entered Adam's spirit. From his spirit, it affected his body and from his body, multiplied generations.

For He made Him who knew no sin to be sin for us, that we might become the righteousness of God in Him.

2 Corinthians 5:21 NKJV

After sin had taken its toll, God sent His Son to pay the ultimate price. God's creation had to be redeemed, yet to do so would require someone *without sin* to pay the penalty *for sin*. God did not send an angel, but rather, He sent His own Son in the likeness of man. He sent the second person of the Trinity. He sent the One by whom all things were made…*and the Word became flesh.*

> **And the Word became flesh and dwelt among us, and we beheld His glory, the glory of the only begotten of the Father, full of grace and truth.**
>
> **John 1:14 NKJV**

The Word of God became flesh, yet it was not enough for Jesus to simply give His life. Sin had taken its toll and humanity needed more than a redeemed body. They needed a redeemed spirit. To accomplish this and to reverse the curse that took place in the Garden, Jesus needed to also die a spiritual death. Only through this sacrifice could men and women become "the righteousness of God in Christ Jesus" (2 Corinthians 5:21).

To die spiritually would mean separation from God. It meant that Jesus would not only endure an unthinkable physical death, but an unthinkable spiritual death. This was the ultimate sacrifice. When Jesus became sin and sickness, He did it *not* because He deserved it, but so that He could take upon Himself the judgment that humanity deserved.

He received the judgment of God into His *total* being.

And Jesus cried out again with a loud voice, and yielded up His spirit (Matthew 27:50).

At the moment of truth, God turned His face from Jesus. As He hung on the cross, suspended between Heaven and Earth, the sky blackened overhead. Earthquakes violently shook the Earth and rocks split open on their own accord. Even the graves were opened and the veil within the temple was torn in two. Christ had paid the price. Just as the first Adam transgressed and died spiritually, so had Jesus died. The sacrifice was complete. The debt was paid.

The Bible refers to Jesus as the "second Adam." He became the antidote to a world that was suffering the effects of the fall. What the first Adam had done, the second Adam reversed through the ultimate sacrifice.

Return From Corruption

Three days earlier Jesus had suffered a brutal physical and spiritual death. Joseph of Arimathea, a secret follower of Jesus, had seen to it that His body was laid in a garden tomb. This day, very early in the morning, the women had come to the tomb with spices and fragrant oils. When they arrived, they were shocked to find that the stone had been rolled away and that the body of Jesus was no longer there. As they stood dumbfounded, two men appeared in bright, shining garments. Trembling in fear, the women bowed their faces to the earth. The angels spoke, saying, *"Why do you seek the living among the dead? He is not here, but risen"* (Luke 24:6).

> **He has raised up Jesus. As it is also written in the second Psalm, "You are My Son, Today I have begotten You." And that He raised Him from the dead, no more to return to corruption.**
>
> **Acts 13:33b-34a NKJV**

Jesus was right all along. Before His death He had said, *"I will give you the sign of Jonah, as Jonah was in the belly of the whale, so will the Son of Man be in the heart of the Earth three days and three nights"* (Matthew 12:39-40).

Not only was His body broken and then buried in the tomb, but His soul was incarcerated so that He might single-handedly pay the price. When Jesus resurrected from the dead, He gained something that Adam had lost thousands of years before. He said, *"All authority, all jurisdiction, all power in Heaven and in Earth is given unto Me"* (Matthew 28:18).

The moment that Jesus left Heaven to become a man, He laid aside His rulership, reign, dominion and deity. He stripped Himself of the glory and splendor of Heaven and came into the Earth as a baby. He came as a man so that He might recover the authority that man had lost.

Having made His soul a sacrifice, Jesus went to the cross and died spiritually. Separated from God, He tasted both Hell and judgment on account of sin. The sacrifice was complete. The price had been paid. The victory had been won.

Three days later, God raised Jesus from the dead. The angles said, *"He is not here, but risen."* On account of that great victory, salvation was made available to all that would call upon His name. Jesus recovered the authority that Adam had lost.

God said, *"Thou art My Son, this day have I begotten Thee."*

Jesus is the firstborn. He is the first to be born of a brand new breed of men and women. He lived as a man and became sin and its sacrifice. On the third day, He threw off the powers of darkness and rose triumphant to be a representative. He rose to be the head and the proprietor of a brand new race, a race that would know divine authority.

He is the *Initiator.*
He is the *Author of life.*
He is the *only begotten Son.*

When the Father said, *"Thou art My Son, this day have I begotten thee,"* Jesus inherited His name.

Authority on Credit

Prior to the resurrection, the only occasion that Jesus' name was used was when the seventy came back rejoicing, saying, *"Lord, even the demons are subject to us in Your name"* (Luke 10:17).

Their success in harnessing the power of the Name was only on *credit*, for salvation had not been made available. Jesus had not gone to the cross and the Holy Ghost had not been released into the Earth. These were simply working off of the authority of the *presence* of the Son of God.

The seventy were operating off of His earthly authority, which was limited. It was limited because Jesus had to walk in accordance with the law. He had to be perfect in order to qualify for answered prayer.

Jesus, of course, did not benefit from any of the temple sacrifices. The blood of bullocks and goats could not wash away His sins. *He didn't have any!*

During His earthly ministry, Jesus' authority was not based upon a defeated devil and a redeemed humanity. His authority was based upon this: If a man's ways would please the Lord and he would walk in perfection towards the Law, God would never deny his petitions.

He sent out the disciples and said, *"Go in My name. Go on credit. Go off of My achievements,"* and the devils obeyed them.

After the death, burial, and resurrection, Jesus said, *"All power in Heaven and Earth is given unto Me. Go ye."* (Matthew 28:18,19). No longer held captive by sin's consequence, the offspring of Adam could become born again and receive the name and identity of the second Adam. In doing this, Jesus made the old nature obsolete, an out-dated relic of the past. He undid the injustice that was rendered in the Garden and re-wrote the heart of man.

The children of the Kingdom, having received the power of the

Name, would also receive the inheritance of the Name. That inheritance would include the *mind* of Christ, the *power* of Christ, the *position* of Christ and the *name* of Christ. They would become engrafted into *Him* and He engrafted into *them*. This is *your* heritage.

Through the new birth, the literal power of the new nature became available to all that would call Him Lord. Within that nature, there is transforming power. In other words, all that believe upon Him can receive His nature and His identity.

People say, *"That was Jesus! That was Jesus!"* The Bible doesn't say that you will be like He *was*. Rather, it says, *"As He is, so are we"* (1 John 4:17).

As He *is*, so are *you*.

Before the resurrection, He had not yet *inherited* the Name above every name. It had not been proven, bestowed, or accomplished. His authority was solely operating on credit, but He spoke His faith ahead of time and said, *"Be of good cheer. I have overcome the world"* (John 16:33). Although He had not yet overcome the cross, He spoke His conviction with the confidence and security of faith. He spoke as if it was already accomplished and the victory secured.

He put Words in motion. As far as Jesus was concerned, He was never going to waver. The victory had already been won in His heart and in His mind. Although the cross was still in the future, the devil had already been defeated. He had already conquered the adversary and He was prepared to walk out His faith into its natural fulfillment.

Spoils of Conquest

He knew no sin, yet He became sin. He knew no condemnation, yet He became the condemned. As such, His victory is our victory. His conquest is our conquest. His inheritance became our inheritance. We were made joint heirs with Christ Jesus.

> **Who being the brightness of His glory, and the express image of His person, and upholding all things by the Word of His power, when He had by himself purged our sins, sat down on the right hand of the Majesty on high, being made much better than angels, as He hath by inheritance obtained a more excellent name than they.**
>
> **Hebrews 1:1-4**

The moment Jesus was begotten from the dead He received a more excellent name. The Bible says that the Father was pleased for Jesus to have preeminence (Colossians 1:18-19). He was given a name that was above every name.

> **"Glorify Me Father. Glorify Me with the same glory I had with You before the world."**
>
> **John 17:5**

> **"Wherefore God also hath highly exalted Him and given Him a name which is above every name."**
>
> **Philippians 2:9**

God highly exalted Jesus. He raised Him from the dead and gave Him a name that was higher than any other. When Jesus sat down in heavenly places, He liberally bestowed His name upon all that would call upon Him.

The name gives the Church the legal authority to enforce the dominion and victory of Calvary. It gives every believer the legal right to exercise the authority of Christ in the affairs of life. There is power in the Name.

Up until this point, this kind of authority and power had not been made available to humanity. When God highly exalted Him, Jesus gave His Body, *the Church*, the legal right to enforce the Word with the power of His name. It was not authority on credit, but rather, it was the authority that held the keys to death, Hell and the grave.

> **And being found in fashion as a man, He humbled Himself and became obedient unto death even the death, of the cross. Wherefore God also hath highly exalted Him, and given Him a name which is above every name.**
>
> **Philippians 2:8-9**

If Jesus had not humbled Himself and become obedient to death, God would not have highly exalted Him. If He had not offered Himself as a sacrifice for sin, He would not have received a Name that is above every other name.

Why is the name of Jesus above every name?

The name was bestowed upon Jesus because He went the extra mile. He did not allow a region to remain untouched by His influence. He took His name from Heaven and brought it down to Earth. *He became a man.* He took His name from Earth and brought it to the lower parts of the Earth. *He became a sacrifice.* Taking the keys of death, Hell and the grave, He established His authority in every realm. On the third day, He rose again. There was no region that was beyond the reach of His reign.

The Name has been given jurisdiction over every corner of the universe.

Through the Word of God, you will discover *your* jurisdiction. You will discover that your jurisdiction goes higher than the stars and deeper than the sea. Through the power of the Name, you can go straight to the throne of grace and into the Holy of Holies. There is no limit. There is no cap on the grace of God. Your jurisdiction is limitless!

Bending the Knees of Opposition

> **Wherefore God also has highly exalted Him, and given Him a name which is above every name, that at the name of Jesus every knee should bow, of those in Heaven, and of those on Earth, and of those under the Earth.**
>
> **Philippians 2:9-10 NKJV**

The key word is "should." Every knee *should* bow. The only time a knee will not bow to the name of Jesus is when the Name is being mishandled.

At the name of Jesus, cancer *should* bow.
At the name of Jesus, poverty *should* bow.
At the name of Jesus, confusion *should* bow.
At the name of Jesus, fear, doubt, unbelief and sin *should* bow.

At the name of Jesus, the onslaught of Hell should bow. The mountain should move. The enemy should fail. The dream should come true and the promise should be realized. Every knee of opposition should bow in the Earth and under the Earth. The name of Jesus is greater and more powerful that any other name in the universe.

Jesus didn't rise empty-handed. Through the conquest of death, Hell and the grave, He has given you His name and seated you with Him in heavenly places. Having won this position of preeminence, He has called you to rule and reign in life, to exercise justice and to punish the disobedience of darkness.

"...at the name of Jesus every knee should bow."

Jesus talked to the fig tree. It wasn't producing, so He spoke to it. *"Let no one eat fruit from you ever again"* (Mark 11:14).

The fig tree was also talking. It was saying, *"I am lord in this situation and I say no fruit."* Jesus said, *"No, I am the Lord of this situation. I say no fruit forever!"*

> **Now in the morning, as they passed by, they saw the fig tree dried up from the roots.**
>
> **Mark 11:20**

When the devil attacks, it is an opportunity for a testimony.

It is an opportunity to demonstrate the preeminence of the Name.

The one who has a revelation of the Name will say, *"In the name of Jesus,"* and the circumstance will bow. The limitation will be subservient. The saint will exercise their authority over all disobedience for *"at the name of Jesus every knee should bow."*

Every contrary situation will make way for the Lordship of Jesus Christ and the heirs of the Kingdom. The one with revelation and understanding will say, *"Bow your knee in my life. I have another Lord and you are not it! Now, move out of my way. His Word is law in my life."* The situation will have to obey the authority of the saint because power backs the Name.

The Name is like a *title*. It grants *influence* and *position*.

Opening the Eyes of Understanding

Look at Paul's prayer for the Ephesian church:

> **That the God of our Lord Jesus Christ, the Father of glory, may give unto you the Spirit of wisdom and revelation in the knowledge of Him: The eyes of your understanding being enlightened; that ye may know what is the hope of His calling, and what the riches of the glory of His inheritance in the saints, and what is the**

> exceeding greatness of His power to us-ward who believe, according to the working of His mighty power, Which He wrought in Christ, when He raised him from the dead, and set him at His own right hand in the heavenly places, Far above all principality, and power, and might, and dominion, and every name that is named, not only in this world, but also in that which is to come: And hath put all things under His feet, and gave him to be the head over all things to the Church, Which is His body, the fullness of Him that filleth all in all.
>
> Ephesians 1:17-22

The Ephesian's were already born again and Spirit-filled. Paul was not praying for anything that Jesus had not already accomplished. Rather, he was praying that they would get a revelation of the things already given. He prays that *"the eyes of your understanding"* may be enlightened and that they may know *"the riches of the glory of His inheritance in the saints."* Paul was praying that they would get a revelation of the greatness of Jesus' power in them and towards them.

They were born again. They had the position and they had the title, yet they did not have a revelation on what this title meant to their everyday experience. Instead of ruling and reigning in life, the circumstance was ruling and reigning over them.

This means that you can have the power, but go without the power. You can sit in the dark and refuse to flip the switch. Once again, your victory in life is dependent upon the revelation you walk in. Your investment and study in the Word of God cannot be overemphasized.

"that you may know…the riches of the glory of His inheritance in the saints"

Jesus was in existence before the world was created. He is without beginning of days or end of life. The Word has always been here, but in the fullness of time, the Word became human. The Word took on the devil as a human. The Word died as a human and the Word rose as a glorified human. One day, we will be glorified just like Him and throughout all eternity, we will owe Him our new identity.

Jesus is seated at the right hand of the Father as a Representative, an Attorney, a Lawyer, a High Priest, and an Intercessor. He represents the redeemed, and those that bear His Name, exercise His authority and wield His power.

Humanity has an ambassador *up there*.
Jesus has representatives *down here*.

CHAPTER 9

WORKING THE POWER WITHIN

---

*You will rise up in the name of Jesus
and walk in fearless obedience.
You will not stay where you are.
You will fulfill your heavenly calling.*

The View From the Throne

The name of Jesus is higher than any other name. When God raised Him from the dead, He highly exalted Him and set Him on high. He set His Son above every principality, power, might and dominion. Jesus not only sits above the principalities of darkness, but He commands the principalities of light. His place of rulership and reign is set high above every angelic position. Gabriel, Michael and all the hosts of Heaven are subject to the name of Jesus.

> **Far above all principality, and power, and might, and dominion, and every name that is named, not only in this world, but also in that which is to come: and hath put all things under His feet, and gave Him to be the head over all things to the Church, Which is His body, the fullness of Him that filleth all in all.**
>
> **Ephesians 1:21-23**

Some 2,000 years ago, Jesus rose from the dead. At the moment of His triumph, humanity was elevated into a privileged position. They were elevated in Him as He was exalted above every principality, power, might and dominion. Those who are *in Christ* are seated with Him. Those who are *not in Christ* have not yet been promoted to this position of preeminence. To be in Christ means to abide in the Name. It is a position of authority, power and prestige. It is an arena of dominion that commands angelic armies.

> **And hath raised us up together, and made us sit together in the heavenly places in Christ Jesus.**
>
> **Ephesians 2:6 NKJV**

Having been raised with Christ, we are seated with Him in heavenly places. God put all things under Jesus' feet and gave Him to be the head over all things to the Body. Of course, the Church is the body. Therefore, it goes without saying, that what is under the feet is also under the body.

The Body of Christ is over all things, yet that rulership must be enforced in the earth realm. In the heavenly realm, the headship of Christ goes unchallenged. However, in the Earth, the renegade forces of Hell will attempt to defy authority that is not enforced.

The saint must be mindful of both the position and the authority given to enforce that position. Through conquest, Jesus gained preeminence and seated the saint with Him in a place of authority. Not only is this a position of *honor*, but it is a position of *responsibility*. The saint is responsible to subdue the powers of darkness. Those things that magnify themselves above Christ must be taken captive and disarmed. They must be brought into submission through the Word of God.

Speaking from the High Places

When Jesus rose from the dead, He inherited a name that is above every name. Having received that Name, He gave it to His own. He gave it to His Body so that the Church might rule and reign through Him.

> **Therefore God exalted Him to the highest place and gave Him the Name that is above every name.**
>
> **Philippians 2:9**

Jesus received a more excellent name. The defeat of death, Hell and the grave promoted Him to the highest place. His conquest earned Him a name that was greater than all others.

He was made a curse, yet He rose triumphant. He was made sin, yet He rose in righteousness. He was made sickness, yet He rose with healing. His *victory* is our victory. His *conquest* is our *conquest*.

The believer can cash in on the benefits of the Name through faith. Jesus won the victory. The price has been paid. The battle has been won. Those that desire it, must only receive the promise and walk in it. Although the Name is exalted, it is not exalted out of the reach of the believer. The Name is *for* the believer. Just as a bride takes on her husband's name, so should the Church take on Christ's name. Within the Name is honor and a divine responsibility to magnify all that the Name stands for.

> **Wherefore God also hath highly exalted Him, and given Him a name which is above every name: That at the name of Jesus every knee should bow, of things in Heaven, and things in Earth, and things under the Earth; And that every tongue should confess that Jesus Christ is Lord, to the glory of God the Father.**
>
> **Philippians 2:9-11**

> **And having spoiled principalities and powers, He made a show of them openly, triumphing over them in it.**
>
> **Colossians 2:15**

The Name stands for the defeat of the devil. It stands for the victory of God. It stands for the provision of the believer. It stands for a new life. It stands for a new relationship with Heaven. It stands for unity with the Father.

When the believer stands in the authority of the Name, they can command obedience. They can decree things. They can exercise justice. They can enforce the Word of God. Those that are seated with Christ in heavenly places, are seated high above powers and principalities. *The view from the throne puts all things into perspective.*

Every part of the planet, down to the most minute atom, knows that Jesus Christ plundered Hell and made a show of it openly. Triumphing over the powers of darkness, Jesus paraded its defeat throughout all eternity. The entire Earth has witnessed the catastrophic failure and humiliation of Hell. It is has been stripped down to what it really is: weak, defeated and wanting.

When the saint says, *"In the name of Jesus,"* they are boldly declaring, *"I come to you in the authority of the Master. I come to you in the certainty of His triumph. I am here with the fullness of His power. I represent your complete defeat."*

Real Power. Real Results.

The power that enabled Jesus to lay down His life and then also to take it back up is the same power that is invested in the Name today. The Name has not lost power. It has not weakened with use. On the contrary, those who exercise their revelation of the Name will access the fullness of its power. That power is not far off, but it is in the heart and in the mouth of the one who speaks it.

The Word is near you, in your mouth and in your heart.

Romans 10:8a NKJV

Jesus is the Word. Those that come in His name, come in the power of the Word. If the Word is near you, the power is near you. The believer does not have to go to Heaven and pull the answer down. Neither must they go down to the deep and draw the answer up.

The *answer*, the *solution*, the *victory* and the *antidote* is near you. It is in your heart and it is in your mouth. When the seed that is in your heart becomes a revelation, you will talk from your place of revelation. You will talk from a realm of victory and conquest. You will speak from the perspective of the Word. That perspective is never an inferior position. It is not a place of *demotion*, but a place of *promotion*.

Those that meditate on the Word, take authority over everything that contradicts the Word. They do not exalt the contradiction, but rather, they exalt the Word and *subdue* the contradiction. The Word of God that is in the heart and the mouth of the believer commands authority and power.

The Name, the Word, and the position that has been given to you in Christ is the *reality* that you live by. Everything that tests this dominion is challenging reality. In other words, your position in Christ is real. It should be more real than anything that counters your authority realm. When you are convinced of this, you will dismiss lying symptoms, situations and imaginations. You will enforce your rule with the scepter of the Word and the power of the Name.

Use the Name. Use the Name to stay happy. Use the Name to build the fruit of the Spirit in your life. Start where you live. Begin to use the Name on the things that directly affect you. As you begin to exercise His Name on the things that are within your immediate reach, you will see your faith work. Do not step out into a fantasyland and try to do something you have not been prepared to do. This is where disappointments are born. Start where you are and as you do, your faith will extend itself into greater realms. Your jurisdiction will get broader and broader as your expectation increases.

Identifying Your Opponent

> **For we do not wrestle against flesh and blood, but against principalities, against powers, against the rulers of darkness of this age, against**

spiritual hosts of wickedness in the heavenly places.

Ephesians 6:12 NKJV

The devil is defeated. The *wrestling* that the Word speaks of is not a physical confrontation; rather it is the wrestling of faith. It is the strong grip that declares, *"No!"* It is the strength that casts down the imaginations of the mind. It is what subdues the thing that exalts itself against the knowledge of God. It is the faith that says, *"No, that is not the truth!"*

If you will fight the good fight of faith, then the enemy will continue to be defeated in your life. Time will no longer matter. You won't pray and wonder, *"When is God going to do something about this?"* Instead, you will stand confident in your expectation. You will stand in the assurance that you have already received the answer. *Wavering does not exist where confidence abides.*

The devil may come and say, *"See, you didn't receive it,"* but he is a liar. He speaks imaginations, but you have the power to douse every fiery dart. You are seated with Christ in the *high places*. Those that will remember this, will not allow the devil to *talk them down* from their delegated place of authority.

> **For the weapons of our warfare are not carnal, but mighty through God to the pulling down of strong holds; Casting down imaginations, and every high thing that exalteth itself against the knowledge of God, and bringing into captivity every thought to the obedience of Christ.**
>
> **2 Corinthians 10:4-5**

You have been given the name of Jesus. That Name carries influence. A person may "drop a name" and that name will get them into certain places. It will gain them access because of the authority or clout behind it. If this is the case in the world, how much more authority is available in the *name* of Jesus? Those who have a revelation of the Name will go places in God.

The Name works in Heaven, in Earth, and under the Earth. There is not a place that is above the authority of the name of Jesus. His name stands for conquest in every arena.

When the believer says, *"In the name of Jesus,"* they must know that the enemy is already defeated. They must know that they possess power to subdue every work of darkness. If they will put their revelation to work, they will overcome every note of opposition. The believer that doesn't *yet* have the full revelation, must go back to the Word and water the seed. *Give greatness a place to grow.*

"For the weapons of our warfare are not carnal…"

Jesus commissioned the Church, yet the devil has so distracted some that they think their warfare is with another person. The Bible says, *"We do not war against flesh and blood, but against principalities and powers"* (Ephesians 6:12). The devil knows that if the Body is divided against the Body, authority will fail to function. Where there is confusion, there is every evil work. The power of God is only available to those who are submitted to the authority of the Word.

In order to operate in authority, one must be under authority. The key to remaining under authority is to *"Love the Lord with all your heart and to love your neighbor as yourself"* (Matthew 22:37-38). Those that obey this commandment will not have a problem submitting to the authority of the Word or in yielding to another in love.

When the Lord deals with us, He deals with us individually, yet He sees our individual triumphs in relationship to the entire Body. Your life is woven into God in Christ Jesus. Although you are one person, you are one with Christ. Christ is one with His Body.

Jesus is saying, *"Listen, you are the Body, My family, and I want every one of you. If you will look after My Kingdom and look after one another, then I will work powerfully in your life. If you would bless somebody and not fight, you would see My power in your midst. If you knew they were wrong but you loved them anyway, I will honor you. I am going to give you authority and I am going to bless the whole Body. I will enable the authority of Calvary to flow through you."*

There is power in authority. There is power in agreement. There is power in faith, love and obedience. When the Church contends as one, all things become possible.

> **And they, continuing daily with one accord in the temple, and breaking bread from house to house, did eat their meat with gladness and singleness of heart.**
>
> **Acts 2:46**

Agreement creates an atmosphere for the miraculous.

> **Insomuch that they brought forth the sick into the streets, and laid them on beds and couches, that at least the shadow of Peter passing by might overshadow some of them. There came also a multitude out of the cities round about unto Jerusalem, bringing sick folks, and them which were vexed with unclean spirits; and they were healed every one.**
>
> **Acts 5:15-16**

Death, Hell and the Grave

> **I am He that liveth, and was dead; and behold, I am alive for evermore, Amen and have the keys of Hell and of death.**
>
> **Revelation 1:18**

What is it that gives Jesus authority in your life? It is the fact that He became a man, died and then rose again. This is what qualifies Him to be a Priest that can be touched with the feelings of our infirmities (Hebrew 4:15). God became a man and did what no man could do.

When did He get the keys of death and of Hell? You cannot get the keys of Hell unless you go to Hell to get them. Jesus died and His soul experienced the condemnation of sin. After three days and three nights, He rose again and forever took the keys.

> **Forasmuch then as the children are partakers of flesh and blood, He also Himself likewise took part of the same; and through death He might destroy him that had the power of death, that is, the devil; and deliver them who through fear of death were all their lifetime subject to bondage.**
>
> **Hebrews 2:14-15**

Jesus destroyed the power of death and took jurisdiction over all that had been stolen.

While Adam walked in the cool of the Garden, the devil fitfully mused, *"Adam has authority over the fowl of the air, the fish, the creeping things and the Earth… so I will take that authority from him."* In a moment of trickery and cunning deceit, the devil talked Adam into forfeiting his God-given authority. Adam and all of creation immediately became subject to the dominion of the curse. Having gained access to the creation of God, Satan perverted and corroded all that God had made good.

At the appointed time, many years later, Jesus was born into the Earth. He became the *last Adam*, the One that had the power to right every wrong. Not only did Jesus recover authority over the fish of the sea, the fowl of the air and the Earth, but He also won jurisdiction for His seed.

Jesus said, *"I will claim the universe. Men and women that believe in Me will be just like Me. They will live forever and ever in an exalted position of oneness and unity with Almighty God. They will rule and reign. They will testify to God's divine purpose in that He predestined them to become conformed to the image of His dear Son."*

When the devil crucified Jesus, he thought that he had thwarted the plan of God. What He did not know, however, was that Jesus only submitted to death so that He might rise again, holding the keys of death, Hell and the grave.

When you say, *"In the name of Jesus,"* you have all the power of Heaven behind you. You have God's *endorsement* behind you. The keys of death, Hell, and the grave are in the hands of your Master.

Communicating with God

Prayer is *communication* with God.

If a person spends a lot of time in the natural, they will become educated on natural things. If they spend a lot of time working physically, they will prosper physically. However, the person who spends much time in the Spirit, will grow much spiritually. Those that invest themselves in a life of prayer, will reap the results of prayer. The Bible says that those who sow to the Spirit, will reap of the Spirit (Galatians 6:8).

Much Prayer. Much Power.
Little Prayer. Little Power.

Those that pray in an unknown language, edify their spirit. They build themselves up on their most holy faith (Jude 20). As a person speaks to themselves in psalms and spiritual songs, they fill themselves to overflowing with the power of the Holy Ghost (Ephesians 5:19). It's not that a person really receives more power through prayer, it's that they *realize* more power. The power was always available. Heaven had not withheld it. However, it took communication with God to open the eyes of their understanding.

Prayer taps into a frequency and a realm of revelation. It bridges Heaven with Earth. It connects the natural with the supernatural. Those who connect with God will see, hear and understand. Their eyes will be accustomed to the glory and they will receive a revelation of the exceeding greatness of His power.

Through prayer, the Spirit of God has the ability to lead the believer into the manifest experience of truth. Those that communicate with the Lord and walk in the Spirit will think the thoughts of God. Their meditations will be charged with life. Revelation will stir in their spirit and the Word of God will become living and vibrant within them.

Prayer enables the believer to see what is already available. Prayer *reminds*. Prayer *positions*. Prayer *revives*. It's not that prayers cause the believer to ascend to the throne. Rather, prayer tunes the believer into their heavenly perspective. It's the perspective from the throne, from the heavenly places in Christ.

> **Now Peter and John went up together into the temple at the hour of prayer, being the ninth hour. And a certain man lame from his mother's womb was carried, whom they laid daily at the gate of the temple which is called Beautiful, to ask alms of them that entered into the temple; who seeing Peter and John about to go into the temple asked an alms.**
>
> **Acts 3:1-3**

Peter and John were walking to the temple for prayer, yet they had already been walking *in* prayer. Having mixed the power of the Word with the power of prayer, they were prepared to do whatever the Lord might ask. They were already dwelling in a realm of communication and fellowship with God. When they came upon the blind man at the gate Beautiful, they did not have to *work up* to the moment or muster Holy Ghost initiative. Rather, they were already *there* in God. They had already been prepared through prayer.

Prayer connects the saint to dunamis, while the Word connects them to exousia. In other words, the miracle working power of God comes through the avenue of prayer, while authority comes through the Word. Those that understand the exousia that the Word gives will understand their authority to say *"No"* to the devil. This kind of authority does not require a miracle. It only requires the badge and a working knowledge of the law.

The believer has the authority to say *"No"* to sin. They have the authority to say *"No"* to sickness and *"No"* to disease. Notice, it does not require a miracle to say *"No"* to sickness and disease. It only requires the authority of the Word. Those that know the laws of the land, have no problem using their authority when the situation demands it. Authority will put the fugitive on notice and the renegade behind bars.

As you spend time in prayer, the Holy Ghost will take the Word that is in you and make it a *rhema* to your spirit. God will breathe on the Word that is *within* and the inspiration of Heaven will fill your heart. That *rhema Word* will become alive and full of divine energy and expectation.

Prayer gives you the ability to tune in with the Holy Ghost. Those that are in synch with the Spirit will walk with the Spirit. Their connection with the anointing will enable them to flow with God. In turn, God will speak through their lips and work though their hands. They will channel the power of God into their everyday life experience.

People miss it in God when they postpone prayer until moments of desperation. They wait to get anointed until they *need* to be anointed. It isn't until they are faced with a crisis that they feel the urgency to touch Heaven. The believer, however, must walk in prayer. It must be a continual practice, as ordinary as eating and breathing. For the believer to maintain victory, they *must* maintain their connection with the power of God. They must stay attached to the source of their inspiration and strength.

Peter drew his sword and chopped off the servant's ear (Luke 22:50). He wasn't anointed when the challenge came. Instead of *acting* in the strength of God, he *reacted* in the flesh. If he had prayed, he would have been prepared to face the opposition. At the point of confrontation, he would have drawn on the power of the anointing and not on the sword.

Prayer is not an option for those who are called to herald the victory of Calvary. Do not say, *"Let's pray"* only when the situation desperately demands a miracle. Instead…*dwell, walk, live, breath* …in a life of prayer and fellowship with God.

Working Miracles

> **And Peter, fastening his eyes upon him with John, said, "Look on us." And he gave heed unto them, expecting to receive something of them. Then Peter said, "Silver and gold have I none; but such as I have give I thee: in the name of Jesus Christ of Nazareth rise up and walk." And he took him by the right hand, and lifted him up: and immediately his feet and ankle bones received strength. And he leaping up stood, and walked, and entered with them into the temple, walking, and leaping, and praising God.**
>
> **Acts 3:4-8**

The devil would like you to believe that hearing God is difficult.

How many have said, *"How do I know that I'm doing the right thing?"*

The believer that has the Holy Ghost and the Word, *will hear God.* They will hear His voice and know how to respond. Jesus said, *"My sheep hear My voice"* (John 10:27). The sheep do not have to strain their ear to Heaven. They do not need an amplifier and God does not need a megaphone. Rather, the sheep's ear has been trained to recognize the voice of the Shepherd. They were born with the ability to identify His voice.

How did Peter and John know what to do with the lame man?

They knew because the same Spirit that had operated in Jesus' life was now operating in their life. That Spirit was bringing to their remembrance the Words that Jesus had spoken. In fact, Jesus encouraged His disciples with this promise just before going to the cross:

> **But the Comforter, which is the Holy Ghost, whom the Father will send in My name, He shall teach you all things, and bring all things to your remembrance, whatsoever I have said unto you.**
>
> **John 14:26**

The Holy Ghost brought the Word to their remembrance. To the untrained eye, it might have looked like Peter and John knew what to do in the natural. Perhaps they had role played the making of a miracle at the gate? This, however, was not the case. Peter and John knew how to hear God and how to obey His commands. They were walking out a supernatural directive in *real time*, as the Holy Ghost was working with them.

"And he gave heed unto them, expecting to receive something of them."

The man at the gate looked at Peter and John and expected to receive something. He was expecting money, but they had something different for him. They had a miracle.

Jesus has already given you what you need. It's like tossing some sliced potatoes in a pan of oil and saying, *"It's on the stove. Why won't it fry?"* God says, *"You have the oil. You have the fire. Turn up the heat so that you get the results!"*

Success is not mysterious. God has given you all the ingredients. All you must do is follow His recipe, *word for word.* You have the Word. You have the Holy Ghost. Connect yourself to the power source and walk in the Spirit. If you *do not* do what you've been trained to do, you will continue to reap the disappointments of the natural realm. Either walk in the flesh and get disappointed or walk in the Spirit and magnify Jesus' name.

> **And he gave heed unto them, expecting to receive something of them. Then Peter said, "Silver and gold have I none; but such as I have give I thee: in the name of Jesus Christ of Nazareth rise up and walk." And he took him by the right hand, and lifted him up ...**
>
> **Acts 3:5-7a**

Peter said to the man, *"I do not have silver and gold for you, but I can give you a divine command based upon the authority of the Man that never failed to do God's will. On behalf of Jesus, I am telling you to get up. He sent me with the divine anointing and authority to impact your life with a gift. I have healing in my hands. When I lay hands on you, if you believe it, something is going to go into your life and God is going to make you whole."*

> **...and immediately his feet and ankle bones received strength and he leaping up stood and walked and entered with them into the temple, walking and leaping and praising God.**
>
> **Acts 3:7b**

Evidently, the man didn't immediately respond to Peter. Peter, therefore, took hold of his hand and pulled him up. When he did, the man immediately received strength in his feet and ankles.

When you step out in God, there will be times that your results will be affected by the atmosphere around you. The lame man's miracle was not only dependent on the obedience of Peter and John, but it also hinged on *his response* to the Word of God. In other words, there are at least two wills involved when a miracle is at hand. If the recipient is *not* in full agreement with the Word, they may *hinder* the flow of God's power in their life.

There have been many sincere believers in the Church that have become disappointed with their results in God. They have obeyed the Word and applied faith, yet the person died. However, it must be remembered that the one on the receiving end has their own faith and their own will. There are other factors involved that may not be outwardly observed. The one that needs the miracle is often the one that is hindering the miracle.

Faith cannot be used in violation of another's will.

Supernatural Initiative

Peter took hold of the man, picked him up and immediately his anklebones received strength. He began leaping, walking and praising God. Those that witnessed this miracle watched the commotion in wonder and amazement. The Bible records that all the people ran together to Solomon's porch to see this wonder (Acts 3:11). Peter and John, seeing an opportunity to preach the name of Jesus, addressed the crowd:

> "And His name, through faith in His name, has made this man strong, whom you see and know. Yes, the faith which comes through Him has given him this perfect soundness in the presence of you all…"
>
> **Acts 3:16 NKJV**

The people stood in amazement, but Peter knew exactly how the miracle happened. He understood delegated authority. He understood the power of the Name and the power of attorney. The Holy Ghost had made the Words of Jesus come alive within his spirit. He knew that He was acting on behalf of the Master. He knew what Jesus would have done, so he reached out, grabbed the lame man, and worked the miracle in His place.

The lame man had obviously heard about Jesus. He was sitting at the temple in the midst of a great revival in the city. People were getting filled with the Holy Ghost and thousands were being added to the Church. The disciples were demonstrating the name of Jesus and His fame was spreading everywhere. The man at the gate had heard the commotion. He heard rumors of miracles and all that was being done in the name of Jesus.

When Peter commanded the man to get up, everything he had heard went into his spirit and he made a decision to receive the power that was extended to him. *He was activated by the Words that he heard.*

If someone that was not a Christian, could receive a miracle based upon faith in the Name, how much more should the believer rise up and become perfectly sound mentally, physically and financially?

> **"Let it be known to you all, and to all the people of Israel, that by the name of Jesus Christ of Nazareth, whom you crucified, whom God raised from the dead, by Him this man stands before you whole."**
>
> **Acts 4:10 NKJV**

How did the limbs get straight? How did the dead rise? It's because somebody talked to them in the name of Jesus. They said, *"Listen, Somebody sent me here. Death, I have been sent by the One that took your keys."*

This is how the dead are raised up. The dead do not rise because people *pray* that God will raise them. The dead are only raised because a person believes that Jesus gave them His name. They believe that they are sent, bearing the authority of His name, to take authority over death, Hell and the grave. Jesus, after all, won the victory and gave the Church the keys.

In the name of Jesus, walk!
In the name of Jesus, rise from the dead!
In the name of Jesus, do not turn back! Live for Jesus!

God does not want you to have an excuse. He doesn't want you to fail. Rather, He has provided for your success and triumph. He has sent you with His divine authority. He has commissioned you with an anointing to conduct business on His behalf. Peter didn't act super spiritual, he just obeyed God from the sincerity of his heart. He heard God and he obeyed God.

By the name of Jesus, the storm was calmed!
By the name of Jesus, the dark clouds have to more out of your life!
By the name of Jesus, the devil has to take his hands off your relatives!

Instead of praying about it, get up and speak your authority. Speak to the situation and say, *"Devil, take your hands off my relatives in the name of Jesus of Nazareth. Loose them and let them go."* Take authority. Bind the work of the enemy so that their minds would have the liberty to see clearly. When they see, they will make a decision for God.

There is power in the name of Jesus. As an ambassador of the Kingdom, you have been commissioned to work on behalf of the Master. You have received a divine mandate to get divine results. He has given you a charge and sent you into the world, equipped with the integrity of His name and the fullness of His power. This day you will rise up, unhindered, and fulfill the call of God on your life. You will do what you were born to do and like Peter and John, you will represent His glory to all the world.

"And all the people saw him walking and praising God…and they were filled with wonder and amazement…" (Acts 3:9,10b)

There is authority in the words that you are reading. Every page of this book is filled with the ability and the supernatural initiative of Heaven. As you read, you are receiving an impartation to act on the things that have been planted within your heart. The Word of God will grow strong in you and you will take hold of your authority. You will rise up in the name of Jesus and walk in fearless obedience. You will not stay where you are. You will not be a failure. You will fulfill your heavenly calling.

Power for Everyday

> "Nor is there salvation in any other (name), for there is no other name under Heaven given among men by which we must be saved."
>
> **Acts 4:12 NKJV**

Jesus is the only name under Heaven that can save. Salvation, of course, is all-inclusive. It not only includes redemption, but also forgiveness, healing, prosperity, rescue and restoration. There is no other name given among men that can procure healing, deliverance and victory.

There is HEALING in the Name.
There is VICTORY in the Name.
There is TRIUMPH in the Name.
There is FINANCIAL BREAKTHROUGH in the Name.

Take the Name and use it where it belongs. Say, *"World, I have the Name of the One who overcame you, reduced you and brought you to a place of inferiority and submission."*

Take up the name and use it in prayer. Use it against the principalities of darkness. Cast out devils and assert your delegated dominion. Heal the sick, deliver the oppressed and address the contrary circumstance. The name of Jesus applies to *victory*. It applies to *success*. It applies to *happiness.* It applies to *accomplishment* and *fulfillment.* The name of Jesus is for everyday life.

> **For He hath said, "I will never leave thee, nor forsake thee." So that we may boldly say, "The Lord is my helper, and I will not fear what man shall do unto me."**
>
> **Hebrews 13:5b-6**

Jesus will never leave you nor forsake you. He sent the Holy Spirit so that His power would be readily available. When you exercise your authority in line with the Word, the Holy Ghost will back you up. He will enforce your victory with His power. In other words, you can confidently do what you have been sent to do. You can stand boldly in Holy Ghost assurance, knowing that He will undergird your every action of faith.

You will say, *"God is my Helper. I am not going to fear what man can or will do to me. Jesus is present with me and I am here in His name."* While you minister (serve, work) in His name, the presence and power of God will help you. He will help you financially. He will help you physically. He will help you spiritually.

Put the Name to *work* in your life.

CHAPTER 10

AWAKENING TO GREATNESS

---

*When a person loses sight of the
will of God, they lose their song.
What was once a shout, becomes a whisper.*

Heavenly Perspectives

And these signs shall follow them that believe…

Mark 16:17a

Jesus said, *"These signs shall follow them that believe."* These are those that get results. They walk on a different plane than mere mortal people. They have an air about them, a boldness that is infused with the divine nature. Instead of cowering in subservience to the dictates of a fallen world, these reign in life through Christ Jesus. They are God's ambassadors to the earth realm.

The Lord has commissioned you to represent Heaven on Earth. You are called to walk in a realm that most people can only aspire to. It's a realm where divine rule takes preeminence and where exploits are performed.

You are not bound. Your hands are not tied regarding the circumstances of life. You are not a victim. All of the resources of Heaven are available to you. If you will be faithful to walk in agreement with the Word, God will see to it that Heaven validates your convictions. Your life will testify to the conquest of Calvary.

Jesus forever changed the status of life for everyone that will believe.

At one time, by nature, we were children of the devil. We were victims of darkness. The taskmaster of this world ruled over us and exercised his dominion in our daily lives. We were oppressed, defeated and in bondage. Through the victory of Calvary, however, Jesus saw to it that the devil was stripped of all power and authority. His sweeping defeat was made a public display and his influence was forever demoted.

Today, within the Church, many look back to the first century Church with a sense of longing. They reminisce of "the good old days," the great victories, and how "they turned the world upside down." *"That was then,"* they say, *"God used to do that for the disciples but it is no longer for today."*

> **Jesus Christ is the same yesterday, today and forever.**
>
> **Hebrews 13:8 NKJV**

Jesus Christ Today

The passage of time has not diminished the authority of the Name. It has not worn out with use, nor has God grown tired of providing power. The name of Jesus is for today. It is for tomorrow. It is for every child of God to freely receive and use. What the Name did for the early Church, it will do in this dispensation. It is not a relic of the past, but it is power for this present generation.

If the Name is for today, then everything that took place in the book of Acts is for today. The Name wasn't just relegated to a dispensation, but it was given to the Church for all ages. The victory that Jesus wrought didn't expire in the first century or in the second, but rather, it is still strong and glorious today. The Name is for anyone who will use it in accordance with the Word of God.

> **And these signs shall follow them that believe; In My name shall they cast out devils; they shall speak with new tongues. They shall take up**

serpents; and if they drink any deadly thing, it shall not hurt them; they shall lay hands on the sick, and they shall recover.

Mark 16:17-18

If the Name is for **today**, then…
"In My name shall they cast out devils"
…is for **today**.

If the Name is for **today**, then…
"they shall speak with new tongues"
…is for **today**.

If the Name is for **today**, then…
"if they drink any deadly thing, it shall not hurt them"
…is for **today**.

If the Name is for **today**, then…
"they shall lay hands on the sick, and they shall recover"
…is for **today**.

If a believer is poisoned, they will not die. The Name includes preservation from plagues, diseases, venomous bites, poison, harmful gasses, bad water or whatever the case may be. The name of Jesus is for the believer 24 hours a day.

The *name* of the Lord is a strong tower. The righteous run into it and they are safe.

Proverbs 18:10 NKJV

There is safety and gladness in the name of the Lord. He is an ever-present help in time of need. He will never forsake His own, nor will He fail to honor the integrity of His name. His name is a strong tower. It will garrison the righteous and they will be preserved from everything that the average man fears.

It does not require a gift to cast out a devil. There is a gift of discerning of spirits, however, a spirit does not need to be discerned before it is cast out. Every believer has authority over *all* of the powers of darkness. Casting out devils is just something that the believer does. It's the same with healing the sick and speaking in tongues. These signs *accompany* those who believe.

You should cast out a devil when you meet a devil. You should lay hands on the sick when you meet the sick. You should speak with tongues when you need to pray.

The believer does not need to *wait* for a special unction, because these things are not dependent on the operation of a gift. They are not manifestations of the Holy Ghost, but rather, they are signs that accompany the believer. These signs are solely dependent upon exousia authority.

Authority never wavers. The name of Jesus does not waver. His name is effective 24 hours a day. It does not waver with feelings and it does not waver with circumstance. If you will do what you have been commanded to do, then God will validate your faithfulness to the Word. He will confirm the Word with signs following. Your life will be accompanied by His performance.

> **The Lord working with them, and confirming the Word with signs following.**
>
> **Mark 16:20b**

Riding the Crest of Revelation

As you grow in your revelation of the Name, you will discover that one could spend a lifetime delving into the many facets of the Name. Each day in God holds higher heights. Likewise, deeper truths lead to deeper truths. One level of revelation opens up to the next level and to the next level, another level. There are countless layers of revelation within the Word of God. As you grow in your understanding of the

Name, you will put your revelation to work in your everyday life. The Name stands for *victory* and if you put the Name to work in your life, it will produce that *victory* in your life.

Apply your revelation.

While studying the power of the Name, E.W. Kenyon had this insight, *"Some of us have experienced the authority vested in the name of Jesus but so far none of us have been able to take a permanent place in our privileges and abide where we may enjoy the fullness of His mighty power."*

By now, you have a foundational understanding of the Name, but there is a place in God that surpasses knowledge. It's the place where *knowledge* becomes *experience*. It's the place where revelation, not only generates expectation, but it obtains the experience of the promise.

There is a permanent place of bliss available to the child of God. It's a place where all of the provisions of the Name are being procured and experienced on a continual basis. Within this generation, there is a remnant that will walk in the fullness of the Word. They will not be satisfied with the 30-fold or the 60-fold, but they will press in and experience the full manifestation of the promise.

In order to know God, one must know His name. When Moses asked God, *"When I go into Egypt and they ask who sent me, who shall I say?"* God said, *"I Am that I Am"* (Exodus 3:13-14). Since that time, God has expanded on the revelation of His name through the ministry of Christ.

"I Am that I Am."

Through a revelation of the Name, you can rise to a place where you will abide on a foundation of stability and strength. Your Christian experience does not need to resemble a roller coaster ride. It does not need to ebb and flow like the tide. Rather, you can stay established in God. You can grow from glory to glory. Like a climber, you can scale peak after peak.

He that dwelleth in the secret place of the most High shall abide under the shadow of the Almighty.

Psalm 91:1

A person cannot *dwell* and *abide* unless they have pressed beyond the revelation. After a revelation, comes a decision. The Word of God demands commitment. It demands a response. *"What will you do with what you claim to know?"*

Revelation that is not fueled with action will remain dormant. There are many within the Church that *know*, but their *knowing* has yet to reach its goal. The goal of revelation, of course, is to produce results in your life. It's not just for the purpose of producing a metaphorical light bulb above your head, but it's so that you would harness the revelation and walk in its experiential understanding.

E.W. Kenyon wrote, *"We have a conviction that before the Lord Jesus returns there will be a mighty army of believers who will learn the secret of living in the Name, of reigning in life, living in the victorious transcendent resurrection life of the Son of God among men."*

The name of Jesus is the property of the Church. The Church has not earned it, but it has been given as a gift. There is more than enough power in the Name.

Many of you that are reading this book will rise to the place in God that Kenyon spoke of. Perhaps you sense the call within your spirit, for you have been commissioned to rise into the ranks of the army of God. God is calling you to live like never before. *Live* in the power of the Name. *Live* victorious. *Live* without fear. *Live* in the fullness of Him that filleth all in all (Ephesians 1:23). The provision of the Name and all that it stands for will be your banner in life. It will be your day-by-day experience. The signs that accompany you will broadcast your victory and herald the obliteration of your adversary.

Melodies of the Heart

> **Let the Word of Christ dwell in you richly in all wisdom, teaching and admonishing one another in psalms and hymns and spiritual songs, singing with grace in your hearts to the Lord. And whatsoever ye do in word or deed, do all in the name of the Lord Jesus, giving thanks to God and the Father by Him.**
>
> **Colossians 3:16-17**

"Let the Word of Christ dwell in you richly..." This is not a suggestion. This is a command and it should lead the Church to a lifestyle. Whenever the Word is taught, some will say, *"I know"* and others will put it off until tomorrow. Still others will prioritize the Word and allow it to dwell richly within them. These will see the Word of God produce the promised performance.

The Word that *dwells richly* will develop, bud, and bring forth a harvest.

Allow the Word to dwell richly and disallow the opinions and reports that contradict the Word of God. A person like this will shake off depression. The enemy may target them. He may try to steal from them. He may try to drag them down, but through the Word that dwells richly, they will thwart every onslaught. The power of the revelation within will well up and overcome the heavy burden.

These will *immediately* think on the Word. They will not give the enemy any headway, but rather, they will quote the Word and refute every lying suggestion. Like David, they will forget *not* all His benefits (Psalm 102:3). They will consider what God has done and they will meditate on His majesty. This alone will bring jubilant shouts and exuberant joy! Like light overcomes darkness, the Spirit of joy will overcome the spirit of depression.

"…teaching admonishing one another in psalms and hymns and spiritual songs, singing with grace in your hearts to the Lord."

The Word that dwells richly will overflow into songs, hymns and spiritual songs. The grace that is in their heart will so fill their mouth, that confession will spill over into an anthem of praise, exaltation and confidence towards God.

In order for a person to admonish another with psalms and hymns, they must live above the circumstances of life. They must have a song in their heart that rises to the occasion. Those that meditate on the Word will always have a song.

> **Those who carried us away captive asked of us a song, and those who plundered us requested mirth, saying, "Sing us one of the songs of Zion!" How shall we sing the Lord's song in a foreign land?**
>
> **Psalm 137:3b-4 NKJV**

If the child of God does not dwell in the name of Jesus or in the Word of God, they are dwelling in a foreign land. They are living contrary to their divine nature. Those that make their home in a land of bondage will *not* carry a song in their heart. The songs of Zion are the melodies that are born out of a heart that has been sown with the Word of God. If the land is barren and without revelation, there will only be the clamor of flesh talking.

Remember, a *land* is never predisposed to barrenness or desolation. The soil of one's heart is meant to be tilled with the Word of God. Meditations will grow into confessions and confessions will spill over into song. Psalms, hymns, and spiritual songs are methods that the Holy Ghost uses to keep the saint *in tune* with the anointing of God.

Say this out loud:

I am not moved by what I see. I know Whom I serve.

I know in whom I have believed. I know what He did and I know what has been provided in His name

How to Touch Heaven

There was once a man named Lazarus, who was suffering with tuberculosis. Bedridden for six years and reduced to skin and bones, all hope had been lost. He was given up to die. As the disease progressed, he had become increasingly angry and bitter towards God. After all, he had served God! Prior to this state, he had labored in the mines during the day, and at night, he served in the church and ministered the Word. After contracting the disease, he prayed repeatedly for healing, yet Heaven seemed to have overlooked his plea.

Six years passed. Lazarus grew increasingly bitter and death drew nearer.

Through word of mouth, Smith Wigglesworth heard of this man and his plight. He asked the Lord about it and God directed him to raise Lazarus up. Going to his house, Wigglesworth began to share the Word of God with the man. He wanted to get him into agreement with the Word of God, but Lazarus would not hear any of it. The man was dying and he did not want to hear about the promises of God.

Just because God told you to do something, doesn't mean that it is going to be easy! This is why *many* are called and *few* are chosen (Matthew 22:14). The chosen ones overcome the obstacles and prevail until the end. *Remember, it's the one that is called that <u>decides</u> to be chosen.*

With Holy Ghost resolve, Wigglesworth left the room and said, *"Can I get seven people to pray with me?"* He did not allow himself to be moved by the man's unbelief. Gathering seven people in the sickroom, they joined hands in agreement. Wigglesworth, speaking to the group, announced, *"We are not going to pray! Instead, we will use the name of Jesus."* They began to say, *"Jesus! Jesus! Jesus!"* and the power of God filled the house.

There is power in the name of Jesus.
His name is above every name.

Some might say, *"I can't praise Jesus, I am in debt."*
JESUS IS BIGGER than debt!

Others might say, *"I can't praise Jesus, I am sick."*
JESUS IS BIGGER than sick!

Jesus is bigger than broke. Jesus is bigger than bound. Jesus is bigger than weak. Jesus is bigger than anything that can come against you. If you will use the name of Jesus in your life, you will not fall short of your position in God. *Your experience in life will testify to the name that you lift up.*

As the power of God began to fall, Smith Wigglesworth said, *"I am not going to help God. This is God! I am going to let Him do it Himself."* Turning to the man, Wigglesworth said, *"Lazarus, that is the power of God in this room and you need to receive it."* Lazarus broke down and said, *"I have been bitter. I have been angry with God because for six years I haven't been healed. I have been mad."* Wigglesworth answered, *"Repent and God will hear you."* With that, they left the man with the Holy Ghost and marched downstairs.

Alone with God, Lazarus asked the Lord to forgive him. When he did, God supernaturally touched him and he rose up out of the sickbed, completely healed. Restored in every way, he walked down the stairs to tell the others of his miracle.

The day has come when the Church will no longer pray long, belabored prayers, begging God to do something. It is a day when the saint will dwell in a life of prayer. They won't pound Heaven when things go wrong, but they will walk in a place of unending communication and fellowship with God. It won't be, *"Gimme, gimme, gimme, my name is Jimmy, I will take what you gimme."* It won't be religious, but from the sincerity and the simplicity of their heart, believers will touch Heaven.

Jesus said, *"Your Father knows the things you have need of before you ask Him"* (Matthew 6:8). He knows that you need clothes. He knows that you need to eat. He knows that you need to abide and reside. The Father will take care of all of these things. He will provide for you, but if you will apply the power of the Name, then the majority of your prayer life will consist of praising God for His faithfulness. Instead of pleading your case, you will be rejoicing in His ever-present help. Instead of pummeling Heaven with an endless shopping list of problems, the saint will walk in the realm of prayer. They will abide in the Presence.

These will say, *"I don't have to see God do one more thing for me to praise Him."*

Jesus said, *"It is finished"* (John 19:30). It has been done for 2,000 years. Jesus finished the job. *"But,"* you say, *"Why haven't I seen it?"* Saint, you need to *get up* and *dwell* in it. You need to rise up and GO THERE in God. Through the Holy Ghost, God wants to give you a working revelation of the Name. He wants you to abide in the strength and power of His presence.

Jesus, Enthroned in Praise

> **I have been crucified with Christ; it is no longer I who live, but Christ lives in me...**
>
> **Galatians 2:20a NKJV**

The Church must relate with Christ in accordance with who He is *now*, not with who He was when He walked the shores of Galilee. Jesus, of course, is the same person, but He was given a better name after His resurrection. Taking the keys of death, Hell and the grave, He was given all power in Heaven and in Earth. His name was made higher than any other. Today, He is on a different plane. He is no longer the carpenter in Galilee. Rather, He is the King of Kings and the Lord of Lords. He is the glorified Master and He has given the Church the crown of His victory. He has given the Church His name.

Not only has Jesus given His name, but He also lives within the saint. Paul called this a mystery and wrote, *"To whom God would make known what is the riches of the glory of this mystery among the Gentiles; which is Christ in you, the hope of glory"* (Colossians 1:27). Christ is *in* the believer. As the Body of Christ, we must identify with the *Person* that has come to live on the inside of us. We must identify with *all* that He is.

"As He is, so are we in this world" (1 John 4:17b).

Jesus is not a boring person; neither is He a religious person! Jesus is a *happy* person! Jesus rejoices in the Lord. He rejoices in the oil of gladness. He sings praises unto God. In fact, Jesus inhabits our praises! This is why *complaining* and *murmuring* makes a person *dry*. When a saint is critical, and they walk in unhealed hurts and wounds, their spirit will become dry because God will not be in it. The Presence will not abide where strife is allowed to fester.

The presence of God is only invited when praise ascends to the throne. This is the atmosphere of miracles. The Bible says, *"God inhabits the praises of His people"* (Psalm 22:3). God does not inhabit the murmuring or griping of His people. These things, rather, drive the Presence away. The saint, who participates in this dryness, will also become dry. Praise then, is like water to the spirit. Just as the farmer knows that a well-watered field will yield abundance, God knows that praise will water every God-Word sown in the life of a believer.

Where praise is, *God is.*

> **For where two or three are gathered together in My name, there am I in the midst of them.**
>
> **Matthew 18:20**

When saints gather in the Name, Jesus promises to be in their midst. He promises to be with those who congregate unto Him and unto the Father. This is why the saint can boldly say, *"Father, in the name of Jesus…"* Those that use the Name are really saying, *"As delegates sent by the Lord Jesus Christ, we know that when You look at us, You are not going to see us, but rather, You will see Christ. Father, because of this, we know that You are obligated to answer every believer in the same way that You are obligated to answer Your Son."*

When the Father looks at Jesus, He sees the Church. He sees the Body of Christ. Even when Jesus, Himself, confronted Saul on the road to Damascus, He didn't say, *"Why are you persecuting My Church,"* He said, *"Why are you persecuting Me"* (Acts 9:4)?

When believers gather together and say, *"Father in the name of Jesus,"* they are standing as delegates of the Lord Jesus Christ. They are approaching the throne of God in the Name that has been given to them. In the midst of such a congregation, Jesus will sing praises unto God. He will declare God's name among His brethren (Hebrews 2:12).

Praise is faith articulated. Many times, praise is thanking God for something that is *yet* to happen. Other times, it may start with something that He has done, but then it will spill over into the things that He *will do* and the things that haven't been seen *yet*. When a saint praises God, they step into the testimony of Jesus. They step into a realm of prophetic foresight.

The testimony of Jesus is the Spirit of prophecy.

Revelation 19:10

Psalms, hymns and spiritual songs are God's way to ensure an anointed lifestyle. If you will keep your heart filled with the Word of God *richly*, then grace will abound in your heart. When you sing and admonish one another with psalms and hymns, the anointing of God will dwell within your life and His presence will accompany you.

Sing out the honor of His name; Make His

praise glorious. Say to God, "How awesome are your works!"

Psalm 66:2,3a NKJV

Positioned for Promotion

And whatsoever ye do in word or deed, do all in the name of the Lord Jesus, giving thanks to God and the Father by Him.

Colossians 3:17

While Jesus walked the Earth, He participated in the fullness of the human experience. There is not a facet of life that has not been touched and perfected by Him. In others words, if Jesus lived *it* and had a testimony *in it*, then so can you.

When you go to work, remember that Jesus also worked. When you serve in the helps ministry, remember that Jesus also served in the helps ministry. He washed the disciples' feet. He preferred others above Himself and He gave of His time. There is not one role in life that Jesus did not fulfill and leave footsteps for you to follow in. He has paved the way so that you might follow in His example, *step by step*.

"And whatsoever ye do in word or deed…"

Whatever you put your hands to, *do it like Jesus would do it*. Serve like Jesus would serve. Work like Jesus would work. Give like Jesus would give. Follow His lead and do what you do in His name.

Jesus did not serve so that He could get something in return. He doesn't look at a saint and think, *"What's in it for Me if I touch their life?"* Jesus is not selfish! His love is entirely unconditional love. He gives without any expectations. He sows the seed because He is confident that the seed will produce. He sows without any pressure or manipulation.

Whatever you do, do it just like Jesus would do it. When you work for an employer, be faithful. There are Christians that will rip off their company. They will justify it and say, *"Well, you don't understand. They don't pay me enough and this is God's way of blessing me."*

"... do all in the name of the Lord Jesus."

Many ministers have fallen because they saw *people* as their key to promotion in God. They looked to *flesh* as their source, and like a ship without bearing, they lost their way. Somewhere beneath the cloudy, starless sky, they deviated from the *"do all in the Name."*

If you catch yourself manipulating, step back and say, *"Wait a minute, I am not doing this in the Name."* If Jesus is not involved in your project, stop yourself before you venture too far out into the flesh. Catch yourself before the fall!

After you catch yourself, get back in the Name. Do what you are called to do in the name of Jesus. Step back into the anointing. Step back into praise, into singing and into giving. When you *do what you do* unto the Lord, *promotion will come from the Lord*.

Many have missed it when they mistakenly thought that advancement would come from another direction. They thought that they could work their promotion according to the flesh. Giving place to the enemy, they allowed him to navigate their judgments. They allowed him to steer their life in a certain way, jockeying themselves for rank or title.

Some people will seek the ordination of a denomination that seems to hold the most open doors. Instead of following the leading of the Holy Ghost, they position themselves in the flesh, and then they get buried in the flesh. Their call becomes suffocated in politics and endless wranglings. Their dream dies and their anointing fades. They become the victim of their own self-seeking.

If you *don't do what you do* in the name of Jesus, then you will do it in *another name*. That name may be religious politics or selfish gain. Whatever it is, it will be a lower level name, a work of the flesh. Those that have veered off into the flesh, will begin to handle the Word of God deceitfully. Instead of telling the truth, they will tell people what they want to hear.

If the devil can't stop you from being a child of God, He will attempt to steer you into a place of barrenness. He does not want you to have the satisfaction of results in God. If He can render you ineffective, then He can neutralize your influence in the Kingdom of God. Resist the devil and he will flee.

Remember: *"God is not unjust to forget your work and your labor of love"* (Hebrews 6:10).

But as for you, brethren, do not grow weary in doing good.

2 Thessalonians 3:13 NKJV

Those that *do good* are not *doing good* in the expectation that they will be repaid for their trouble. If this were the case, the *do-gooders* would only *do good* in the prospect of compensation. They would evaluate their good works in terms of reward and gain.

"Whatsoever ye do ... do all in the name of the Lord Jesus."

Whether it is in word or in deed, do all that you do in the name of Jesus. Don't base your good works on the hope of remuneration. It is not wise to put your results in life within the reach of your own intellectual ability to manipulate. As the redeemed of God, such a level is beneath you. You are called to walk in the high places in God, to heed His spirit and to represent the integrity of His name. Do not grow weary in well doing, but do everything in the name of the King of Kings.

Make a decision to once and for all, place your destiny in the hands of God. Promotion comes from the Lord. If you will put Him first and live by the anointing and by the Word, God will highly exalt you. You will excel in life and people will wonder what the secret to your success is.

> **Delight yourself also in the Lord, and He shall give you the desires of your heart. Commit your way to the Lord, trust also in Him, and He shall bring it to pass.**
>
> **Psalm 37:4-5 NKJV**

The Secret to Success

The *anointing* is both your secret to success and your reward.

> **Now the Lord is that Spirit: and where the Spirit of the Lord is, there is liberty.**
>
> **2 Corinthians 3:17**

The anointing is for action. It will produce *results* in your life. After all, it was the anointing that brought the coin from the fish's mouth. It was the anointing that multiplied the loaves and the fishes. It was the anointing that made provision for the Word of God. Therefore, the anointing will even work on your behalf monetarily. If you are laboring on behalf of the name of Jesus, the anointing will attract the resources that you require. When you seek first the Kingdom of God, all of these things will be added unto you (Matthew 6:33).

If you are not *doing what you do* in the name of Jesus, you are doing it in *your* name. A person that is seeking after their own, will be without divine enablement. The Holy Ghost can best help the saint who has allowed the Word of God to dwell richly in them. All things become possible in an atmosphere that is fertile with the Word of God. Allow the Word to dwell *richly* in you.

Make the Name your common denominator in life. *Whatever* figures into your day, allow the Name to be the deciding factor. Allow Him to be your point of agreement in everything that you do. When you submit your life to the authority of the Word, the Name will keep you on track and in check. You will walk in the character of Christ, the fruit of the Spirit and the nature of the Word of God. Everything within your life will magnify the divine nature that dwells richly within you.

Where do wars and fights come from among you?

James 4:1a NKJV

Wars start when people split. Contentions erupt when individuals become absorbed with their own selfish pursuits. These go to war because of *differences* that have crept into the church. Somewhere along the line, someone stopped serving in the name of the Lord. Instead of speaking the Word always, they gave place to words devoid of power and life.

When this element is allowed to come in, it becomes a leaven that will leaven the whole lump. It will pollute the whole Body. Jesus said that a kingdom that is divided against itself cannot stand (Matthew 12:25).

Finding Your Song

Wherefore he saith, "Awake thou that sleepest, and arise from the dead, and Christ shall give thee light." See then that ye walk circumspectly, not as fools, but as wise, redeeming the time, because the days are evil. Wherefore be ye not unwise, but understanding what the will of the Lord is. And be not drunk with wine, wherein is excess; but be filled with the Spirit; Speaking

> to yourselves in psalms and hymns and spiritual songs, singing and making melody in your heart to the Lord; Giving thanks always for all things unto God and the Father in the name of our Lord Jesus Christ.
>
> **Ephesians 5:14-20**

"Awake thou that sleepest." An awakening takes place when one heeds a call. It's a stirring that occurs when a distinct sound has been made. Like the dawning of a new day, an awakening revives what was asleep. God is awakening the Church. He has sounded the alarm to arise, for He will give light. He will give the light of direction and it will shine on the path of the just.

"Walk circumspectly, not as fools but wise."

In order to walk wise and to redeem the time, the saint must understand the will of God. They must understand that the will of God *is* the Word of God. Jesus is that Word. He is the will of God in motion. His life is the pattern for victorious living. He is the ultimate example of ATTAINABLE SUCCESS.

"Don't be unwise in understanding what the will of the Lord is."

Know the will of the Lord. In order to sing and praise God, the saint must recall what Jesus did on their behalf. They must know their benefit package in God. They must be familiar with the promises. If a person does not know the will, they cannot contend for the promises. This is why it is imperative to understand *what* the will of the Lord is.

"...singing and making melody in your heart to the Lord."

Why do people lose their song?
Why do people lose their praise?

When a person loses sight of the will of God, they lose their song. What was once a shout, becomes a whisper. *What happened?* The devil came and they were unwise concerning the will of God. Instead of standing upon the Word and resisting enemy lies, they allowed a fiery dart to penetrate their heart. In the end, they gave up their song.

There was a decision involved. They gave place to the enemy, but it didn't have to end there. In the face of opposition, they could have said, *"That will never happen to me. Jesus defeated you. You have no power in my life. I am under the influence of His divine nature."*

You can stand for your divine rights.

"Be filled with the Spirit, speaking to yourselves in psalms and hymns and spiritual songs, singing and making melody in your heart to the Lord, giving thanks always for all things unto God and the Father in the name of our Lord Jesus Christ."

If you can see it in His will, you can thank Him for it. If there is a situation in your life that needs some special attention, take authority and say, *"Thank You Father that no weapon formed against me shall prosper."* You can thank the Father for the promises and resist those things that are less than His will. You do not have to put up with substandard results. You can take a stand. If the Word of God is living on the inside of you, then you should expect and contend for the very best. Anything that falls short, can be easily addressed.

God has given us precious promises to safeguard our lives from the adversary. Therefore, when you wake up, walk circumspectly. Be watchful and let your wisdom be the will of God, which is the Word of God. *Articulate praise.* Speak to yourself in psalms, hymns, and spiritual songs. Use your mouth to thank God. In all that you do, give thanks unto the Lord, and contend for the promise before you.

Chapter 11

Advancing in Victory

---

*Where there is single-mindedness,
there is clarity of direction.
Where there is double-mindedness,
the paths are too many to choose from.*

Namesake Results

The name of Jesus is living and powerful because Jesus is *alive*. His name embodies the nature, person and power of the Lord Jesus Christ. Therefore, when an individual comes in the Name, they come in the *person* of the Lord Jesus. The Bible says, *"My people who are called by My Name..."* (2 Chronicles 7:14). These are the people who are walking in the person of the Lord. They have taken on His identity and become His namesake.

The Word of God is alive and powerful. It is filled with exceeding great and precious promises. Through these promises, the child of God becomes a partaker and an inheritor of the divine nature. As an associate and a carrier of the will of God, they rule and reign as representatives of the Kingdom.

The name of Jesus is the key that accesses the performance of Heaven. Everything that is miraculous and supernatural stems from a proper understanding of the Name. Just as an ambassador's influence is built upon the authority of backing powers, the Name is built upon a foundation of agreement with the living Word of God. That foundation, *the Word of God*, is the basis for its power and influence.

As an ambassador of the Kingdom, you will only see *Name-results* if you are standing on a platform that has been shored up by the Word of God. That platform, of course, is your faith in the integrity of the Word. This is where the Name gets its strength in your life. If you will allow the name of Jesus to have His will in your life, you will obliterate the influence of the devil in your realm of influence. Give NO PLACE to the enemy.

> **Is any sick among you? Let him call for the elders of the church; and let them pray over him, anointing him with oil in the name of the Lord, and the prayer of faith shall save the sick, and the Lord shall raise him up; and if he have committed sins, they shall be forgiven him.**
>
> **James 5:14-15**

Forget everything that you have ever learned that contradicts Scripture. If it is not in line with the Word of God, you can dismiss its influence in your life.

The Name stands for the *Person*. When believers gather in the Name, the *Person* is there. If the *Person* is there, then the *power* of that person is there. Jesus, *the person,* is just as powerful today as He was when He walked the planet. Given the availability of His power, James instructs the believer to call for the elders if they are sick. *"Let the elders pray over the sick, anointing him with oil in the name of the Lord."* Notice, that although Jesus had completed His earthly ministry, His name was still being used to produce results in the earth realm. Jesus is the same yesterday, today and forever.

"And the prayer of faith shall save the sick."

The prayer of faith is a solid conviction. God is not *"Yes"* and *"No."* His Word is definitive. Therefore, the prayer of faith can be definitive as well. It is not a passive, hope for the best, *"Well, I'm believing God"* petition. It's a prayer that has a conviction. It has a confidence in the outcome. Anything less, is not the prayer of faith.

> **Now faith is the substance of things hoped for, the evidence of things not seen.**
>
> **Hebrews 11:1**

The Word says, *"Let them anoint him with oil in the name of the Lord."* In other words, James is saying, *"Let them anoint him with oil on behalf of Jesus, as if He was there doing it personally."* The logical outcome, of course, would be: *"And the Lord shall raise them up."* Jesus was never short on results! Therefore, in His stead and having been vested with His delegated authority, we should get the same results as Christ. The Word of God leaves no room for failure in the prayer of faith.

However, the *only person* that can pray the prayer of faith is the person that knows that they are there on behalf of Jesus. A person like this cannot be talked out of who they are in Christ. They know *who* they are and *who* they've been sent by. Their faith will say, *"I am talking to you in the person, position, nature, victory, and strength of the Lord Jesus Christ. Sickness and disease, you have to come out of this body right now. We are in agreement with the Word of God that says the prayer of faith shall save the sick and the Lord shall raise him up."*

"...and if he have committed sins, they shall be forgiven him."

The same God that said, *"it shall be forgiven him"* also promises that, *"the prayer of faith shall save the sick and the Lord shall raise him up."* God both forgives *and* heals. Both are miraculous and neither are obsolete. The same God did it. The Name that guarantees the forgiveness of sins is also the Name that guarantees healing for those that have need of it.

There is no need to suffer when the solution is in the Word of God. If the believer will walk in the Spirit and use the Name, they will see *real* results. The Church understands forgiveness; they know how to use the Name in conjunction with repentance. No one would dare say, *"Well, I don't know if it's the Lord's time to forgive me of my sins."* It is universally understood that the Lord is not a respecter of people. He will forgive everyone 100% of the time if they meet the criteria of true repentance. On the other hand, many freely speculate, *"It just may not be the Lord's time to heal me."* The *same* Name that does the *forgiving* also does the *healing*. God's arm does not shorten with regard to purpose. His power works the same for each of His promises.

Unlocking Kingdom Rule

> **And I will give unto thee the keys of the Kingdom of Heaven: and whatsoever thou shalt bind on Earth shall be bound in Heaven: and whatsoever thou shalt loose on Earth shall be loosed in Heaven.**
>
> **Matthew 16:19**

"And I will give unto thee the keys of the Kingdom of Heaven." The Church does not need a key to get into Heaven. Those that are born again are *already* in the Kingdom of God. Keys, rather, are a symbol of authority. They are representative of an endowment that accesses power. They give the possessor the ability to lock and to unlock. They can say *"yes"* and they can say *"no."* Jesus said, *"and whatsoever thou shalt bind on Earth shall be bound in Heaven: and whatsoever thou shalt loose on Earth shall be loosed in Heaven."*

A kingdom has laws. It has rules that govern its realm and a ruler that enforces those laws. Different rulers, of course, have different methods. The devil is the ruler of the kingdom of darkness. His subjects are those that submit to him. As the sovereign of his realm, the devil doesn't wait for people to invite him into their heart. Rather, he will take opportunity and force his way in through trauma and terror. Using a traumatic experience as a point of access, he will take advantage of an individual and overcome them in a moment of distress.

He is an oppressor and his kingdom is governed by the principles of hate and fear. He does not wait until an individual believes on him. In fact, he couldn't care less what a person's *will* is, but if he can violate it, *he will*. This is his *modus operandi* or method of operation.

The Bible teaches that the devil takes people captive at his will (2 Timothy 2:26). He lays a snare through trickery and deceit and enslaves the children of disobedience. This, however, is not how God operates. The children of God dwell in the Kingdom of Light and the

Holy Ghost leads those who follow. *He leads.* In other words, God won't force you to pray in tongues. The Holy Ghost will not take you captive at His will!

God is a God of inspiration. He doesn't *push*. He doesn't *drive*. The believer must, therefore, develop a sensitivity and an awareness to the Holy Ghost. The children of the Kingdom operate under the laws of the Kingdom. Those that know the law of the land will resist enemy rule. If the enemy does attack with symptoms of sickness, those that know better will declare, *"By His stripes, I am healed"* (1 Peter 3:24). They will assert their rights and refuse outlaw influence.

The devil is an outlaw and a renegade. His destiny may be forever sealed in the flames of Hell, but his desire is to take as many with him as possible. If he cannot take the believer, he will try to pressure them into relinquishing their divine rights. This is why God has given the believer authority. This is why Jesus said, *"I give to you the keys of the Kingdom."*

Shutting the Door to Darkness

For we do not wrestle against flesh and blood, but against principalities, against powers, against the rulers of the darkness of this age, against spiritual hosts of wickedness in the heavenly places.

Ephesians 6:12 NKJV

People are not your problem. In fact, the moment you start wrestling flesh and blood, you step out from operating under the Name. You leave the strong tower and vacate the secret place of the Most High. The weapons of your warfare are not in the arm of the flesh. They are in the strength of the Name.

For though we walk in the flesh, we do not war

> according to the flesh. For the weapons of our warfare are not carnal (fleshly), but mighty in God for pulling down strongholds, casting down arguments (thoughts, imaginations) and every high thing that exalts itself against the knowledge of God (the Word), bringing every thought into captivity into the obedience of Christ.
>
> **2 Corinthians 10:3-5 NKJV**

Imaginations come from the kingdom of darkness. They are *arguments* from another realm. Those that heed demonic suggestions will find themselves outside of the provision of the Kingdom. Just as the devil talked Adam and Eve out of their inheritance, he will attempt to talk the believer out of the divine will. The devil would like to rob you of all that Jesus has *won* for you! Therefore, Wisdom would say, *"Cast down the imagination and bring it under the arrest of the Word of God."* Enforce obedience. These are your divine rights.

"And I will give unto thee the keys of the Kingdom of Heaven."

The keys of the Kingdom open and close doors. Jesus says, *"I am giving you the keys so that you will see to it that the only things that access your life, are the things that come from God. When you see a contrary force invading, use the key and shut the door."*

Heaven's gates are locked to the enemy. In fact, Jesus said, *"Lay up for yourself treasures in Heaven where no thief can break in and steal"* (Matthew 6:20). The enemy cannot access what is locked with Kingdom keys.

God is saying, *"I give to you the keys of the Kingdom and you have the ability to place your life, your possessions, your family members, your ambitions in God, your visions and God-given dreams in the realm of the Kingdom."*

Everything that you stand for can be placed under the protective umbrella of Jesus' name. Therefore, when the devil solicits you with an imagination, rise up and say, *"No, devil, I won't take that out of God's hands so you can steal it. Everything I have is in the heavenly realm, and through the authority that God gave me, I am locking you out of the storehouse that houses everything that I stand for. You can't steal my call. You can't steal anything from me because I will not give you a right to get in."*

> **These things saith He (Jesus) that is holy, He that is true, He that hath the key of David, He that openeth and no man shutteth, and shutteth, and no man openeth.**
>
> **Revelation 3:7b**

How does Jesus open and shut doors? The hand must cooperate with the head. In other words, Jesus is the head of the Body. The *Head* instructs the *hand* and the *hand* uses the *key*. Jesus has given the Church the key. He has said, *"Now go ye. This belongs to you."* When the Church works in agreement with the Head, doors open and things happen for the furtherance of the Gospel.

The key of David is the key of the Kingdom. When David was king, he prophetically foresaw a Kingdom that would have no end. That, of course, was fulfilled in Jesus. Therefore, the keys of David or the Kingdom, enforce Kingdom law. They have the power to bind and loose, to open and close. Those keys are not way up in Heaven, beyond the reach of the child of God, but they are in the hands of the believer. Jesus won them and has instructed the Church to use them.

This means that there are certain things that you *do not need to pray about*. Paul, for instance, did not pray that the snakebite wouldn't kill him. He shook it off into the fire and went back to work. The moment the snake bit, he was most likely solicited with this imagination: *"You're going to die. It was a venomous snake."* Rather than giving heed to the thought, he cast it down and shook the snake into the fire. He used a Kingdom key. That is called *binding* or shutting a door.

It isn't always necessary to say a lot to the devil. Authority doesn't come in a multitude of words. Many times you can just say, *"No, I will live and not die."*

When you say *"No!"* to the devil, based on the law of God, you are utilizing the keys of the Kingdom. Take the key and say, *"No, devil, you can't make me sick because by His stripes I am healed."* Use your authority and declare, *"No, you can't steal from me because when a thief is caught he has to repay sevenfold."* Know your divine rights and utilize the key to safeguard what belongs to you. Use the Name and put the devil where he belongs: UNDER YOUR FEET.

If you tell a tumor to *dissolve*, it has to do what you say. If you say *no* to a disease, it has to stop. Jesus has given the believer the keys to enforce the Kingdom of God on Earth.

Building Upon Bedrock

Turning to His disciples, Jesus asked, *"Who do men say that I am?"* The group produced many answers. Some said, *"They say you are John the Baptist."* Others responded with, *"Elijah,"* and still others said, *"Jeremiah or one of the prophets."* After all had spoken, Jesus asked, *"But who do you say that I am?"* Peter was the first to respond. He answered, *"You are the Christ, the Son of the Living God."* Jesus immediately addressed Peter and said, *"Blessed are you, Simon Bar-Jonah, for flesh and blood has not revealed this to you, but My Father who is in Heaven"* (Matthew 16:13-17).

Jesus continued:

> **"And I also say to you that you are Peter, and on this rock I will build My Church, and the gates of Hades shall not prevail against it. And I will give you the keys of the Kingdom of Heaven and whatever you bind on Earth will be bound**

in Heaven, and whatever you loose on Earth will be loosed in Heaven."

Matthew 16:18-19 NKJV

Peter got a revelation of *who* Jesus was. He said, *"You are the Christ, the Anointed One."* When Peter received that revelation, Jesus said, *"You are PETROS (Greek meaning: little rock), but upon this PETRA (Greek meaning: big rock), I will build my Church and the gates of Hell will not prevail against it."* In other words, Jesus is saying to Peter, *"Upon this immovable stone (upon this revelation you just spoke, upon the Word of God, upon Christ) I will build My Church."*

Once you know *who* Jesus is and *what* He has done, you will be able to appreciate *what* He has given you.

"And I will give you the keys of the Kingdom of Heaven..."

When a child approaches a parent and says, *"Thank you that you are going to do this,"* that child must have a *basis* for their thanksgiving. They must have a *foundation* for their confidence.

Why do you believe what you believe?
What is the basis for your convictions?

When you approach the Father and ask for something, what is the basis for your boldness? If it's *"for Christ's sake,"* that's not good enough! If it's because, *"I gave to the church"* or *"If anyone deserves healing it's 'Sister So-and-So',"* your prayer will not be answered! The believer must pray according to the authority that is given in the Word. Begging and manipulation simply will not move God. Remember, faith pleases God. It's the *substance* that moves mountains.

Authority does not work when people say, *"thou art John the Baptist"* or *"thou art Elijah."* Authority will only work in the name of Jesus: *"thou art the Christ."*

If God were to say to the believer, *"On what basis should I answer your prayer for healing,"* the believer's response should be, *"Father, it's because Your Son, the Word of God, Jesus Christ—died on Calvary and by His wounds I am healed. Healing is a promise that belongs to me in Jesus' name."* When a believer's petition is backed by a *Word-conviction*, God is obligated to answer that prayer. The person who utilizes the keys of the Kingdom, has grounds to praise and thank God for the manifestation of the promise.

Praise does not manipulate God. Praise demonstrates to God and to the enemy that the believer has an *internal conviction* that the thing hoped for is a *done deal*. In fact, praising the Lord will bind depression. Such a person doesn't need to spend time binding the spirit of depression; they can just lift up their hands and praise the Lord. Sometimes an *action* in the *right* direction, *stops* something that is going in the *wrong* direction.

Obedience brings breakthrough.

Reporting On Your Perspective

Refuse to be moved by what you see. Sometimes a believer may go through a season of contradiction. Perhaps, everything looks like it's going wrong in the natural. People get off course, however, when they begin to talk about the affliction. They say, *"Well, you know, there's a lot of warfare. We are fighting and the devil has been doing some stuff. Everything is just wacko."*

The more they talk about it, the more they magnify the devil! In the same way that God inhabits the praises of His people, the devil inhabits praises to him. How many people have watched a horror movie and then had nightmares following? The devil inhabits the glorification of his works. If you give him room, he will move in. The more a person talks about him, the more he fills the space given to him.

Here's a good rule: *Don't talk about what the devil is doing!*

Somebody may say, *"But can't you see what is happening in my life?"*

Whose report will you believe and magnify? God's report says that He is an ever-present help in the time of need. God's report says that Jesus is a friend that sticks closer than a brother. God's report says that if God is for you, then who can be against you?

If the believer understands the keys to the Kingdom, they will not confess or tolerate any enemy activity. They will exercise their dominion and confess their rights.

At this point, someone invariably says, *"But that's lying!"*

Declaring your God-given rights is *not* lying. It's called giving the report of another realm. Don't report the *situation*, but report your *position*. It doesn't matter what the circumstance says, because beyond the circumstance is victory in Christ. His name is still above every other name. In fact, once the situation turns around, Jesus won't be any more King than He is already! Jesus has already done it all. He said, *"It is finished."* He sat down and gave you the keys of the Kingdom.

The Word of God says that you are seated with Christ in the heavenly places (Ephesians 2:6). This is far above any circumstantial inconsistencies of the earth realm. From the perspective of the heavenly places, your horizon in Jesus is lit with endless victories and testimonies of triumph.

The natural contradiction can't take one thing *from you* unless you *choose* to lay your keys down. It's easy to recognize when a person has stopped using the keys of the Kingdom. These will begin to speak words that are laced with demonic propaganda. They will confess the situation, and in doing so, they will give voice to demonic innuendoes and lying imaginations. Remember, if you talk about it, you give it power.

The Bible instructs the believer to gird up the loins of their mind and to tighten the belt of truth around the waist of their thought life (Ephesians 6:14). Be sober in the Word of God. Don't vacillate between natural opinions. Speak the Word only. Speak from your heavenly perspective.

Authority never works where there is double-mindedness or confusion. Such a person is without a foundation because they are not grounded in the integrity of the Word. As a result, they waver, not having a basis for their confidence. Without the Word, true faith cannot operate. Without faith and an understanding of the Name, authority will not function.

Authority never works in the presence of confusion, for God is not the author of confusion (1 Corinthians 14:33). Rather, the devil authors confusion. He said to himself, *"If I give them multiple choices, chances are, they will make the wrong decision!"* Through powerless theology, the devil has offered the Church a smorgasbord of theologies.

"Yes, the Lord sometimes heals, but…"
"Yes, the Holy Ghost is somewhat available, but…"
"Yes, you have all power in Heaven and Earth, but…"

Confounded by multiple choices and without an understanding of the Word, these flounder in a puddle of double-mindedness and confusion. Beguiled by murky doctrine, their faith becomes short-circuited.

Where there is single-mindedness, there is clarity of direction. Where there is double-mindedness, the paths are too many to choose from. There is, however, only one direction in God. His answer is not *"Yes"* and *"No,"* but it is definitive.

Kingdom Space Occupied

Neither give place to the devil.

Ephesians 4:27

The devil is after a place. God purchased you and said, *"I want all the space that you have in your life. I want it to be filled with Me and filled with My Word. To safeguard this, I am giving you the keys to lock the door to the devil and to unlock the door to Heaven's provision. You have the power to make the Kingdom of God the reigning Kingdom in your life."*

The Kingdom of God, of course, will come in literal form when Jesus returns. However, to the disciples Jesus said, *"Some of you standing here will not see death until you see the Kingdom of God come with power"* (Mark 9:2). Six days later, Peter, James and John were on a mountain with Jesus and they saw the *dunamis power* of God. To the believer today, this means that the *dunamis power* of the Holy Ghost is available to enforce all of the promises of the Kingdom. Those who believe, have the power to make the Kingdom of God the influential force in their life. The disciples tasted of it on the mountain, but every believer can walk in the experience of *dunamis power* today.

If the Word says, *"Do not give place to the devil,"* that must mean that the believer has taken territory *from* the devil. Therefore, the Holy Ghost warns, *"Don't give it back!"* The devil is after territory in your life. He is looking for space to occupy.

Wherefore take unto you the whole armour of God, that ye may be able to withstand in the evil day, and having done all, to stand.

Ephesians 6:13

"Stand" is a military term. It means, after you have conducted battle according to the Word of God and gained territory, *stand prepared* to do battle again. God warns, *"Do not give place to the devil."* The believer must always be sober and vigilant. They must not be slack concerning the promises because in so doing, they leave room for the enemy to advance.

Can you imagine if the devil had no place in your life?

This doesn't mean that contradictions won't come, but rather, you will be victorious in them. The Bible says, *"Many are the afflictions of the righteous but the Lord delivers him out of them all"* (Psalm 34:19). If the righteous are confident in the promise, they will praise God in spite of the circumstance. Standing on the Word, they will see victory in the midst of challenge. This is called spiritual warfare. It is the good fight of faith.

Standing in the Stature of Christ

> **Epaphras, who is one of you, a servant of Christ, saluteth you, always labouring fervently for you in prayers, that ye may stand perfect and complete in all the will of God.**
>
> **Colossians 4:12**

One who serves is a minister. Epaphras, who was a Colossian and a minister of Christ, was laboring or wrestling in prayer so that the Colossian Church would stand mature in all the will of God. He was struggling in prayer or striving so that they would be perfect and complete.

"For we wrestle…against principalities and powers, against rulers of darkness" (Ephesians 6:12a).

There is a certain degree of warfare in prayer. This doesn't mean that prayers are directed toward Satan, for we do not pray to the devil. It does mean, however, that during times of promotion and breakthrough, there may be an intensified psychological, physical and situational warfare in a person's life. While we do not deny these things, we don't give them praise either. When a person praises the warfare, they will only stretch it out. Remember, what you give voice to is what you glorify.

The devil will try to oppose you in the prayer closet. He will try to hinder your prayers through distraction. You may walk into church, feeling disconnected, almost out of tune. The devil will whisper, *"See, the Word is not working for you. Nothing has changed."*

Why the intensification? Why the heat? The devil is seeking a *place*. He is standing against the believer's progress, trying to convince them of certain defeat. If he can get them to *give ear* to his lies, he will successfully take *back* the place that was taken from him.

> **Casting down imaginations and every high thing that exalteth itself against the knowledge of God.**
>
> **2 Corinthians 10:5a**

Bring every renegade thought into captivity. If the thought isn't born out of the Word of God, *dismiss its influence*. Do not give place to an imagination that exalts itself against God. This is best done through the power of the Holy Ghost. Therefore, walk in the Spirit. Speak the Word only. Praise God only. Allow the Holy Ghost to give you the perspective of Heaven on the situation. Rise above the contradiction and report on it from the heavenly perspective. When you do this, the situation will pass.

Epaphras was fervently laboring in prayer that the Colossians would be able to stand mature in all of the will of God. The will of God is the Word of God or the person of Jesus Christ. One that *stands* in all of the will of God, *stands* in all of the victory of Jesus. They are living in the power of the name of Jesus and in the power of the divine will.

Those that stand mature in the full will of God, are standing in the full measure and stature of Christ. This means that when the devil faces you, he faces the fullness of the Godhead bodily. The Church is the Body of Christ, and God has made Jesus the head of that Body. *"He has put all things under His feet and made Him to be the head over all things to the Church, which is His Body, the fullness of Him which filleth all in all"* (Ephesians 1:22).

However, we speak wisdom among those who are mature, yet not the wisdom of this age, nor of the rulers of this age, who are coming to nothing.

1 Corinthians 2:6 NKJV

It is the wisdom of God to agree with the will of God. Rebellion to the Word is unwise, for it gives place to the enemy. In fact, the kingdom of darkness operates off of rebellion and demonic spirits work in the children of disobedience.

James says that the tongue will set on fire the course of life. It defiles the body (James 3:6). The Christian that chooses to speak outside of the Word of God is kindling iniquity and strife in their life. Their words will set the course of their existence on fire.

The tongue should be giving praise to God for the position of provision. Those that have a rebellious tongue that is given to murmuring and complaining, will grant access to the enemy. Disobedience always gives place to the devil.

This is what obedience looks like: *"God said I should be saved and I am saved. God said I am healed and I am healed. I don't care if I have pain in my body, I am healed. I don't care if the doctor diagnoses me with a condition, I am healed."*

Obedience is when the child of God is wise concerning the will of God. They recognize that what the enemy brings is *temporary*, but what God has provided is *eternal*. These stand assured in all of the will of God. When they wrestle in prayer, *they wrestle to win*. They do not become weary in well doing or forgetful of the Name, but they tenaciously speak the wisdom of the Word. They give praise to God and magnify His promises at all times. These do not become sidetracked or distracted by natural inconsistencies, but they weigh everything in life against the reality of their position and power in Christ.

Chapter 12

Manifest Wisdom

*If you do not use what you have been given,
your good intentions will fall short of producing
Heaven's best in your life.*

The Wisdom of the Age

> **Howbeit we speak wisdom among them that are perfect; (or mature) yet not the wisdom of this world, nor of the princes of this world, that come to nought.**
>
> **1 Corinthians 2:6**

The Word of God is the wisdom of God, and the reverence of the Lord is the beginning of wisdom (Psalm 111:10). A person who reverences the Lord will seek the wisdom of the Word. They will study, meditate and speak the Word of God. As they saturate their lives with this wisdom, they will begin to dwell in the mind of Christ. *They will think God thoughts!* In turn, this Word will become so alive within them that they will be led into all knowledge. The Bible says, *"For who hath known the mind of the Lord, that he may instruct him? But we have the mind of Christ"* (1 Corinthians 2:16). The mind of Christ is available to the believer so that they might walk in divine wisdom. God does not want His will to be mysterious.

> **Not a wisdom belonging to this passing age, not to any of it's governing powers which are declining to their end.**
>
> **1 Corinthians 2:6 NEB**

It's not the child of God that is *passing* and it's not the wisdom of God that is *declining*. All that is of God is abiding and increasing. The wisdom of this age, however, is fading into extinction. The governing powers are declining to their end. Ever since its cataclysmic defeat, the powers of darkness have steadily lost strength and viability. Calvary's victory forever sealed their demise.

When Jesus returns to set up His Kingdom on Earth, the things that most people consider to be intelligent and wise, will be obsolete and outdated. What was once considered state-of-the-art, will be archaic. Jesus will govern and rule with a rod of iron for 1,000 years. His saints will reign with Him, but the princes of this age and the carnal wisdom of it will have reached their end. In its place will be the full expression of the manifest wisdom of God.

The child of God *does not* need to wait for the millennial reign to put the wisdom of this age out of commission. Jesus has already done it all. He took the keys of the Kingdom and gave the Church authority and power to exercise dominion. The child of God must only receive the keys and govern by the wisdom of the Holy Ghost. That wisdom is not far off, but it is in the Word and it is resident in the believer. *"But we have the mind of Christ"* (1 Corinthians 2:16b).

Taking *Charge* of Your Life

It is not the wisdom of this world nor of the dethroned powers who rule this world.

1 Corinthians 2:6 Moffat

Jesus dethroned the devil, but it is up to the believer not to invite him back. If the child of God will refuse his wisdom, they will disallow his power. If they will keep their thoughts in agreement with God, the devil will not have a place in their life. The Word says, *"Neither give place to the devil"* (Ephesians 4:27).

The devil is a spirit of fear. Therefore, reject fear and do not permit its influence to ascend the throne of your life. God has not given you the spirit of fear, but of power, love and a sound mind (2 Timothy 1:7). *Dwell in these things.*

Allow the wisdom of God to be your guide in life. That wisdom is revealed at length within God's Word. More simply stated, the will of God for your situation, is as near as the Word of God. Therefore, allow the Word to be a lamp unto your feet. Allow it to illuminate the path of your life.

Those that know the *Word* on the subject, will enforce the *Will* on the subject. Those that enforce the Will, enforce Satan's defeat. If the believer will allow the Word to have His perfect way in the affairs of their life, then the devil will not have a space to call his own. When the believer rises to this place of *always contending* for the Will, they will begin to see *Word-results* in their life.

Late night infomercials market self-help programs, teaching people to *"Take Charge"* of their lives. The Christian watches these and cringes at the *"Take Charge"* message. They say, *"Well, I only want God to take charge of my life."* While this is the right desire, *passivity* is not the right method! God has already provided the tools that will enforce His *charge*. The Christian must only pick these tools up, exercise their God-given dominion and take charge of what God has freely given.

Jesus has given the keys of the Kingdom to His Body. If God is to take charge, the believer must rise up in delegated authority and say, *"Hey, wait a minute! Devil, I'm in charge and I'm putting you out of my life!"* The gift of Calvary made this provision available over 2,000 years ago. The believer does not have to be taken captive by the devil at his will, but they can take charge and enforce their divine rights. They can enforce the Kingdom of God on Earth.

Take charge of your mind. *Take charge* of your body. *Take charge* of your finances. Allow the will of God and the plan of Heaven to rule in each of these areas. Do not tolerate defeat by default. God has given you the keys, but only *you* can pick them up and use them. If you do not use what you have been given, your good intentions will fall short of producing Heaven's best in your life.

It's as if you stand at the threshold of a door. One side opens up to the spectacular views of God's best. The other side is simply the much-traveled terrain of good intentions and unrealized dreams. God has given you the key to access His best. As you stand at the threshold of expectation, only you can determine if you will use the key to unlock the desire and ability of Heaven in your life.

The true message of the Gospel is the most positive message in the world. This is why it is called the *Good News*. Religion has distorted it and foolish people have twisted it, but in the end, *truth remains truth*. The Word of God is wisdom for all who will receive it.

The message of the world is channeled through principalities of darkness. These have long been dethroned, but they will still attempt to access your life. *Will you give these defeated powers a throne?* Only you can decide if you will give the devil a place or if you will use your God-given authority to take charge. *The door stands before you.*

Take control of your life through the anointing. Take authority over your thought life and bring every thought captive to the will of God. If *you* are not in control of your life, *God* is not in control of your life. Remember, the devil is not a gentleman. He is not standing passively on the sidelines, waiting for your vote. You must be proactive in God. Go after divine results! Contend for God's best!

Wisdom for the Mature

> **However, we speak wisdom among those who are mature…**
>
> **1 Corinthians 2:6a NKJV**

The mature can handle strong wisdom. The baby Christian,

however, will run from the presence of such teaching and seek milk. Unable to digest the full Word, these will look for what they have *grown* accustomed to. They will seek elementary principles.

> **For everyone who partakes only of milk is unskilled in the Word of righteousness, for he is a babe. But solid food (strong meat) belongs to those who are of full age (mature), that is, those who by reason of use (practice), have their senses exercised to discern both good and evil. Therefore, leaving the discussion of the elementary principles of Christ, let us go on to perfection (maturity)…**
>
> **Hebrews 5:13-6:1a NKJV**

A child that is given strong meat will spit it out. Whimpering they will cry, *"This is bad!"* Those that are mature know that the food is not *bad*, but that the *baby* is still a *baby*. There will be a day when that baby will be ready for solid food. However, until that day arrives, the spiritual child will refuse those things that they are not familiar with. They will refuse the wisdom of the mature and the advanced teaching of the wise.

The mature are those who are already walking in the will of God. These can stand in the presence of wisdom and not stumble over strong Words. They are not foolish or unwise concerning the divine will, but they have allowed the Holy Ghost to lead them into the fullness of truth. Having an ambition to push past every limit, these say, *"Father, I am going to believe Your will and I am going to see to it that Your will is enforced in my life."* The mature take charge of their lives through the Word of God.

The greatest opportunity to believe God comes when the promise hasn't yet manifested. If a person is "believing God," it means that their faith will see the promise *through* to performance. This is not a job for those that have not been established in the Word, for it takes faith and patience to inherit the promise.

If a believer does not contend for the performance of the promise, then the seed will be stolen. The devourer is always at hand to steal, kill and destroy. He waits for an opportunity to steal that which has been disregarded. If he can steal the seed, he can rob the believer of productivity in God. This is why the child of God must *know* and *fight* for their divine rights.

The Dawning of a New Breed

For if by one man's offense death reigned by one; much more they which receive abundance of grace and of the gift of righteousness shall reign in life by one, Jesus Christ.

Romans 5:17

Through Adam's offense, death reigned. Through the abundance of grace and the gift of righteousness, those that were once held captive by the reign of death, will reign in life by Jesus Christ. One man brought the dominion of death and the other heralded the dominion of life. The Amplified Bible translates "reign in life" as "reign as kings in life."

"…they shall reign as kings in life…"

The moment Adam and Eve sinned, the nature of Satan entered into them. When their first child came into the world, he was *by nature*, a child of the devil. Although the child was innocent, he willingly turned to sin at the age of accountability. His bloodline had been contaminated with the nature of darkness. In turn, this darkness was transmitted through the bloodlines of each successive generation.

The sacrifice of Calvary heralded a new day and the dawning of a new breed. Jesus became the head of a new race and His gifts of righteousness and grace were made available to all. Today, these gifts are freely given, but it takes faith and authority to lay hold of them.

The divine nature is available to all who will appropriate it.

In many cases, the child of God has not been taught about their new nature. Instead of tapping into the divine, they have been instructed to control and restrain their appetites. Ignorant of promise, these live outside of their rights and below their nature.

It takes faith to appropriate the nature of God. A person who has been taught that they are a sinner, will have faith to live as a sinner. The child of God, however, has not received the sin nature, but the divine nature. The one that is born again, *is saved*. They are saved from the nature of the devil and instead of darkness; they are inheritors and heirs of the nature of God.

If death reigned in the old life, how much more should the gift of grace and righteousness reign in the lives of God's children today? The child of God is called to rule and reign as *kings in life* by Christ Jesus. They are called to overcome adversity with the rights and privileges of the divine nature.

Christ is not like the devil. He freely gives the gift, but He will not impose His will on another. God respects the will of His children because He created freewill. Therefore, the believer can rise up and make a quality decision of faith and trust in God.

Those who rise up in the confidence of this new nature will grow in wisdom and strength. Whereas in the past they might have said, *"If God doesn't do something, I'm going down,"* now their faith declares, *"Wait a minute! I have authority over that situation. It's not like it used to be; I have the gift of God living in me! I am a king and a priest and I rule in life!"* These have the Name, possess the Nature and walk in the divine Will.

Commanding Your Helm

The anointing destroys the yoke of bondage, but that yoke can only be destroyed by the one that exercises authority. A person like this will boldly pronounce judgment on bondage. They will say, *"You lying spirit of bondage, you cannot rule in this life! I know who I am in Christ."*

Jesus said, *"It is finished!"*
The *devil* has been *defeated.*
The *curse* has been *broken.*
The *blood* has been *shed.*
The *price* has been *paid.*

When all has been said and done, it is up to men and women of faith to stand up and profess, *"God, we will believe You no matter what. If You say this nature is ours, then we will walk in the fullness of it."*

When the devil says, *"It's impossible to forgive,"* do it anyway, for God has said, *"Forgive men their trespasses"* (Matthew 6:14). God would never give a command that the believer doesn't have an ability to fulfill.

When the devil says, *"Give up, you can't do it,"* do it anyway, for God has said, *"We can do all things through Christ which strengthens us"* (Philippians 4:13). There is divine ability packaged within the Word of God.

When the devil says, *"You are going down in defeat,"* laugh at him, for God has said, *"No weapon formed against us shall prosper"* (Isaiah 54:17). Victory is inherent within the divine nature.

Believe God and lay claim to the Will. Put your revelation to work and grow into maturity. Those who use what they know will grow into greater levels of understanding and promotion in God.

Remember, God is only pleased with faith. Without faith, it is impossible to please Him (Hebrews 11:6). Therefore, do what He has said and yield to His nature.

Humility is doing what God has commanded. Rebellion and pride say, *"I just believe it's up to the Lord to do whatever the Lord wants to do."*

True humility, however, sides with God and says, *"I am going to yield to the Word."* The person who submits to God's commands will receive grace or God's divine ability.

> **God resists the proud, but gives grace to the humble. Therefore, humble yourselves under the mighty hand of God.**
>
> **1 Peter 5:5b-6a NKJV**

When a person resists God's Word and insists on their own way, they are refusing divine responsibility. Instead of taking the helm of their life, they leave it to the "sovereignty of God." Yet in doing so, they give the enemy clearance to their realm of influence. Instead of rising up in the authority of the Word, they stand in the wayside waiting for *someone* to take the lead. The humble person is the one who obeys God, even in what seems insignificant.

Those that put God's Word in their mouth, put Him in the driver's seat of their life. Those that refuse wisdom, even passively through inaction, allow the *devil* to drive the course of their life. Abandoning the wheel of their authority, their adversary will steer them clear of destiny and fulfillment.

God's Will and Testament

> **For this cause we also, since the day we heard it, do not cease to pray for you, and to desire that ye might be filled with the knowledge of His will in all wisdom and spiritual understanding.**
>
> **Colossians 1:9**

"For this cause…we do not cease to pray for you." God never commands anything in vain. In other words, every command necessitates an expected end. Performance is always attached to

obedience. Obedience acts and God responds. For this reason, Paul did not cease to pray. He believed that his prayers would secure what God had promised.

"...that ye might be filled with the knowledge of His will..."

Paul continually prayed that the Colossians would be filled with the knowledge of God's will. If this was his never-ceasing prayer, then Paul must have been thoroughly convinced that "the knowledge of His will" was available. He knew that the will of God was not locked away in a heavenly vault, but that the child of God should know their Father's intentions.

Paul believed that the Colossians could abound in this knowledge, yet in churches all over the world, believers pray, *"If it be Thy will."* If you know something, there is no "if" in it. God does not work in "mysterious ways." He works in *revealed* ways.

I run into people all over the world who are dying and desperately need a miracle. Their only hope is God, yet their knowledge of His will comes short in the area of their greatest need. When I tell them, *"I'm going to pray for you. Do you believe God will heal you?"* they will often reply with *"Well, if it be His will."*

God's will IS to heal; yet, these have not been filled with the knowledge of His will or His wisdom. For some reason, they have not been taught the will of God. Instead, they were given a *catchall phrase* that conveniently sweeps everything under the carpet of God's sovereignty. They were given a theology that was not based on Bible, but was born out of religious tradition and ignorance. Those that hold onto such error, will die early, stoutly defending their belief that God has ordained their death.

God will hold the teacher responsible. The one that handled the Word deceitfully will be held accountable for Kingdom casualties. They knew that it was God's will to heal, but it was easier to preach God's sovereignty on the subject. Instead of raising God's children up into spiritual maturity, they reiterated a super-spiritual, formulated-theology to make the message palatable to the hearer. In the end, ignorance produced physical death.

"...that ye might be filled with the knowledge of His will."

Contend for the knowledge of His will. Go after wisdom and spiritual understanding. Continually mediate on the Word of God and do not settle for anything less than the divine will. *Fight for truth.*

When someone writes a *Will and Testament*, it is the final authority. After they die, that document will end all debate and settle all questions. If your name is included in that will, there is no more cause to doubt. The worry is over. In the same way, the Lord Jesus Christ has left His *Will and Testament* in your care. He has called you *by name* and you have become an inheritor of divine promise.

> **That ye might walk worthy of the Lord unto all pleasing, being fruitful in every good work, and increasing in the knowledge of God.**
>
> **Colossians 1:10**

Those that know the *Will*, will walk worthy of the Lord. They will please God and their spiritual understanding will enable them to be fruitful in every good work. God is always pleased by faith. Faith hears God's promise and believes it—*just like it is.*

If somebody says, *"Well, are you going to live?"* the one that has spiritual understanding will *not* say, *"If it be His will."* Rather, they will confess their faith. They will say, *"Doesn't the Word say that God will satisfy us with long life? Therefore, I will live and not die"* (Psalm 91:16).

Once the promise is revealed, it is foolishness to believe two reports. God is not the one *that healeth thee* and then also the one *that maketh thee sick*. The Wisdom and Will of God says, *"by His stripes we are healed"* (1 Peter 2:24b). The child of God must therefore, dismiss fables and contend for truth.

Faith that Finds its Fulfillment

The fastest way to grow in God is to start exercising your faith. Speak His promises and hold onto them. Guard the Word in your heart and water it with your meditations and with the power of prayer. *Think on God.* As you do this, you will increase in the knowledge of God. Not only will you know God's *will*, but you will know *Him*. You will walk worthily and God will be pleased with your faith.

Jesus said:

He who has My commandments and keeps them, it is he who loves Me. And he who loves Me will be loved by My Father, and I will love him and manifest (reveal) Myself to him.

John 14:21 NKJV

"He who has My commandments and keeps them..." The commandments are the will of God. Those that know the Will, *walk worthy* of the Will. These are pleasing to God because their actions are born of unconquerable faith. To these God says, *"and I will love him and reveal Myself to him."*

Where there's more *presence*, there's more *power*. Those that walk close to the Lord will find the strength to resist every fiery dart. When the devil knocks, they will rise to the occasion and he will flee.

Strengthened with all might, according to His glorious power, for all patience and longsuffering with joy.

Colossians 1:11

"Strengthened with all might..." Not only is the believer increasing in the knowledge of God, but they are strengthened with all might. It is the glorious power of God that strengthens them unto all patience.

Faith and patience inherits the promises.

Patience is the substance of longevity. It's what defines steadfastness. Those without patience will wilt beneath the heat of adversity. They will find themselves unable to stand in the presence of headwinds. However, those *possessing patience* will persevere where others fall short. They will stand where others drop. They will not cast away their confidence, but they will remain unmoved in unshakeable assurance. Their spiritual fortitude will garner the harvest of their faith.

"Strengthened ... unto all patience and longsuffering with joyfulness."

Strength will produce joy and joy will produce ever-increasing strength. The Bible says, *"The joy of the Lord is my strength"* (Nehemiah 8:10). Those that know His will, know His presence and wherever the Presence is, there is joy unspeakable and full of glory.

Looking into the Light

Giving thanks unto the Father, which hath made us meet to be partakers of the inheritance of the saints in light.

Colossians 1:12

"Giving thanks unto the Father..." The child of God gives thanks to the Father for His benefits. They say, *"Father, thank You for Your benefits. I haven't seen the full measure, but I know there's more coming into my life than ever before. I know You are faithful and I'm full of joy."*

These rejoice in the fulfillment of the promise, even before the manifestation. They say, *"Thank You that You have healed me, and provided for me! Thank You that You will direct me, anoint me, and use me!"* Having confidence in the God of promise, their faith finds its fulfillment in the expression of thanksgiving. There is power in thanksgiving.

"...partakers of the inheritance of the saints in light..."

The child of God nas been translated out of the kingdom of darkness and made to be a partaker of the inheritance of the saints in *light*. Light, of course, is where the Word is. It's the source of all revelation and understanding. The Psalmist wrote, *"The entrance of Thy Words giveth light"* (Psalm 119:130). Light illuminates the path of the just.

Jesus said, *"I am the light of the world. He who follows Me will not walk in darkness, but shall have the light of life"* (John 8:12). Jesus is the light of the world and God's Word is the light of life. The *"inheritance of the saints in the light"* is the inheritance of all that God has promised within the Word.

There is no room for darkness in light. Therefore, those that say, *"If it be Thy will,"* are in the dark. When the will is known, there is the light of understanding. Those that say, *"I don't know why the Lord won't do it,"* are participating in darkness. The inheritance of the saints is in the light. Those that will delve into the Word will discover the light of promise.

The Bible says that the god of this world has blinded the eyes and the minds of those which don't believe (2 Corinthians 4:4). The devil knows that darkness gives him an advantage among the ignorant, for in darkness the individual will stumble and grope for truth. In the absence of light, revelation cannot shine and faith will not have a foundation.

> **The path of the just is like the shining sun, that shines brighter unto the perfect day. The way of the wicked is like darkness; they do not know what makes them stumble. My son, give attention to my Words...**
>
> **Proverbs 4:18-20a NKJV**

Only under the explicit brightness of revelation, will the promises of God take their true form. The light of revelation will illuminate the path of the just, shining brighter and brighter unto a perfect day. However, those that are without the penetrating light of revelation will stumble beneath the heavy shroud of darkness. The god of this passing age has worked to blind the minds of those who refuse truth; for fear that the brilliant light of the Word will penetrate their darkness (2 Corinthians 4:4).

> **For God, who commanded the light to shine out of darkness, hath shined in our hearts, to give the light of the knowledge of the glory of God in the face of Jesus Christ. But we have this treasure in earthen vessels, that the excellency of the power may be of God, and not of us.**
>
> **2 Corinthians 4:6-7**

When you have the Word on a subject, you have light on the subject.

The inheritance of the saints is *in* the light. Those that look into the light will see truth, for the light of the knowledge of the glory of God will shine upon them. These hold onto the promises in the undefeatable expectation of faith. Having looked into the face of glory, they are assured in confidence, believing that God will do what He said He would do.

> **But we all, with unveiled face, beholding as in a mirror the glory of the Lord, are being transformed into the same image from glory to glory...**
>
> **2 Corinthians 3:18a NKJV**

The inheritance of the saints is kept in the light of glory. Anything outside of the light is subject to the thievery of the enemy. The devil, however, cannot access what is safeguarded within the light of the Word. He cannot touch glory for his realm encompasses the deepest of darkness. As a creature of the night, he shuns truth and works to invalidate the Word of God. He specializes in misinformation and demonic propaganda. In the shadows, he whispers, *"God is mystical," "God is mysterious," "His ways are beyond understanding."* Those that teeter between light and darkness will find themselves given over to demonic suggestions. The ignorant and the indecisive will be taken captive at his will.

God is not mysterious. Neither are His ways beyond understanding. In fact, God has brought the hidden things of darkness to light (1 Corinthian 4:5). There is nothing hidden that will not be revealed by the light of His glory.

The Great Salvation Experience: Escape from Darkness and Defeat

Who hath delivered us from the power of darkness, and hath translated us into the Kingdom of His dear Son.

Colossians 1:13

The child of God has been delivered from the power of darkness and translated into the Kingdom of God's dear Son. Having received such a great deliverance, Paul exhorts the Colossian's to give thanks to God. At the same time, he prayed that they might see and know the divine Will. Those that know the Will, can enforce the Will.

How does one enforce the Will?

Give thanks to God for His great salvation. When you are confronted with a work of darkness, like poverty, remember *Whose* Kingdom you belong to. Stir yourself into remembrance and thank God that you have been delivered from the power of poverty. In the same way, thank God that you have been delivered from the power of sin, sickness and disease. Speak the language of your new nature.

Say, *"God, thank You that I'm delivered and I give You praise that I'm already free. Thank You for delivering me from the old nature, from the old man and from the things that are behind me. I am free and I am new in God."*

Praise God in the *name* of Jesus! When you do so, you will put the anointing to work in your life. Everything that Christ stands for will work on your behalf. There is power in the Name.

Neither is there salvation in any other; for there is none other NAME under Heaven given among men, whereby we must be saved.

Acts 4:12

There is power in the name of Jesus to save. The Name has been given to all those that are under Heaven. It has been made available to every man, woman and child that will receive the headship of Jesus Christ. Those that have the Name, have the authority to enforce the will of God with power. They are God's representatives in the earth realm.

The Hebrew and Greek words for salvation literally imply deliverance, safety, preservation, healing and soundness. Salvation is not one-dimensional, but rather, it is inclusive of everything that pertains to life and godliness. Therefore, this Scripture could be expanded in the following manner: *"Neither is there deliverance, safety, preservation, healing and soundness in any other; for there is none other Name under Heaven given among men whereby we must be delivered, saved, preserved, healed and made sound."*

A student of the Word would never dare say, *"The Name will save some, but it might not save others."* It is universally understood that those who claim the Name will receive the salvation of the Name. Therefore, given the literal translation of *salvation*, those who claim the provision of preservation will receive preservation. Those that claim the promise of healing will receive healing. Those that call on soundness and deliverance will not be denied. Just as the Name procured salvation from sin, it will procure safety, healing, soundness and the like. The Name will provide for everything that pertains to life and godliness. There is not one thing, *that is good*, that the Name cannot reach for the child of God.

The Name given among men packs all the power of Heaven. God has injected the entirety of His *person* and all of the resources of His *nature* into the name of the Lord Jesus. In His earthly ministry, Jesus never turned faith away. All that came to Him *believing*, received from Him *rejoicing*. He didn't play favorites, but He manifested the perfect will of God in every situation.

In light of the resurrection, God turned to the Church and said, *"I'm going to give you a gift, Church. The gift is a Name that carries power to enforce the delegated authority I have given you. When you stand for something in Me, know this: the name of My Son Jesus has the power to back up the authority that I have given you. His name seals the thing that you have petitioned Me for. It is the assurance and the security that you will receive exactly what you have asked for."*

The name of Jesus is above every other name. It will save everybody. Whosoever shall call on the name of the Lord will be saved, healed, preserved and delivered. There is no shame in the Gospel of Christ, for it is the power of God unto *salvation*. It is the power of God unto *healing*. It is the power of God unto *prosperity*. It is power unto *preservation, soundness* and *unending victory*.

CHAPTER 13

PURSUE AND RECOVER ALL

---

*Remember, your victory is not based upon
what God is going to do.
Your victory is based upon what God has already done.*

Spoils of Conquest

And David enquired at the LORD, saying, "Shall I pursue after this troop? Shall I overtake them?" And He answered him, "Pursue: for thou shalt surely overtake them, and without fail recover all."

1 Samuel 30:8

David occupied the position of prophet, priest and king. Under the Old Covenant, the anointing for these three positions was reserved for three very special people. It was not something that was accessible to the average Old Testament person. David, however, was the one exception. He was anointed to fill all three divinely appointed offices. For this reason, David is a type of *Christ* and also a type of the *believer*.

Jesus Christ paved the way for every saint to have access to the Spirit of God. As a New Testament believer, the child of God can utilize the anointing in both word and deed. The power in the office of the prophet, priest and king is the same power that is available through the anointing of the Holy Ghost. The Old Testament layperson did not have the privilege and access that the Church enjoys today.

David was anointed as a spiritual leader, a governmental authority and a prophetic voice. In fact, he was one of the most powerful voices in heralding the messianic prophecies. When the anointing of a prophet would come upon him, he would prophetically declare things that no man could know. It was David who prophesied, *"For thou wilt not leave My soul in Hell; neither wilt thou suffer Thine Holy One to see corruption"* (Psalm 16:10).

Time after time, the Spirit of God would settle on him and he would speak as the oracle of the Most High. He would sing psalms, prophesy out of his spirit, dance and declare God's praise. With his words, he painted verbal portraits of a Messiah that would forever change the nature and destiny of man. He was 900 years removed from the birth of Jesus Christ, but he saw it as if he was living in the day of promise.

> **And it came to pass, when David and his men were come to Ziklag on the third day, that the Amalekites had invaded the south, and Ziklag, and smitten Ziklag, and burned it with fire; And had taken the women captives, that were therein: they slew not any, either great or small, but carried them away, and went on their way. So David and his men came to the city, and, behold, it was burned with fire; and their wives, and their sons, and their daughters, were taken captives. Then David and the people that were with him lifted up their voice and wept, until they had no more power to weep. And David's two wives were taken captives, Ahinoam the Jezreelitess, and Abigail the wife of Nabal the Carmelite. And David was greatly distressed; for the people spake of stoning him, because the soul of all the people was grieved, every man for his sons and for his daughters: but David encouraged himself in the LORD his God. And David said to Abiathar the priest, Ahimelech's son, "I pray thee, bring me hither the ephod." And Abiathar brought thither the**

ephod to David.

1 Samuel 30:1-7

David and his men were just returning home to Ziklag after tending to some kingdom business in a distant land. As they approached their city, they found that it had been burned to the ground. All that remained was the smoldering of ashes and the charred remains of a life that once was. The livestock, the goods, and each man's family had been plundered and taken as spoil. Even David's wives had been carried away as trophies of conquest. The sight was enough to make the strongest of men weep in anguish and loss. The Bible records that David and his men wept, *"until they had no more power to weep."*

"the Amalekites had…smitten Ziklag"

Israel had a long and tumultuous history with the Amalekites. In fact, they were the first nation that Israel had gone to war against. Moses had led the Israelites out of the bondage of Egypt, but the Amalekites withstood them and their passage to the land of promise. In the midst of this epic battle, Moses stood upon a hill with the rod of God and his hands lifted high. While his hands were raised, Israel prevailed, but when exhaustion weighed heavy upon his arms, the enemy prevailed.

> **But Moses hands were heavy; and they took a stone, and put it under him, and he sat thereon; and Aaron and Hur stayed up his hands, the one on the one side, and the other on the other side; and his hands were steady until the going down of the sun.**

Exodus 17:12

Israel learned a valuable lesson that day. In fact, after the victory had been won, God told Moses to record their conquest as a memorial. He said, *"rehearse it in the ears of Joshua"* because Israel will fight against Amalek from generation to generation (Exodus 17:14-16).

Although Israel fought a natural enemy, this battle between God's people and Amalek is a type of spiritual warfare. It's the assurance of victory over every tactical maneuver and strategy that the opposition can launch. Amalek is the face of *your* enemy. It's the face of everything that contradicts your high call. Israel's great conquest was forever recorded so that each successive generation would be versed in the tenets of victory.

The victory is knowing that *"No weapon formed against you shall prosper"* and that you are *"more than a conqueror through Christ"* (Isaiah 54:17; Romans 8:37). It does not matter what you feel like or what the enemy may look like. The truth, in Christ, is that you are seated above principalities, powers, might and dominion. If you will take your stand, as Moses did, you will witness the utter defeat of everything that sought to plunder you.

After your victory and breakthrough, realize that Amalek will come back again. He will find another way, another angle to fight the land of promise that God has given you. Amalek will not go away, for he is a type of the flesh. He is a type of the devil that will always seek opportunity. Therefore, embracing the surety of success, take dominion and live in the Name and walk in the Spirit. Plunder your enemy and prove that he is just as defeated *today* as he was *yesterday*.

Charging Destiny

> **So David and his men came to the city, and, behold, it was burned with fire; and their wives, and their sons, and their daughters, were taken captives. Then David and the people that were with him lifted up their voice and wept, until they had no more power to weep.**
>
> **1 Samuel 30:3-4**

As long as you live on the Earth, the enemy will fight your call.

Those that think they will grow to a place in God that is removed from the warfare are mistaken. While victory is assured, spiritual warfare will remain until Satan is dealt his final blow.

Whenever a person makes a decision to attend to Kingdom business, the enemy will go after home base. This tactic is as old as the war games of the Amalekites. If the enemy can tamper with the home front, he knows that he can distract, and possibly turn back, those that are advancing on his kingdom. This tactic has been used for ages to turn the gaze of God's elect.

Instead of marching on in the confidence of victory, the *elect* remove their hands from the plow and fall from formation. It's not that they wanted to forsake their commitment to God, but home base was hit with the flaming arrows of enemy fire. The smoke that ascended into the horizon distracted them from their spiritual course and from the path of imminent victory. Instead of advancing in the expectation of triumph, they became disheartened, disenchanted and defeated by the harassment of enemy forces.

"So David and his men rose up early to depart..." (1 Samuel 29:11a).

David and his army are on their way home. Everything is good. They're doing what God has called them to do. They're serving the Lord, prophesying, singing songs and preparing to rule and reign under the Name and with the key of David. It's the *David Movement*.

The journey has been long and the men are excited to return to those they love. They trek homeward. *Smoke looms ominously in the horizon.* In all probability, even before they could distinguish the charred outline of their city, they could see the blackness of smoke draping the distant sky. Fearing the worst, but hoping for the best, they pressed forward into the foreboding darkness.

"...and, behold, it was burned with fire..."

The enemy came while they were about Kingdom business. He

came to thwart the advance of God's elite forces and to frustrate their progress. His strategy was to simply break their spirit so that the child of God would be without strength to continue.

The wayside today is paved with men and women who failed to advance in their call. At some point, they were dealt the crippling blow of disappointment and despair. Instead of shaking it off and pressing forward, they became faint in their minds and surrendered the banner of their mandate. These did not have to fall by the wayside or become casualties of war. Had they known their authority and the age-old tactics of their adversary, they would have gathered their strength and overcome every obstacle.

The devil's only artillery is his big mouth. He doesn't have anything to launch other than fiery words. Jesus Christ defeated him over 2,000 years ago and ransacked his kingdom. He stripped him of the keys of death, Hell and the grave and made his defeat a matter of public spectacle. Today, he is no match against the authority of the believer. Those who are committed to *charge destiny* will not be turned from their pursuit. The enemy is powerless to deter the one that knows their *identity* and their *divine commission*.

Diversion on the Wayside

"So David and his men came to the city…"

After much travel, they arrive in their city. Instead of a hero's welcome, their eyes are met with the stinging of smoke and the acrid smell of defeat. David leads his mighty men. Perhaps they canvassed the remains of their city, looking for some sign of hope in the midst of despair. Recoiling in shock, they say to one another, *"Our city… what happened? It's burned up with fire…nothing but ash…The devil, he destroyed it all."* Looking further, the men ask, *"Where are the women? The devil has taken the women! And the children…where are they? The devil has taken our sons and our daughters!"* Beside themselves in sorrow, they lament, *"The money…where's the money? And our flocks and our herds…where have they gone? The devil has taken it all!"*

Does this sound familiar to you?

The enemy's strategies are not new! Originality is not one of his attributes. What he did *then*, he will do *now*. The Bible admonishes, *"We are not ignorant of his devices"* (2 Corinthians 2:11b).

And this is how it happens…

Men and women that are consumed with the things of God will tenaciously advance in the Kingdom. With the fire of purpose, these will run and contend for divine destiny. In the midst of their pursuit, a distraction will beckon them to the sidelines.

"Give no place to the devil" (Ephesians 4:27).

Veering off course, they fix their gaze on the *diversion*. Captivated by the spectacle on the wayside, they lose direction and purpose. They had been pressing forward and performing exploits, but now they feel lost in confusion. They feel like they have lost their bearing.

"We are not ignorant of his devices" (2 Corinthians 2:11b).

Distracted and disoriented, they feel at *loss*. In fact, they begin to feel like they're *losing*. They're going to *lose* their job. They're going to *lose* their business. All is *lost*. It's all sinking. It's all going down. It's going downhill. *The thoughts are relentless.*

"For we do not wrestle against flesh and blood" (Ephesians 6:12).

Behind the scenes, the devil is working hard to convince them that defeat is inevitable. *"Fill their eyes with impossibility. Fill their ears with the sounds of despair,"* he whispers from the wayside.

"…they are taken captive by him at his will" (2 Timothy 2:26b).

The child of God, overcome with the suggestions of darkness, falls. They are unable to press forward into divine destiny. As David's men, they lament, *"Everything is gone. It's all gone. There's no hope."*

It is for this reason that the Word of God reminds believers to *"cast down imaginations"* and bring into *"captivity every thought to the obedience of Christ"* (2 Corinthians 10:5).

Conquer Your Mountain

Are you ready to count the cost?
Have you considered the price?

The price is not backing down in the face of apparent defeat. It means not changing your mind or diluting your convictions. It doesn't matter how much smoke the enemy blows into the horizon, not even the flaming arrow can move you from your course. You will not back down from the divine mandate. Holding the banner of your victory high, you press forward in all that God has commanded.

> **Then David and the people that were with him lifted up their voice and wept, until they had no more power to weep.**
>
> **1 Samuel 30:4**

Perhaps you have faced a mountain that seemed impossible to move. At one time or another, you have lifted up your voice to God and wept. You said, *"God, I just don't understand. Why is everything going so wrong? You said one thing, but all I see is another."* Like David and his men, you were overcome with the sight, sound, and smell of defeat. The circumstance was bigger than anything you had ever seen.

It's all right to lift your voice and weep, but after you're done, *rise up*. Pick yourself up and set yourself back on course in the plan of God. The devil would like to keep you weeping and mourning on the wayside. God, however, would like to turn your weeping into *joy* and your sorrow into *victory*. Disregard enemy propaganda. Put your thoughts on God. Fix your gaze on the promise and move forward in faith and steadfast determination.

Champions like you, *will dry their tears.* They will dust themselves off and rise from where they fell. They will gird their loins and determine in their heart that the "sitting" is over. Putting aside immobility and fear, they once again press forward in *faith*.

Faith is not fantasy.

The Bible says that through *faith*, the elders obtained a good report (Hebrews 11:39). Enoch was translated by faith. Abraham came out of his kindred by faith. Sarah conceived by faith. Shadrach, Meshach and Abed-Nego would not burn because of faith and Daniel shut the mouths of the lions by faith. Faith is not a poetic outlook or an allegorical sentiment. Faith, rather, is a tangible expectation and a conviction that is founded on the unshakeable foundation of truth.

The devil would not be the devil if he did not attack you; and God would not be God if He didn't deliver you when you believed. Therefore, *let the devil be the devil.* We are not impressed. We know what God has said and that He will never fail to perform.

For God has said, *"I will never leave thee, nor forsake thee"* (Hebrews 13:5).

Know Your Enemy

> **Then David and the people that were with him lifted up their voice and wept, until they had no more power to weep. And David's two wives were taken captives, Ahinoam the Jezreelitess, and Abigail the wife of Nabal the Carmelite. And David was greatly distressed...**
>
> **1 Samuel 30:4-6a**

David was distressed because his own people were speaking of stoning him. So great was their anguish, that they sought to retaliate against their leader. The enemy had carried away their wives, their children and all of their possessions. Even David's two wives had been taken captive. Nothing was left behind.

The people mourned until they were exhausted by their sorrow. *"David speaks of promise and a Kingdom that will have no end,"* they murmur. *"But then after we have fought for the promise and pursued the call, we came home only to find it destroyed."* Looking toward the smoldering rubble, they continue, *"Yes, David speaks of great things, but the city lies in ruin."* Overcome with discouragement and mounting fury, they accuse God's anointed. *"Blame the leader!"* they rally.

Strengthened with a *new* cause, they unite in ungodly opposition.

> **And David was greatly distressed; for the people spake of stoning him, because the soul of all the people was grieved…**
>
> **1 Samuel 30:6a**

These men didn't join David's army to see their families taken and their city destroyed. Rather, they joined his side because they believed in the vision of their leader. They believed that they had aligned themselves with a great call, yet despite their valiant intentions, the enemy wreaked havoc on the home front. Now they had no more power to weep.

It is at this point, once an individual has *spent their sorrow*, that they will choose to go one way or the other. They will either *unite* or *divide*. They will press forward in the vision *or* they will heed a suggestion to oppose it.

In other words, you can cry about it and then *walk away from God* or you can *draw closer to God* and *move back into formation*. The world is populated with Christians who say, *"I was hurt in church."* They say, *"There's too many hypocrites there."* They have abandoned their rank and fallen to the wayside.

I grew up in the streets of Los Angeles, California. I was both shot at and stabbed, but I never woke up in the morning and said, *"That's it. I'm leaving the world. You can get killed out there!"* I believed too much in the streets to leave them. I enjoyed the world even in the midst of challenge and adversity! The Church, however, is much safer than the world! The backslidden Christian can't say, *"Oh well, I was shot at and stabbed in church…that's why I left. It's dangerous out there!"*

> **For we do not wrestle against flesh and blood, but against principalities, against powers, against the rulers of the darkness of this age, against spiritual hosts of wickedness in the heavenly places. Therefore take up the whole armor of God…**
>
> **Ephesians 6:12-13a**

God never changes His Word; neither does He change His mind about the elect. Your destiny will never change for the gifts and callings of God are irrevocable (Romans 11:29). However, in the heat of battle, you will always have a decision to make.

David's men were about to make a wrong decision. *"Stone him,"* they said. The Bible records that *"David was greatly distressed."* Nevertheless, in the face of the most disparaging of circumstances, David made a quality decision to get back on course. His city was gone, his wives taken captive and his men were plotting to stone him, yet in the midst of all this, David encouraged himself in the Lord.

Garnering Strength for Battle

> **But David encouraged himself in the LORD his God.**
>
> **1 Samuel 30:6b**

David found the strength to encourage himself, yet Christians all over the world are waiting for *God* to encourage them. God has already given them the tools, but they are waiting for Him to do something about their situation.

The circumstance will talk. It will tell the believer that the Word doesn't work and that the situation is insurmountable. The saint's eyes, ears and feelings will parrot that same report. It is at this point that the believer must make a decision to either believe the circumstance or believe the Word. They will have to choose allegiance to either the promise or the natural report.

David, seeing the devastation at hand and the contention in the ranks, made a decision to align himself with God. Turning from the diversion, *he encouraged himself in the Lord.*

Those that have read the Psalms will understand *how* David encouraged himself. Shutting his ears to the divisive chatter of enemy fire, he wrote and sang songs of hope and faith. He didn't sing according to the natural, but he sang according to the inspiration of God. He sang, *"Bless the LORD, O my soul: and all that is within me, bless His holy name. Bless the LORD, O my soul, and forget not all His benefits: Who forgiveth all thine iniquities; Who healeth all thy diseases; Who redeemeth thy life from destruction…"* (Psalm 103:1-4).

Looking past the insurmountable, he hummed to the sure sound of what resonated within: *"The Lord is my shepherd, I shall not want. He maketh me to lie down in green pastures. He leadeth me besides the still waters"* (Psalm 23:1-2). David encouraged himself in the Lord.

While David meditated on God's faithfulness, the enemy continued to launch fiery words. He said, *"Your men are going to kill you!"* but David said, *"The Lord is my refuge and my fortress, in Him shall I trust."* *"As you say…"* continued the voice, *"but look around you! The city is burned up, David. Everything is gone. There's no hope."* David remained unmoved. *"The city may be gone,"* he replied, *"but I know of a city that can never be burned."* Working from another angle, the enemy softly whispered, *"Tell me what happened to your mate David. Where is she now?"* but David continued to encourage himself, *"I know somebody that will never leave me nor forsake me and He has promised me that what God has put together, let no man put asunder"* (Psalm 91:2; Psalm 145:13; Hebrews 13:5; Mark 10:9).

The devil will fight your every step. No matter the direction, he will propose defeat. He will rehearse the impossibility of the situation. However, those that encourage themselves in the Lord will rise above the insurmountable. They will scale the mountain of the impossible.

In the face of opposition, you will want to rehearse the situation, but restrain yourself and do as David did. *Encourage yourself in the Lord.* When you do, you will rise above the harassment of a lower realm. From the summit of your heavenly perspective, you will begin to see your situation from the viewpoint of Heaven. In other words, *altitude* determines *perspective*. Remember, God raised us up together with Jesus and made us to sit with Him in the *heavenly places* (Ephesians 2:6).

When the devil says, *"You're going to die,"* remember the One that died for you and then rose again! Pull yourself together and say, *"Wait a minute! The Bible says, 'With long life shall He satisfy me and show me His salvation'"* (Psalm 91:16). Encourage yourself in the Lord! Feed yourself with Words that will disarm fiery darts and strengthen your spirit.

Speaking to one another in psalms and hymns and spiritual songs, singing and making melody in your heart to the Lord.

Ephesians 5:19

The anointing is on the report of the Lord. When the devil says, *"There's nothing to sing about today,"* get up and say, *"This is the day that the Lord has made! I will rejoice and be glad in it"* (Psalm 118:24).

Why encourage yourself? The Word of God packs the power and the anointing to bring supernatural strength into your life. When you speak what God has said, you garner strength to persevere in the midst of battle. This is why Scripture exhorts the believer to be strong in the Lord and in the power of His might. That might and power is in the Word of God.

> **Finally, my brethren, be strong in the Lord, and in the power of His might. Put on the whole armour of God, that ye may be able to stand against the wiles of the devil.**
>
> **Ephesians 6:10-11**

Putting Your Armor to Use

> **Wherefore take unto you the whole armour of God, that ye may be able to withstand in the evil day, and having done all, to stand. Stand therefore, having your loins girt about with truth, and having on the breastplate of righteousness; And your feet shod with the preparation of the gospel of peace; Above all, taking the shield of faith, wherewith ye shall be able to quench all the fiery darts of the wicked. And take the helmet of salvation, and the sword of the Spirit, which is the Word of God: Praying always with all prayer and supplication in the Spirit, and watching thereunto with all perseverance and supplication for all saints.**
>
> **Ephesians 6:13-18**

"Stand therefore…having on the breastplate of righteousness…"

The breastplate of righteousness says, *"I know that I am the righteousness of God in Christ Jesus"* (2 Corinthians 5:21). It doesn't say, *"Well, we're not worthy"* or *"You know, we're all just sinners."* The breastplate of righteousness is for those who have a revelation of the blood of Jesus. They know that the blood did not come short in recreating their new nature.

When an individual has a revelation of righteousness, they will know that *nothing* can short-circuit the power of the blood in their life. The Word of God says, *"But if we walk in the light as He is in the light, we have fellowship with one another, and the blood of Jesus Christ His Son cleanses us from all sin"* and *"If we confess our sins, He is faithful and just to forgive us our sins and to cleanse us from all unrighteousness."* (1 John 1:7,9). When the sin has been cleansed, righteousness remains.

"Stand therefore, having your loins girt about with truth…"

In order to deal with the devil boldly, the believer must not only have a revelation of their right standing, but they must be wearing the belt of truth. The one that wears *truth* speaks the Word only and disregards the report of the world. They aren't moved by the sights and sounds of natural impossibilities, but rather, they stand firm in the Word. The devil knows that if he can get the believer to walk away from the Word of truth, they will *surrender* both the race and their right to win.

"Above all, taking the shield of faith, wherewith ye shall be able to quench all the fiery darts of the wicked."

The shield of faith will quench all the fiery darts of the wicked one. It will douse every word he launches in the path of the just. However, if the devil can convince the believer to lay down their shield, those fiery darts will penetrate their life.

Faith comes by hearing and hearing comes through the Word of God (Romans 10:17). Therefore, the shield of *faith* is the byproduct of the Word of God. That shield is not built out of editorials, commentaries or best selling books. Rather, the shield of faith finds its substance and strength in the Word of the Living God.

The Word of God will *not* give the hearer faith for cancer, high blood pressure, leukemia, unemployment, divorce, misery or pain! In fact, there is not one promise that says, *"I am the Lord Thy God who burns your city, steals your wife, abducts your children and robs you of all that you own."* Only the true Word of God will produce faith. Anything less will produce apprehension and fear.

If there's *something* working on your life that doesn't fit within the parameters of Bible faith, then douse it and dismiss it. Use the Word of God—*the shield of faith*—to quench every fiery dart.

"Wherefore take unto you the whole armour of God, that ye may be able to withstand in the evil day…"

As a real person living in the midst of a real world, you will face an evil day. Don't fear the evil day, just remember to put on the armor. Don't whine, *"But why won't the Lord help me?"* Mature children dress themselves. Therefore, put on the whole armor of God that you may be able to stand against the wiles of the devil.

Inquiring of Light and Perfection

But David encouraged himself in the LORD His God.

1 Samuel 30:6b

There are two groups of Christians. One group is waiting for God to do something. They weep and say, *"When God, when?"* The other has finished weeping and has made a decision to encourage themselves through the Word of God.

After people have encouraged themselves in the Lord, *they are ready for action.*

And David said to Abiathar the priest,

> **Ahimelech's son, "I pray thee, bring me hither the ephod." And Abiathar brought thither the ephod to David.**
>
> **1 Samuel 30:7**

Once David had encouraged himself, he was no longer fearful of the circumstance. Turning to the priest, he said, *"Bring me the ephod."* The ephod was the garment of the high priest. Upon this garment was the *breastplate of judgment* (or *righteousness*) and four rows of precious stones, representing each of the twelve tribes. According to the law, only a priest could wear such a garment. David, however, was anointed as priest and king.

"Bring me the ephod."

As a child of God under the New Covenant, you are also anointed as a priest and king unto God (Revelation 1:6). Therefore, after you have encouraged yourself, pull on your armor and drape yourself in the *robes of righteousness* and the *garments of praise*.

Adorning the breastplate of righteousness was also the *Urim* and the *Thummim*. The Urim and the Thummim represented *light* and *perfection*. So therefore, the ephod not only contained the breastplate with the twelve precious stones, but light and perfection was set in it as well. After the man of God had donned this priestly garment, he would inquire of God and the Word of the Lord would come.

The Bible says the steps of the righteous are directed or ordered of the Lord (Psalm 37:23). They are only directed, however, after the *righteous* have encouraged themselves. After a person is encouraged, they are ready to inquire of the Lord.

David said, *"Bring me the Urim and the Thummim. Bring me Light and Perfection."*

In the New Testament, Light and Perfection are types of the Word and the Spirit. Therefore, after the saint has encouraged himself or herself in the Lord, they are ready to inquire, *"Okay Lord, what does your Word say?"* Walking in the Spirit, they ask, *"All right Holy Ghost, where should I go from here?"*

David put on the garment and said, *"Let me inquire of Light and Righteousness. Let me consult the Word and the Spirit."*

And David enquired at the Lord, saying, "Shall I pursue after this troop? Shall I overtake them?"

1 Samuel 30:8a

For every day that you live beneath your privileges, *you allow* the devil to rob you of days of divine fulfillment. However, the day has come for YOU to encourage YOURSELF in God. Think and speak His report. Walk in His ways. Do what you have been trained to do.

David asked, *"Shall I pursue this troop? Should I go after the thief?"* The unlearned would answer, *"Well, David…you know, it's all in the Lord's time…"*

And the Lord answered him:

"Pursue: for thou shalt surely overtake them, and without fail recover all."

1 Samuel 30:8b

Times of Restitution

"The Lord planted a garden eastward in Eden…" (Genesis 2:8a). Adam and Eve walked in the Garden and had dominion over all of the Earth (Genesis 1:28). There was grass in the field, beasts on land, waters that teemed with life, the sun in the day, the moon in the night and stars that spread out over the sky. Everything was exactly as God created it. The Lord looked at His creation and said, *"It is good."*

During a moment of opportunity, the devil broke in on Eden and not only carried away Adam and Eve, but he stole the nation that God had created to be His wife and bride. He took all of God's children and all of the property of the Earth. In turn, everything was brought under the dominion and reign of darkness.

David is a type of Jesus.

Jesus said to God, *"Should I pursue this troop? Should I go down to Earth?"* Light and Perfection replied, *"Yes, go after them. Overtake them and You will recover all without fail."*

Determined to thwart the plan of God, Satan took Jesus to the highest of mountains and showed Him the kingdoms of the world. He made this proposition: *"All these things I will give Thee, if Thou wilt fall down and worship me"* (Matthew 4:9). Setting His face as flint towards destiny, He rejected the fiery words of opposition and ran the race that had been set before Him.

Jesus came to seek and to save the lost. He came to the Earth to recover all that had been stolen. He came to reclaim all that was His.

> **"Pursue: for thou shalt surely overtake them, and without fail recover all."**
>
> **1 Samuel 30:8b**

Heeding the divine direction, David and his men went after the enemy. He found the Amalekites eating, drinking, dancing and reveling in the spoils of conquest.

> **Behold, they were spread abroad upon all the Earth, eating and drinking, and dancing, because of all the great spoil that they had taken out of the land of the Philistines, and out of the land of Judah.**
>
> **1 Samuel 30:16b**

God told Jesus, *"You're going to recover all without fail."* When Jesus came, the demon spirits were spread abroad, all over the Earth, eating drinking and gloating in the spoil of humanity.

> **And David smote them from twilight even unto the evening of the next day: and there escaped not a man among them, save four hundred young men, which rode upon camels and fled. And David recovered all that the Amalekites had carried away: and David rescued his two wives.**
>
> **1 Samuel 30:17-18**

For this purpose the Son of God was manifested, that He might destroy the works of the devil" (1 John 3:8b).

Jesus not only recovered the Jews, but He rescued the Gentiles. Jesus rescued His His people and His Church. Walking in upon the profane merrymaking of the Amalekites, Jesus said, *"You stole something from Me."* He smote the devil, making him a public spectacle of defeat and triumphing over him in the cross.

Jesus recovered all who would believe. He reclaimed every bit of property, all the gold, all the silver, all the divine health and every other blessing that belongs to the believer. He took the captive and said, *"See, you're free now! You're not a slave. You've been redeemed from darkness."* Pointing to the spoil, He said, *"And look! I have given you everything that you need with regard to life and godliness."*

Jesus recovered all.

> **And there was nothing lacking to them, neither small nor great, neither sons nor anything that they had taken to them. David recovered all.**
>
> **1 Samuel 30:19**

Pursue What Belongs to You

As a believer, you must encourage yourself in the Lord. Encourage yourself in the victory that Jesus already accomplished! Remember, your victory is not based upon what God is *going to do*. Your victory is based upon what God has *already done*.

When the devil says, *"Your city is burned,"*
tell him that Jesus bought you back from destruction.

When the devil says, *"You're sick in your body,"*
tell him that Jesus bought you back from sickness and disease.

Your victory is based on what Jesus has already done. Therefore, God's Word to you today is this: **PURSUE what belongs to you**. It's yours. Jesus paid for your victory.

The Bible says, *"How shall we escape if we neglect so great a salvation"* (Hebrews 2:3a)? In the last chapter, you learned that salvation is inclusive of certain provisions, such as deliverance, safety, preservation, healing and soundness. A person that neglects the salvation of the soul, will not escape the judgment of Hell. In the same manner, a person that neglects the provisions of salvation, will not escape the consequences of thievery and lies. If the believer does not know the Word of truth, then they will be powerless to exercise dominion over the enemy.

PURSUE what belongs to you. Go after *every* promise. If the devil stole your peace of mind, pursue the mind of Christ. If you are in confusion and feel tossed to and fro on the seas of emotional wavering, *pursue the thing and recover all without fail*. Don't gawk at the enormity of the mountain. *Move it!* Recover and claim what belongs to you.

There's men and women, like yourself, rising up all over the world. These will walk by faith and they will pursue and recover all. Even the children will pursue the devil. Little ones will walk into school, and the devils will tremble at their authority and power. Throughout the

Earth, a great army will rise up and walk in the fearless conquest of Calvary. This isn't a vision for the distant future, for *you* are among those that have been called to such greatness.

> There's going to be
> AN ARMY MARCHING through the land.
> DELIVERANCE is going to be in their SONG.
> HEALING is going to be IN THEIR HAND.
> EVERLASTING GLADNESS is
> going to be IN THEIR HEART…
> … and in this army YOU HAVE A PART.

PURSUE what belongs to you. Not only will you overtake your enemy and recover all, but the wealth of the wicked will be delivered into your hand. When Jesus Christ is your motivation in life, *abundance will come.*

> **And David took all the flocks and the herds, which they (the Amalekites) drave before those other cattle, and said, "This is David's spoil."**
>
> **1 Samuel 30:20**

God's army will meddle in what the devil calls *his* kingdom. Champions from far and wide will not be impressed with his methods or his show. They will rise up and take back what belongs to the Church. They will take back the anointing, the truth, and the revelation that the Church has lost. Yet, they won't stop there, they will press further and recover more revelation, more rights, more privileges, more truth and more anointing. They will recover more than they ever thought possible.

It's the hour of abundance and the time of restitution of all things.

Do you believe it? You have a purpose. In fact, you are living in the greatest hour of human history. This victory, this mandate, belongs to you. God won't get any bigger in Heaven, but you are rising to a place that resonates with the fulfillment of prophetic purpose.

Before you go any further in this book, make this your prayer:

Lord, thank You for MAKING ME A PART of the army.
A SOLDIER of *righteousness*…
A *child* of the KINGDOM…
A saint *called* and *chosen* for destiny and purpose…

Forgive me for getting my EYES on the CIRCUMSTANCES.
Remind me *daily*, through the Holy Ghost…
to ENCOURAGE MYSELF in the Lord…
and to *fight* the good fight of faith.

I am *committed* to YOUR PURPOSE.
MY GAZE IS FIXED on the Kingdom.
I am a *soldier* in Your work AND I WILL PURSUE.
I WILL OVERTAKE and *without fail*…
I will recover all.

I am coming IN THE NAME of Jesus!
Oh, I'm coming IN THE POWER of the Word!
I am claiming *what belongs to You*, God!
I am claiming *what belongs to the Church*!
…and without fail…
I will recover all!

Chapter 14

Instructions for Building

*Whatever is not built on faith,
will fall apart under pressure.*

Build with the Word

Therefore, whoever hears these sayings of Mine, and does them, I will liken him to a wise man who built his house on the rock.

Matthew 7:24 NKJV

Are you wise? The person who builds with the Word of God will withstand the winds of contradiction and the tremors of challenge. When opposition shakes the ground of the righteous, they will remain unmoved. While a thousand may fall at their side and ten thousand at their right hand, they will not go down (Psalm 91:7).

Jesus said that those who *hear* His Word and *do* His Word are like a house built on a foundation of rock. Even when the rains descend and the forecast looks bleak, the righteous will stand with a testimony. Not even the floods will carry their victory away.

And the rain descended, the floods came, and the winds blew and beat on that house; and it did not fall, for it was founded on the rock.

Matthew 7:25 NKJV

The rains will descend, the winds will blow and the floods will come.

Just as surely as storm clouds gather, opposing forces and destroying spirits will come against your position, property and God-given rights. The enemy *will* attack, but through the Word of God, you are well equipped to withstand the deluge. He may come against you one way, but he will flee before you in seven (Deuteronomy 28:7).

When the believer builds upon the Word of God, no weapon in the kingdom of darkness can move them from their foundation. What you build in God will withstand the test of time. In the end, everyone who mocked and prophesied demise will have to testify to your triumph. After the smoke has settled and the dust has cleared, you will remain standing, just as steadfast as before the rain.

Those that are built upon the Word can never fail.

> **But everyone who hears these sayings of Mine, and does not do them, will be like a foolish man who built his house on the sand: And the rains descended, the floods came, and the winds blew and beat on that house; and it fell. And great was its fall.**
>
> **Matthew 7:26-27 NKJV**

Those that build on sand will shift with the passing wind. When the circumstance boasts of downpour and feelings rise and swell beyond their banks, those that are built on shaky ground will see calamity and destruction. Their downfall will be swift.

The Word of God is a rock that cannot be moved. It is a fortress of preservation, safety and security. The one that builds their life on it will stand against the storm. However, those that build on the principles of the world, will find themselves shaken and floating downstream.

"And great was its fall."

Bussing Your Table

The champions of today are going to fight with the Word of God. The Bible calls the Word of God, the *Sword of the Spirit*. God's Word is living and powerful and sharper than any two-edged sword. Jesus said, *"The Words I speak to you are Spirit and life"* (Ephesians 6:17; Hebrews 4:12; John 6:63).

Those who are well trained in the Word will win every battle. Even when Jesus fought the devil with the Word, He said, *"Man shall not live by bread alone, but by every Word that proceeds from the mouth of God"* (Matthew 4:4). Jesus quoted the Pentateuch or Deuteronomy 8:03! If the Word, Himself, waged war with the sword of the Word, how much more should the believer?

Jesus Christ is the same yesterday, today and forever. Heaven and Earth will pass away but God's Word will never change. The truth of God will always remain.

Truth will continue to be Truth.

The days that you are living in are perilous times. What you do with the Word of God will determine how you stand in this hour. In fact, the natural realm will be affected by your spiritual decisions. Those that base their decisions upon the volatile market of natural principles will experience the highs and lows of that realm. However, those whose decisions are grounded upon the foundation of spiritual principals will never fail to prosper and increase.

Words have the power to either make you or break you. This is why it is *life or death* what church you go to. The sermon that you hear, whether it's from the pulpit of the church or the pulpit of the world, has the power to produce after its *kind* in your life. Just as the *apple seed* will produce after the *apple tree*, so will the *poverty word* produce after the *poverty message*. The Bible calls the Word of God a seed (Luke 8:11).

The word that you lend your ear to will determine your victory or your defeat.

> **Then the twelve called the multitude of the disciples unto them, and said, "It is not reason that we should leave the Word of God and serve tables."**
>
> **Acts 6:2**

There are two kinds of ministries in the earth realm today. One of those is the *Word Ministry* and the other is the *Table Ministry.*

A great revival had begun in Jerusalem. People were coming to the Lord in thousands. The Bible records, *"And believers were increasingly added to the Lord, multitudes of both men and women"* (Acts 5:14).

As the Church grew and people were added, natural problems began to arise. One such problem was that certain individuals were being neglected. In today's modern language, we would say, *"Some people were falling through the cracks."*

> **And in those days when the number of the disciples was multiplied, there arose a murmuring of the Grecians against the Hebrews, because their widows were neglected in the daily ministration.**
>
> **Acts 6:1**

Looking for a solution to the mounting problem, the people began to pull on the ministry gift. They said to the Apostles, *"Leave the Word of God and deal with this natural situation. Counsel us, Pastor."* The Apostles, however, refused the soulish pull of the people. Instead, they said, *"It does not make sense for us to neglect the preaching of the Word in order to attend to your natural needs."*

The Word of God is relevant to today. It is the answer and the solution to every situation that mankind will face. However, what transpired in the early Church, has repeated itself many times over since that date. Those that have not learned to draw on the Word of God for encouragement and strength will pull on their pastor for natural attention. They will say, *"Pastor, step away form the Word and talk to us where we are at. Leave your prayer closet and come down to Earth. You see, we just have some needs that we'd like you to address. To begin with, we would like you to be a jack-of-all-trades to us. Be our psychologist, be our politician, and be our priest. Marry us, bury us and mention our name when you pray."*

The Apostles said, *"It is not reason that we should leave the Word of God, and serve tables."*

In many churches today, the pastor has left the Word of God to wait on tables. Instead of preaching the pure Word, they have diluted their message with the ideologies of the world. Responding to the soulish pressure of immature saints, they have backed off of the Word of truth and catered to the demands of the pew.

As a child of God, you have been equipped to hear God. You do not need a counseling session and you do not need natural direction. Rather, your solution is in the Word of God. Instead of giving an ear to the natural report, meditate on God's thoughts and immerse yourself in His counsel. Jesus, after all, is the Great Counselor (Isaiah 9:6). The answer that you seek is in Him.

You have a house to build, but only you can choose how to build it.

The House That's Built to Last

The Word of God is consistent. What God said over 2,000 years ago, He is still saying today. The immature will say, *"But I want to know what God is saying right now,"* and the slothful will complain, *"But I want to hear from the prophets!"* The child of God must build their life on the Word. It is not enough to get it second hand; they must personally invest themselves in the Word of God.

There is direction in the Word of God. The Bible said, *"Thy Word is a lamp unto my feet, and a light unto my path"* (Psalm 119:105). Those who turn to the Word will see by the Word. If you need direction, *get a Word from God.*

People approach me and say, *"I need direction."* I want to tell them, *"What's wrong with going forward?"* Yes, I stand in the office of the prophet, but the revelation of that office is not for giving personal direction. You will never hear me say, *"The Lord would have you marry So-and-So."* Prophecy is for edification, exhortation and comfort (1 Corinthians 14:3).

Neither is the gift meant for correction or rebuke. While correction is biblical, under most circumstances, it should not be addressed through the ministry of the prophetic gift. God did not give prophecy for the purpose of correction. Rather, He gave the *Word* to correct, rebuke and reprove.

You are responsible to build your own house.

The Psalmist said, *"Thy Word have I hid in my heart that I might not sin against Thee"* (Psalm 119:11). Paul went on to say that *Christ* or *the Word* is near you. It is both in your heart and in your mouth. Paul called this *"the Word of faith, which we preach"* (Romans 10:8).

Faith only comes through hearing. It is the byproduct of the ministry of the Word. Therefore, faith is the language of God. Those that approach God must speak His language. This, and only this, is pleasing to the Lord (Romans 10:17; Hebrews 11:6).

If the Word Ministry produces faith, then the Table Ministry only produces those things that are acquainted with the world. Table ministries don't generate faith because they are busy bussing tables! *"Well, I like to keep my ear to the ground and keep tabs on what's happening."* If you would keep your ear to the Spirit realm, you would find out what's happening in God.

What kind of CHURCH are you building?
What kind of MARRIAGE are you building?
What kind of BUSINESS are you building?
What kind of HOME are you building?
What kind of LIFE are you building?

The foundation you build on will determine how long the edifice of your work will last. As long as there are sunny days, the things that are built on the rickety principles of the world will stand tall. Even the Table Ministries will shine for a time on the mountaintop. However, in the presence of strong winds and rain, these edifices will collapse from the pressure of the storm. Their foundation will give way from beneath them and they will slide down the mountain of natural presumption.

Whatever is not built on faith, will fall apart under pressure.

God did not make you a king and priest unto Him so that you would be trampled by the world. The Word says, *"If God is for you, who can be against you"* (Romans 8:31)? In the realm of the Spirit, you have *everything* going for you in God. He has given you authority, power, jurisdiction, His name, His Spirit and everything that pertains to life and godliness. As His ambassador in the Earth realm, you have been given the tools to build an edifice in God that is strong and that shines as a city set upon a hill.

In these last days, Christians will be the happiest people on Earth. They will be the richest, the most anointed and the most envied people on the planet. The world will look on and say, *"Man, what is going on with that person? They look like they live in another world!"* The Church will shine like a city that cannot be hid.

Those that build on the rock will not suffer loss. The Apostles told the people that it didn't make sense for them to wait on tables. They knew that great works are built with the Word of God. Those things that aren't built with the Word will crumble under persecution. The Bible says, *"Except the Lord build the house, they labour in vain that build it"* (Psalm 127:1). Jesus is the Word. The Word should build the house.

"It is not reason that we should leave the Word of God and serve tables."

Strategies for Church Growth

Wherefore brethren, look ye out among you seven men of honest report, full of the Holy Ghost, and wisdom, whom we may appoint over this business. But we will give ourselves continually to prayer and to the ministry of the Word.

Acts 6:3-4

Within the Church world, leaders will point to statistics and current research on church growth. They will cite studies and expert opinions. The experts recommend, *"Keep the Word short. Make the people comfortable. Have them drive in and have them drive out."* Their opinions are published and pastors from all over the world build on their principles.

These principles, however, cannot be found in the Word of God. Anything that is not built on the rock will not stand. Jesus said, *"Upon this rock, I will build My Church"* (Matthew 16:18).

And the Word of God increased; and the number of the disciples multiplied in Jerusalem greatly; and a great company of the priests were obedient to the faith.

Acts 6:7

If the Apostles had not delegated the natural things to others, they would have become preachers controlled by the spirit of the people. Instead of ministering the Word and giving themselves to prayer, they would have become administrative worker bees, buzzing about as problem-solvers and soulish bridge-builders.

In the beginning, the people may like the social pastor. They may enjoy the natural bonding and the chicken dinners. However, if the pastor continues to wait on natural tables, the people will lose respect for their spiritual office. They will lose respect for the Word that they speak.

Why?

Those that put down the Word and leave the prayer closet will become naturally minded. Instead of relating to the people on a spiritual level, they will relate to the people on a natural level. Rather than speaking Words of life, they will speak out of the flesh. In so doing, the man or woman of God will have turned their pulpit into a platform for the flesh or a *Table Ministry*.

In Jerusalem, however, this was not the case. The early church leaders did not forsake the Word of God and prayer. Their first priority was the Word of God. Having built upon the foundation of the Word, the number of disciples multiplied and the platform of the Gospel increased.

"And the Word of God increased; and the number of the disciples multiplied…"

Building to Code

Building is a process. It involves laying brick upon brick. It is a labor that requires the work of faith, the mortar of patience and the application of the Word of God. While it takes little effort to construct castles in the sand, a work of faith must be built upon the rock. It must be built upon the sure foundation of the Word of God, lest the tides wash the work away.

Therefore, whoever hears these sayings of Mine,

and does them, I will liken him to a wise man who built his house on the rock.

Matthew 7:24 NKJV

It's easy to build on the sand. However, it takes faith to build on the rock. It takes not being moved by what you see and refusing the natural report. For the believer, the most gratifying place in God is to live according to the Word. Anything less, will leave the believer dissatisfied and grumpy.

All Scripture is given by inspiration of God, and is profitable for doctrine, for reproof, for correction, for instruction in righteousness: That the man of God may be perfect, thoroughly furnished unto all good works.

2 Timothy 3:16-17

Every Word of God is God-breathed. It is literally filled with the life and power of God. The Bible teaches that these *God-breathed Words* are profitable for doctrine. Therefore, any doctrine that is not derived from Scripture is a misappropriation of the Word.

"Well, I just believe that the Lord makes you sick to teach you."
"Well, I just believe that we're all sinners."
"Well, I just believe that God works in mysterious ways."

Subtle religious lies like these are not only inaccurate and unbiblical, but they are dangerous. Demonic propaganda has been used for centuries to rob the Christian of their authority. The consequences of these *doctrines of devils* have not only produced paralyzed saints, but also death and backsliding within the Body.

Do not build on sand, but build on the rock of the Word.

The Word of God will reprove, correct and instruct. It will perfect, mature and thoroughly furnish the man or woman of God for every good work. Those that train under a Word and prayer ministry, and who partake of a strong diet of the Word of God, will grow into the fullness of all that God has called them to be.

Laying Sound Doctrine

> **Preach the Word; be instant in season, out of season; reprove, rebuke, exhort with all longsuffering and doctrine.**
>
> **2 Timothy 4:2**

Preach the Word. This is what grows a *strong* church! This is what *nourishes* a body into maturity! Paul told Timothy, *"Be instant in season."* In other words, don't be double-minded. Don't be occasional or seasonal, but always walk full of the Word of God. Be *ever-ready* in God for whatever comes your way!

"Well, I just believe that we go through seasons in God." Be instant. Don't be a seasonal Christian. Don't go through a dry spell. Life may be seasonal, but this should never dictate how a Christian lives. *You are called to live above the seasons.*

"But I'm going through a dry spell," they say. No, you're going through backsliding! For the Christian, it does not matter how dry the natural realm is. When you have the anointing, seasons do not matter. The one that walks in the anointing, walks in the victory. They're strong in the Lord and in the power of *His* might.

The Christian's face should not reflect the global economy. Neither should it mirror the medical report, a relative's opinion or the word on the street! Paul told Timothy, *"Be instant in season, out of season."* Be *instant* in victory. Be *instant* in the anointing. Be *instant* in your call. Be *instant* in joy. Be *consistent* in God. Your security is based on a higher realm. Your confidence is invested in a higher power.

When you build on the Word, you don't waver.

For the time will come when they will not endure sound doctrine; but after their own lusts shall they heap to themselves teachers, having itching ears.

2 Timothy 4:3

By and large, most believers are unable to handle sound doctrine. Jesus has given the believer the healing power of God. Their body has been made a temple for the Holy Ghost and they've been given the mind of Christ. Even more, the believer has been granted the Name. When darkness opposes them, that devil is facing the living, breathing representative of the Lord Jesus Christ!

God has done all this, yet *Pastor Table Waiter* will stand in the pulpit and hem and haw on everything but sound doctrine. They will say, *"We just want you to know that we are humble here. We're sinners and we don't have any power, but we know of Someone who does."* The people that sit under their teaching, numbly bob their heads in agreement! Not having been raised in sound doctrine and never having experienced the unadulterated Word, they do not know enough to *know better*.

"For the time will come when they will not endure sound doctrine."

The day will come when those who have handled the Word deceitfully will turn the tables around. They will persecute the Word Ministry and call them heretics. These will not endure sound doctrine, but having itching ears, they will heap to themselves teachers. They will run after those who will cater to their soulish desires. These teachers will tell them exactly what they want to hear.

I've been in churches where I preached the Word and watched people grind their teeth in disagreement. They sat with their arms folded, fuming, yet when I gave the altar call for healing, they got in the line and received their healing. They received a miracle, but immediately after the gathering they qualified it by saying, *"Well, I received my miracle today, but it's not because of that man. I went up to the Lord."*

Why didn't they just go up to the prayer line of the Lord in their house?

The Bible said that men and women would not tolerate sound doctrine, but would run after their own lusts, seeking a voice that would echo their own. "Lusts" are simply *desires*. They are the things that people want. They are the things of the natural realm. Those that are well acquainted with the natural realm and its lusts will say, *"I have struggles, flaws and weaknesses. This old nature is obstinate. I want to do what God says, but I'm so weak. I tell you what, this sinful flesh gets the best of me."*

Those that refuse sound doctrine are really saying, *"I want the salvation without the responsibility of using my faith to step into transformation."*

When you build, build on the Word.

CHAPTER 15

WALKING IN AGREEMENT

Where there is great agreement, there is great power.

Vote with Your Feet

Christianity is the byproduct of a miraculous encounter with God. The child of God isn't born into the Church through natural means, but rather, the Spirit of God gives these the experience of the new birth. Through this supernatural miracle, the *sinner* becomes a *saint*. The *old* man is recreated into the *new*. What was steeped in *darkness* becomes the brilliance of *light*. Those that are born of the Word, shine with the glory of that Word. God is light and *in Him* there is no darkness (1 John 1:5).

The miracle of the new birth takes place in an *instant*, however, the outward transformation is in most cases, *a process*. In other words, the child of God grows as they are *renewed in knowledge* to the Word of God. Prior to their new birth, these were groomed in the ways of the world. Through training and sensory learning, they became accustomed to natural living. Once a person is born into the Kingdom, however, they must learn Kingdom principles. They must learn to live and walk by the Spirit and the Word. If they do not, they will always live on a substandard level.

Nevertheless, the moment a person receives Jesus, everything becomes new. By virtue of the new nature, the child of God receives all the tools of that new nature. They receive everything that they need to live like God has called them to live.

Everything that you need for life and godliness is already on the inside of you. You may not have "arrived" yet, but your life is a journey in God. It's a journey from glory to glory! If you will continue to train under the Word of God, you will continue to grow into all that God has called you to be. It may not be an overnight transformation, but as you renew your mind to your new nature, you will walk in newness of life.

> **As newborn babes, desire the sincere milk of the Word, that ye may grow thereby.**
>
> **1 Peter 2:2**

Those that are nourished by the sincere milk of the Word will grow into spiritual maturity. They will walk with God in agreement with His Word. The Bible says, *"How can two walk together except they be agreed"* (Amos 3:3)? Those that walk with the Word are in agreement with God. On the contrary, those that are *not* in agreement with the Word, are *not* walking with God.

The child of God can be saved while at the same time, refusing to walk in the Word. They can be on their way to Heaven, but not walking in agreement with the Lord. *How can two walk together except they be agreed?*

> **But if we walk in the light, as He is in the light, we have fellowship one with another, and the blood of Jesus Christ His Son cleanseth us from all sin.**
>
> **1 John 1:7**

"We have fellowship." Fellowship is not available to the sinner. In the Scripture above, God is not exhorting the sinner to walk in the light and have fellowship. Rather, it's impossible for darkness to dwell in the light. Darkness calls to darkness.

Fellowship is only available to those who have been born of God. Only these can walk in the light of the glory of God. The one that walks in the light *as He is in the light* will be cleansed from all unrighteousness. However, the Christian that deviates into darkness cannot also walk in the light. Neither can they participate in the benefits of the light.

> **If we say that we have fellowship with Him, and walk in darkness, we lie, and do not the truth.**
>
> **1 John 1:6**

The saint that walks in the light as He is in the light has fellowship with Him. However, the saint that chooses to walk in the dark as the devil is in the dark, will only fellowship with darkness. Light cannot fellowship with darkness, for only *light* can fellowship with *light*.

Those that are fellowshipping with the wrong realm must repent before they can fellowship with the right realm. If these change their course and walk right, He is faithful and just to cleanse them from all unrighteousness.

> **If we confess our sins, He is faithful and just to forgive us our sins, and to cleanse us from all unrighteousness.**
>
> **1 John 1:9**

Walk in the light as He is in the light.

God is not walking the path of defeat. He is not having problems in His life. Therefore, those who walk in the light *as He is in the light* are walking the same path of victory and triumph.

There are benefits available to those who will walk with God in the light.

This book was written so that you might receive a revelation of things already given. In fact, the words that you are reading have the supernatural ability to destroy the yoke of bondage and to forever change your life. This is a prophetic declaration from the heart of God to *whosoever will.* God is saying, *"Anybody who is willing and obedient will be able to eat of the good of the land"* (Isaiah 1:19).

This is the day where anyone can take the limits off of God. You can advance faster than you thought possible. You can escalate in God. While others stand along the wayside, you can move forward in God, allowing Him to change your life in dramatic proportions.

YOU are the one standing at the voting both of your life. YOUR PRECINCT is within your jurisdiction. In the end, when every vote has weighed in, only your ballot will determine the results in your life. It doesn't matter what the news said, what the odds said, what the relatives said or what the opinion said. When all has been said and done, this fact remains: **God has given YOU the ability to DETERMINE YOUR RESULTS in life.**

Agreeing with God

How can two walk together except they be agreed?

Amos 3:3

If I were to ask most Christians, *"Are you in agreement with the Word?"* they would quickly answer, *"Oh yes!"* If I were to ask them, *"Are you walking with God?"* they would immediately respond, *"All the time!"* Not having received sound doctrine, the average Christian may mistakenly believe that walking in agreement is an automatic provision of salvation.

If agreement with God was automatic, the Christian would never need to be reproved, rebuked or corrected. In fact, every believer would be fully mature and walking in the full measure and stature of Christ. This, however, is not the case. Like the child that grows into adolescence and then into adulthood, so must the Christian grow in God.

> **The steps of a good man (righteous) are ordered (or directed) by the Lord.**
>
> **Psalm 37:23 NKJV**

God will direct you, but ultimately, you choose your steps. Each day involves a decision to step in one direction or the other. Paul described it in this way, *"Redeeming the time, because the days are evil"* (Ephesians 5:16). Redeem your days and walk in agreement with God. When you do so, you will participate in God's best.

Divine results are available to those who operate in the power of faith. However, those things that are not built upon the secure foundation of faith's agreement with the Word, will fail to endure the test of time. What is not built on the Word of God, will fall short of results in God. Therefore, use your faith to walk in agreement with the Word of God.

If you don't use your faith, it can't profit you.

As you already learned, faith comes by hearing and hearing comes by the Word of God (Romans 10:17). Notice, however, that faith does not *work* by *hearing*. It *works* by *doing*. In other words, you can be a hearer and not a doer.

Remember, faith without works is dead (James 2:26).

When the Word of God is preached, *faith will come.* However, the Bible says that faith must be mixed with the Word in order for it to profit the believer. Faith that is received, but not released, is *dead faith*.

> **For unto us was the Gospel preached, as well as unto them: but the Word preached did not profit them, not being mixed with faith in them that heard it.**
>
> **Hebrews 4:2**

Work your faith in agreement with God's Word. When you hear the Word, agree with God. Say, *"That Word is talking about me! That Word is mine!"* When you come into agreement with God, you are mixing *His Word* with *your faith*. A Word that has the stamp of faith's agreement will profit the hearer.

Thinking God Thoughts

> **This book of the law (the Word of God) shall not depart out of thy mouth; but thou shalt meditate therein day and night, that thou mayest observe to do according to all that is written therein: for then thou shalt make thy way prosperous, and then thou shalt have good success.**
>
> **Joshua 1:8**

God told Joshua, *"that you may learn to observe all that is written therein."* The only way to learn to observe all that is written, is to meditate on the Word day and night. God gave this command: *"This book of the law shall not depart out of your mouth."* If you will give the Word of God first priority in every facet of your life, it will make your way prosperous and give you good success. There is strength in the Word of God.

Once a believer is strengthened, they are ready for action. Having heard the Word and received the Word, they are ready to act on their faith. They are in a place of agreement with God. It is at precisely this point that the devil will seek to dismantle their faith. Waging his war on the battlefield of their mind, he will suggest lying accusations and thoughts of condemnation. If he can get them to believe his word over God's Word, he will successfully render their faith ineffective.

This is why the Bible says to fight the good fight of faith (1 Timothy 6:12).

The good fight of faith is the fight that the believer prevails in. The devil may lie, but the child of God has the power to fight and *win* 100% of the time. Those who fight with the Word, will always have a testimony. Nevertheless, the strategy of the enemy has remained consistent since the beginning. Even in the Garden, he suggested to Eve, *"Hath God said* (Genesis 3:1)? If he can discredit the Word of God in the heart and mind of God's creation, then he can ascend to the throne of their life.

The enemy is after the believer's agreement. He knows that if the child of God will think like he thinks, then they will follow him into darkness. The Bible says, *"We are not ignorant of his devices"* (2 Corinthians 2:11b). His methods are not new. However, those that *know* and *enforce* truth cannot be taken captive.

This is how the enemy works:

Launching a thought at the saint's mind, the devil will whisper, *"See! You're a bad person for thinking that!"* If the person graces this fiery dart with their meditations, he will fill their life with condemnation. He will say, *"Well, you know...you wouldn't have thought that unless you really wanted to do it."* Before long, the one that has not been established in sound doctrine will surrender themselves to the suggestions of their adversary. Not knowing enough to rebut the thought, they will give credence to its influence.

This is why the apostle Paul tells the believer, *"For the weapons of our warfare are not carnal, but mighty through God to the pulling down of strongholds: casting down imaginations, and every high thing that exalteth itself against the knowledge of God, and bringing into captivity every thought to the obedience of Christ"* (2 Corinthians 10:4-5).

Don't believe the devil. Don't listen to him. Don't meditate on his thoughts. The suggestions may feel like they belong to you, but remember, his battlefield is in the soulish realm. Extinguish every fiery dart with the Word of God. Fight the good fight of faith and stand on the foundation that God has laid for you.

If the devil can get you to take ownership of *his thoughts*, you will participate in his results. Therefore, do not allow him to meddle with your emotions. Do not allow lying physical symptoms. Rather, stand your ground on the Word. Comfort your spirit and bring every renegade thought captive to the obedience of Christ. If you resist the devil, he will flee.

Those who walk with God must agree with what He has said.

United We Stand...
...Divided We Fall

Now I beseech you, brethren, by the name of our Lord Jesus Christ, that ye all speak the same thing, and that there be no divisions among you; but that ye be perfectly joined together in the same mind and in the same judgment.

1 Corinthians 1:10

Paul was writing to the Corinthian church, saying, *"I'm begging you, in the name of Jesus, that all of you speak the same thing."* When a body speaks the same thing, they contend together as one. They stand in agreement and are perfectly joined together in the same mind and the same judgment. United in one accord, there is no room for division within the ranks of God's elect.

If the Holy Ghost says that the Church can speak the same thing, then it is so. He said, *"Speak the same thing so that there will be no divisions among you and that you would be perfectly joined in the same opinion."* In the presence of agreement, God can work powerfully. In fact, agreement around the Word of God is a catalyst for the miraculous.

In the absence of agreement, God cannot bring His will into fulfillment. Agreement in the home, church, family and thought life is of the utmost importance in procuring divine results. Jesus said, *"For where two or three are gathered together in My name..."* There must be *a gathering* around the Word of God. When there is, Jesus says, *"...there am I in the midst of them"* (Matthew 18:20).

Without perfect agreement and union upon the Word, little will be accomplished according to the will of God. Those that think they have a right to assert an opinion contrary to the Word, are instead, giving place to the enemy. Their discord with God is saying, *"Devil, I'm granting you access to rob me of all that God would have for me."*

Therefore, agreement will fail when people are not in one accord. When the saints begin to speak contrary to the Word of God, division will settle into the Body. Where there is division, there is broken fellowship and separation from God. Jesus said that a kingdom divided against itself cannot stand (Matthew 12:25). God wants His people to think, talk and act like Him! When the believer steps into agreement with the Lord, in both word and deed, all things become possible. This is the place of miracles. Agreement is the place of power.

"Now I beseech you, brethren, by the name of our Lord Jesus Christ, that ye all speak the same thing..."

The apostle Paul told the Corinthian's to speak the same thing. Those that believe the *same thing* have all been taught the *same thing*. Therefore, it stands to reason that the Corinthian's were taught *what* to believe in God. Paul instructed them in the Word of God. Following up with them, he says, *"Don't speak different things. Stay in agreement with the Word."* Those that talk the same thing are perfectly joined and without divisions. "Division" in the Greek means "split," "gap," or "rent."

Division is what causes churches to split. It's a gap or rent in the area of agreement. On the West side of town, it's *The First Church of the Christian Olive Tree*. However, on the East side of town, it's *The Second Church of the Christian Olive Tree*. What happened? The elder of the first church stopped talking the same thing as the head. Garnering support for division, they assembled a following. These followed that elder all the way across town to start another church.

> *"...and that there be no divisions among you; but that ye be perfectly joined together in the same mind and in the same judgment."*

The Christian is entitled to their views as long as they are the Lord's views.

Following the Voice of God

How can two walk together except they be agreed?

God is not pleased with division in His Body. The Lord knows that division brings suffering and He is not the author of such things. In fact, it is written, *"For God is not the author of confusion, but of peace, as in all churches of the saints"* (1 Corinthians 14:33). God is an author of peace and agreement in His Word. If there is division, it is a work of darkness. This is why the Spirit of God said, *"And I sought for a man among them, that should make up the hedge, and stand in the gap before me for the land..."* (Ezekiel 22:30a).

> **And ye shall know the truth, and the truth shall make you free.**
>
> **John 8:32**

This is why God has given us a mandate to train people like you. The army that God is raising up will walk with one mind and one opinion. Their persuasion will be the Word of God and they will contend together in agreement. Speaking the same things, they will grow up as mature sons and daughters of God. While every child of God is unique and creative, these will find their inspiration in the power of God. Where there is great agreement, there is great power.

> **But the natural man receiveth not the things of the Spirit of God: for they are foolishness unto**

> **him: neither can he know them, because they are spiritually discerned.**
>
> **1 Corinthians 2:14**

The natural man does not grant access to the things of the Spirit of God. Those that are naturally minded cannot receive the things which are spiritually discerned. Instead, he or she regards these things as foolishness. They look, but they don't really see, at least not according to God. They only see according to the realm they have invested themselves in—*the natural realm*. However, if they will bring themselves into agreement with the Spirit of God, they will see as God sees.

> **But he that is spiritual judgeth all things, yet he himself is judged of no man. For who hath known the mind of the Lord, that he may instruct Him? But we have the mind of Christ.**
>
> **1 Corinthians 2:15-16**

"But he that is spiritual judgeth all things..." The spiritual man investigates the will of God. He searches the Word of God and walks according to the mind of the Lord. Those that walk as such will baffle the unlearned. *"...yet he himself is judged of no man."* The unsaved will fail to judge such a person for they do not have access to what is spiritually discerned. This does not mean, however, that the Christian is exempt from correction. It simply means that the naturally minded person cannot discern the spiritually minded person.

The spiritually minded individual lives in the experience of the mind of Christ. The mind of Christ, of course, is the Word of God. If you really want to know what God thinks, then read His Word!

The apostle Paul commanded the Corinthian church to *"all speak the same thing."* He pleaded with them in writing that they would not permit divisions, but rather, that they would be *"perfectly joined together in the same mind and in the same judgment"* (1 Corinthians 1:10).

Within that same letter, he reminds the Corinthian's that they have the mind of Christ. In other words, those that share the same mind, share the same agreement. Where there's agreement, division cannot bring separation.

"But we have the mind of Christ."

You can have the mind of Christ, but not use it. You can know the truth, but fail to employ it. This is why it's so vitally important for the believer to maintain their connection with God. If the saint will stay prayed up and in the anointing, then their feet will follow the voice of God. God will direct their steps and they will spiritually discern His voice. He will say, *"This is the way, walk in it"* and they will follow (Isaiah 30:21). They will *follow His voice* into marrying the right person. They will *follow His voice* into seeing their kids grow up to serve Him. They will *follow His voice* into prosperity. They will *follow His voice* into all joy and contentment in God. Instead of running around, searching for satisfaction, they will follow the voice of God into all fulfillment.

If you will walk in agreement with God, your life will become a portrait of God's divine ability. People will marvel and say, *"My God, how can they be so happy?"* They will inquire as to the secret of your success and you will have to tell them the truth. The truth is simply this: the Word of God works and those who walk with God, will walk within the sphere of His results.

Agreement with God is the secret to success. Those that walk with the Word cannot fail to participate in the Word. With God, *success is inevitable.*

Becoming of Christ

Only let your conversation be as it becometh the gospel of Christ: that whether I come and see you, or else be absent, I may hear of your

> affairs, that ye stand fast in one spirit, with one mind striving together for the faith of the gospel.
>
> **Philippians 1:27**

"Let your conversation be as it becometh the Gospel of Christ."

God wants His children to put the Good News in their mouth. Those that will speak His report, will see Heaven validate their words. The Word of God is alive and powerful. It is active and effective and it will produce after its kind. Those that will agree with the Word of God, and confess it as such, will partake of the fruit of their confession.

Similarly, those who speak words that *do not agree* with the Gospel, will inaugurate the dominion of darkness in their life. They will initiate a rule that is contrary to the divine will. There is power in the spoken word. That power will produce results that are consistent with the origin of that word. It makes no difference whether that origin is founded in light or darkness. The principle is the same.

Remember this principle:

What is *heard* will become what is *meditated* on. What is *meditated* on will eventually find its way into *action*. It will produce *decisions* that are in *agreement* with what was *first heard*. In the same way that a seed cycles from germination, to flower, to fruit and to pollination, so will words cycle. What is sown in the heart will ultimately spring forth in the form of words, bringing forth both fruit and seed. Speak Words of life and guard your heart with all diligence, for out of it flows the issues of life (Proverbs 4:23).

> **Behold also the ships, which though they be so great, and are driven of fierce winds, yet are they turned about with a very small helm, whithersoever the governor listeth. Even so the tongue is a little member, and boasteth great things. Behold, how great a matter a little fire**

> **kindleth! And the tongue is a fire, a world of iniquity: so is the tongue among our members, that it defileth the whole body, and setteth on fire the course of nature; and it is set on fire of Hell.**
>
> **James 3:4-6**

Great ships are directed by a small helm. Wherever the captain steers the ship, the ship will go. The one that navigates the helm, or chooses the coordinates, navigates direction. These control the wheel and have the power to choose *destination*.

The tongue, although small, directs the course of your life. It navigates your path. Your words, therefore, determine your destination. If you arrive at a destination that is "south" of God's best, it is only because you did not speak the *coordinates* of God's Word.

God cannot control your tongue…BUT YOU CAN!

> **Only let your conversation be as it becometh the Gospel of Christ…**
>
> **Philippians 1:27a**

Paul said that he was not ashamed of the Gospel of Christ because it is the power or *dunamis* of God unto salvation (Romans 1:16). As you learned previously, salvation includes the salvation of the soul, deliverance of the mind, healing of the body and prosperity of the finances. It's an all-inclusive word that encompasses both spiritual and natural needs. When the Lord provides, He doesn't skimp on His blessing. Rather, His promises are comprehensive and pertain to both life and godliness (2 Peter 1:3).

Since God has provided this great deliverance, *"let your conversation be as it becometh the Gospel of Christ."* Speak as it *becomes* a believer. In other words, there is a certain vocabulary that should grace the lips of a saint. Anything other than the *vocabulary of God* is not *becoming* to the one who has received such a far-reaching gift. Paul exhorted believers in this manner: *"Let no corrupt word proceed out of your mouth, but what is good for necessary edification, that it may impart grace to the hearers"* (Ephesians 4:29). Pronounce Words that *build* on the promises of God. Speak words of *grace* and *power*.

There is power in the Word of God. Those that put the Good News in their mouth are putting the *dunamis* in their mouth. They are speaking Words that are filled with grace and power. Those that complain, *"Well, the Lord just never blesses me,"* would do well to consider their words and the meditations of their heart. Rather than embracing and nurturing opinions that did not originate in the mind of Christ, these need to instead, embrace and nurture the Word of the Lord in their heart. If they do this, they will see the results that only God can give.

Put grace and power in your mouth.

Infrastructure of Agreement

> …that ye stand fast in one spirit, with one mind striving together for the faith of the gospel.
>
> **Philippians 1:27b**

Those that stand fast in *one spirit* are those that stand in the *circle of agreement* around the Word of God. They are speaking the same things and contending in the same direction. Having put on the mind of Christ, these are united in a common purpose and vision. They cannot be moved for they have one mind in the plans, purposes and intents of God.

Get in agreement with the vision of God for your church.
Get in agreement with the vision of God for your family.
Get in agreement with the vision of God for your life.

If you will speak what God speaks in these areas, there will be no schism. Where there is no schism, there is no opportunity for the enemy to gain access or foothold.

How does the devil rob the believer of their destiny?

He robs the saint through their confession. Those that speak words that do not impart grace are only sowing for unfulfilled dreams. It is in the devil's best interest to pressure the believer into becoming disgruntled and discouraged *with what is.* The one that will think *thoughts of discord,* and speak *words of disagreement,* will derail their call. Through the power of their own vocabulary, they will create a breach in what was meant to lead them into all victory. Instead of following the voice of God into that place of fulfillment, they jumped the tracks of destiny and bypassed their destination in God.

> **And the Lord said, "Behold, the people is one, and they have all one language; and this they begin to do: and now nothing will be restrained from them, which they have imagined to do."**
>
> **Genesis 11:6**

Having one language and one speech, the people came together to build the Tower of Babel. They were sinners, but they said, *"Let us build a city and a tower, whose top may reach into Heaven; and let us make us a name, lest we be scattered abroad upon the face of the whole Earth"* (Genesis 11:4). Together, they laid brick upon brick, building upon the infrastructure of their agreement.

When the Lord came down to see their work, He said, *"Behold the people is one."* Striving together in one purpose, they had built a tower that reached into the sky. Although they were sinners, their agreement enabled them to contend under the banner of one purpose. Each spoke the same thing and there was no schism among them.

God said, *"Let Us go down, and there confound their language, that they may not understand one another's speech"* (Genesis 11:7). The Lord brought diversity to their language and they ceased to contend as one unit. Instead, they dispersed across the Earth and the city was left unbuilt. Notice, however, that God had said, *"The people is one and nothing will be restrained from them, which they have imagined to do."* Their unified language and sphere of agreement enabled them to build as one. Together, they were able to accomplish a tremendous natural feat. God said, *"Nothing they have imagined will be impossible for them."* There is power in agreement. There is power when people contend as one.

If God's people will *think* and *talk* the same thing, nothing will be withheld from them. What transpired under the Old Covenant is limited by the provisions of that covenant. However, as a New Testament believer, you are a partaker of a *better* covenant. The accomplishments of Calvary have given you rights and privileges that exceed anything previously experienced. Those that are filled with the Spirit of God have the substance and ability of the divine nature.

If you will CONTEND AS ONE with the Word, *nothing will be impossible for you.*

The Prerequisite for Blessing

> **If there be therefore any consolation in Christ, if any comfort of love, if any fellowship of the Spirit, if any bowels and mercies, fulfill ye my joy, that ye be likeminded, having the same love, being of one accord, of one mind. Let nothing be done through strife or vainglory; but in lowliness of mind let each esteem the other better than themselves.**
>
> **Philippians 2:1-3**

Paul said, *"If there is any comfort of His love, any fellowship of the Spirit, any mercy or compassion, then fulfill my joy and be in one accord."*

In other words, all these things are available in God, so therefore, be of one mind.

Agreement will produce results. If one will put a thousand to flight and two will put ten thousand to flight, then corporate agreement will form an impenetrable barrier against the devil (Deuteronomy 32:30). For this reason, the husband and wife should not let the sun set on their wrath (Ephesians 4:26). When agreement is broken for any reason, a breach is created. It is this *breach* or *schism* that gives access to the enemy. Where he has been granted access, he will steal, kill and destroy.

> **Behold, how good and how pleasant it is for brethren to dwell together in unity! It is like the precious ointment upon the head, that ran down upon the beard, even Aaron's beard: that went down to the skirts of his garments; as the dew of Hermon, and as the mountains of Zion: for there the Lord commanded the blessing, even life for evermore.**
>
> **Psalm 133:1-3**

The *precious ointment*, the *dew* and the *blessing* are all representative of the anointing. God says, *"for there the Lord commanded the blessing."* The blessing is commanded where brethren dwell together in unity. It is at this place of agreement that the anointing flows down from the *head* to the *toe*.

When there is a breach in agreement, the anointing will be short-circuited. Instead of covering the body, it will stop at the schism. The Lord does, indeed, command the blessing, but the saint must dwell with the brethren in unity. In other words, *agreement* is a prerequisite for the *anointing* and the *anointing* is a prerequisite for the *blessing*.

God does not want the devil to take advantage of His children. This is why He has admonished the child of God to walk in agreement and to close every gap. Where there are divisions and disagreements, the power of God cannot flow. However, if saints will strive together for the faith of the Gospel, they will see the miraculous in their midst.

The key to unity is agreement.

> **Finally, be ye all of one mind, having compassion one of another, love as brethren, be pitiful, be courteous: not rendering evil for evil, or railing for railing: but contrariwise blessing; knowing that ye are thereunto called, that ye should inherit a blessing.**
>
> **1 Peter 3:8-9**

Be of one mind. Talk the same thing. Be courteous. Do not return evil for evil.

At one point or another, you have been wrongly treated. Injustices will take place, but you have the power to rise above them. Refuse to hold a grudge. The Bible says, *"And when ye stand praying, forgive, if ye have ought against any: that your Father also which is in Heaven may forgive you your trespasses"* (Mark 11:25). Do not allow an offense to short-circuit your connection with Heaven. Remember, unity is as *"the precious ointment upon the head, that ran down upon the beard"* of Aaron. When you stand praying, forgive so that there will be no breach or hindrance in the anointing.

I specialize in not letting "it" get to me. When a person allows *nonsense* to penetrate their heart, it will drain the strength from their life. Don't count the times you've been wronged. Don't tally your war stories. Don't testify to situations that went bad. *"Neither render evil for evil or railing for railing"* (1 Peter 3:9a). The Holy Ghost is saying, *"Never mind what they've done or what they're doing, but rather, be of one mind. Return blessing for evil and speak the Word only."*

There is *no one* that can stop YOU from being in agreement. No amount of evil can separate you from the agreement that is found in God. If you will return good for evil and speak according to the mind of Christ, you will participate in the inheritance of the saints.

"...knowing that ye are thereunto called, that ye should inherit a blessing."

Do not let the devil rob you of the blessing that you're called to inherit. Those that are robbed are those who return evil for evil and railing for railing. Do not sow discord, lest you reap discord. Rather, sow blessing and you will reap blessing. *You will reap what you sow.*

Sow the right seed.

Shaping the Future

For he that will love life, and see good days, let him refrain his tongue from evil, and his lips that they speak no guile.

1 Peter 3:10

"Those that will love life and see good days" is stated in the future tense. It is the outcome of those who have kept their *tongue from evil* and their *lips from guile*. In other words, what you speak will affect your future. Your words will shape your destiny. God has called you to a certain place, but you can either abort that call or accelerate that call through the vehicle of your confession.

Those that will speak evil, will end up hating life. Their confession will catch up to them and bring the despair that they had spoken. They will say, *"My worst fears have come upon me."* They sowed for that future. Their confession preceded their experience.

"For he that will love life, and see good days, let him refrain his tongue from evil..."

Keep your mind in line with God. Remember, what you think,

you will eventually speak. When a thought comes that isn't of the Lord, recognize it as warfare. Recognize it as a fiery dart and cast it down. Douse it with the Word of God and tell that devil to shut up. Stop the thought in its tracks and make a decision to meditate on the promises of God. Participate in the mind of Christ. When you contend for agreement with God, nothing will be withheld from you.

Stand your ground on the never changing, never shifting foundation of the Word of God. If the devil sends someone to fan the fire of discord, *close the door.* If they say, *"Oh girl, I know what you're going through because I saw him look at you like that,"* halt the conversation! Do not allow the devil to stir the embers of contention. He would like to rob you of the love of life and good days, but if you will resist him, he will flee.

> **Let him eschew evil, and do good; let him seek peace, and ensue it. For the eyes of the Lord are over the righteous, and his ears are open unto their prayers: but the face of the Lord is against them that do evil.**
>
> **1 Peter 3:11-12**

Lay hands on yourself and say this:

> *I'm a child of the Living God. I've been born from above. I've been bought with a price. The Spirit of God lives in me. The mind of Christ and the wisdom of Christ live in me by the Holy Ghost. I have God-given abilities to be in agreement with the Word, to be in agreement with God's vision and to prosper and succeed in life. Right now, I make a decision to be educated by the Lord, to think His thoughts, to speak His words and to walk in His path.*
> *I believe that my victory is manifested now.*

CHAPTER 16

THE WAY OF A CHAMPION

―◆―

*Fight the good fight of faith.
The good fight is the fight that you win.*

Opportunities to Overcome

> **Casting all your care upon Him; for He careth for you. Be sober, be vigilant; because your adversary the devil, as a roaring lion, walketh about, seeking whom he may devour: whom resist steadfast in the faith, knowing that the same afflictions are accomplished in your brethren that are in the world.**
>
> **1 Peter 5:7-9**

Those that traverse the Earth according to natural principles will find themselves living according to natural law. As an inhabitant of the Earth, you will encounter the threats of a lower realm. Each of these threats, however, are merely *opportunities* to take territory and enforce the will of Heaven. Although you live in the world, you are not of the world. Jesus has given you the keys to the Kingdom and your authority precedes you. Even the devils tremble in *fear* of the *dominion* that you bring.

You are an ambassador of the Kingdom.

As a representative of a higher realm, you are called to live above the influences of the lower realm. Although influences like worry, anxiety and fear may beckon at the door of your life, you have the God-given ability to take authority over these things and to cast them out. It is *possible* to walk on the Earth, yet walk above the things of the Earth.

This is only available, however, to those who will walk according to the Spirit. Those who walk with God will be able to *cast their care* upon God. The one that doesn't walk with God, will carry and participate in the burdens of the world. In all things, the believer has a choice. They can choose the realm they will partake of. They can live in the flesh or they can live in the Spirit.

"Casting all your care upon Him…"

The devil will tell the believer, "*The reason you're in the flesh is because of your cares and your burdens. If you didn't have these things, you would be really spiritual.*" Those that know the ways of the Spirit, know that this couldn't be further from the truth. The truth is that those who make a *decision* to walk in the Spirit will walk above both "care" and "burden." Remember, the name of Jesus is above every *name*.

Challenges will come, but in God, a challenge is nothing more than an *opportunity to overcome!* The ones that overcome are those who have made it a practice to walk in the Spirit. So often, people mistakenly think that those who walk in the Spirit do so because they are somehow mysteriously exempt from natural nuisance. This, however, is not true. All those who live on the Earth will face *opposition, burden* and *care*. The defining difference between a champion of faith and a mere mortal is that the champion has made a decision not to submit to defeat.

What will you do when you face opposition, burden and care? Your answer to this question will determine your level of victory in life. You have the making of a champion on the inside of you, but ultimately, the decision of championship is yours.

Do not submit to defeat.

For the child of God, the throne of grace is only a decision away. If they will boldly approach it, they will find grace to help in time of need. The power and presence of God is extended toward all those who will walk according to the Spirit.

> **Let us therefore come boldly to the throne of grace, that we may obtain mercy and find grace to help in time of need.**
>
> **Hebrews 4:16 NKJV**

If you feel like you've been run over by a bulldozer or your mind is swimming in confusion, get up and make a decision to use the tools that God has given you. Draw from the well of salvation! Come into agreement with God! Speak the Word and testify to your godly convictions! Praise and thank God. Tell Him, *"Thank You, Lord that I've been saved! Thank You that I'm delivered! Thank You for filling me full with the Holy Ghost!"* Begin to quote God's Word and to stir yourself into remembrance. Like David, *encourage yourself* in the Lord!

As you do what you've been taught to do, you will rise up from under the circumstance and topple its influence. Standing in that place of power within the presence of God, you will see clearly and think accurately. Strength will come upon you and confusion will cease. As God's ambassador in the Earth realm, you will once again exercise dominion and enforce authority over every natural irritation.

Mounting Up on Wings of Eagles

In the same way that it is impossible to *walk in the flesh* and *cast your cares upon the Lord*, so is it impossible *to walk in the Spirit* and *carry anxiety and care*. Those who walk in the Spirit are not carrying *their burdens*, but the *Lord's burdens*.

> **Come unto Me all ye that labor and are heavy laden and I will give you rest. Take My yoke upon you and learn of Me, because I'm meek and lowly in heart and you will find rest unto your souls.**
>
> **Matthew 11:29**

Burdens like anxiety and care are not *becoming* of the ones who have been given dominion over the Earth realm. Over 2,000 years ago, Jesus paid the price, took the heavy burden and said, *"Child of God, I will give you rest."* Therefore, come unto Jesus and cast your care upon Him. Trade in your heavy yoke and take His and *"you will find rest for your souls."*

"Take My Yoke upon you and learn of Me."

People have said to me, *"Oh brother, it must be a heavy load to carry all of the responsibilities of the ministry."* Quite frankly, I wouldn't know because *I don't carry that care!* Rather, I have *Someone* bigger and better that said, *"I will carry it for you."*

As a believer, you do not have to carry the responsibilities and anxieties of life. *"But you don't understand what I'm going through, Dr. Harfouche!"* Child of God, if you are weary and heavy laden, then cast your burden upon the Lord and allow Him to carry it for you. He cares for you!

> **Even the youths shall faint and be weary, and the young men shall utterly fall: but they that wait upon the LORD shall renew their strength; they shall mount up with wings as eagles; they shall run, and not be weary; and they shall walk, and not faint.**
>
> **Isaiah 40:30-35**

If *"even the youths shall faint and be weary"* and the *"young men shall utterly fall,"* then God is saying that no one possesses the NATURAL STRENGTH to overcome the battles launched against them. There is not one person that has the *natural ability* to overcome the spirit of the world system. Those that *walk in the flesh* will be run down and worn out by the opposition.

However, the Bible says, *"Those that wait upon the Lord shall renew their strength."* If there are cares bearing down upon your shoulders,

Jesus said, *"My yoke is easy, My burden is light."* Turn the cares and the heavy yoke over to Jesus. Allow Him to bear the responsibility that weighed heavy. Trust in Him and as you do, He will break the yoke of the world from your neck.

>   Rise up in HIS STRENGTH!
>   Rise up in HIS POWER!
>   Rise up in HIS AUTHORITY!
>   Rise up in HIS NAME!

Don't take on the world according to the world, but walk according to the Spirit. Walk according to the power that has been invested in you. This is the secret to walking in the high places in God.

"They shall mount up with wings as eagles…"

Those that wait upon the Lord, steadfast in faith, will mount up with wings as eagles. They will climb with the wind and soar high above the burdens of life. Uninhibited by the pressures of the world, these will run and not be weary, they will walk and not faint. Having given their burdens to the Lord, they will RISE UP unencumbered into the expression of Godly freedom.

>   GIVE GOD the RESPONSIBILITY.
>   GIVE GOD the BURDEN.

CAST YOUR CARE upon Him.

The Simplicity of Faith

Just as it takes faith to obey the Word, it takes faith to be delivered from anxiety. The Bible says that unless the believer becomes as a little child, they will not see the Kingdom of Heaven (Matthew 18:3). *Have you ever seen a small child desperately wringing their hands in anxiety, wondering where breakfast will come from?* The baby trusts that provision will be made. Their outlook on life is blissfully uncomplicated by the cares of the world. *Babies don't carry burdens.* Rather, it takes a lot of growing up before the baby will become a *burden-bearer*.

The world has trained men and women to be anxious about their tomorrows. Gone are the days of childlike simplicity! Instead, it has groomed its children to be driven by the frenzied momentum of anxiety and fear. Overridden by the onslaught, those that once walked in childlike simplicity, are instead overcome by ulcers, heart conditions, mental torment and irrational fears.

Like the surf that relentlessly pounds the rocks, so does anxiety take its toll on its victims. Therefore, *resist the temptations of the natural world*. Take up Jesus' offer and release the cares to Him. In so doing, you will once again recover the childlike simplicity of faith.

Faith in God is not complicated.

> **But I fear, lest somehow, as the serpent deceived Eve by his craftiness, so your minds may be corrupted from the simplicity that is in Christ.**
>
> **2 Corinthians 11:3 NKJV**

Do not allow your mind to be corrupted from the SIMPLICITY that is in Jesus. Do not allow your emotions to be sucked into the convoluted undertow of the world. Resist those things that are beneath the nature of CHRIST IN YOU. Instead, walk in the simplicity of faith according to the power of your *new nature*. Rise up above the lower levels of *human inadequacy* and walk according to the supernatural power that abides within you.

"...*which is Christ in you, the hope of glory*" (Colossians 1:27b).

Casting Cares

Stress will affect the natural person. Theme parks often post warning signs on rides which caution visitors with pre-existing medical conditions. "*WARNING: Do not board this roller coaster IF YOU*

HAVE..."

Do not board the *flesh ride*. Do not board the *doubt ride*. Do not board the *fear ride*. Get off of the roller coaster of double mindedness, and board the ride that goes from glory to glory! Choose the *faith ride!* Leave the limitation behind and ascend to a realm that is free from care.

"Casting all your care upon Him; for He careth for you."

Once you've given your cares to God, don't pick them back up. Trust the Lord that He cares for you. The devil will try to talk you into heavy burdens, but resist him and he will flee. Remember, worry doesn't solve any problems. It only drags the worrier into the throes of mental torment.

Don't worry over what God has promised to carry. If you have obeyed His Word in *"casting your cares"* then God will see to it that His power provides for your need. Jesus said, *"For your Father knoweth what things ye have need of, before ye ask of Him"* (Matthew 6:8).

God knows that there are legitimate needs in your life. He is not too lofty, as to overlook your provision. In fact, Jesus says, *"Therefore I say unto you, take no thought for your life, what ye shall eat, or what ye shall drink; not yet for your body, what ye shall put on"* (Matthew 6:25). In other words, Jesus is saying, *"Don't give these things even one anxious thought. Your heavenly Father has it all covered."*

For your heavenly Father knoweth that ye have need of all these things.

Matthew 6:32b

Those that *invest their care,* in lieu of *casting their care,* will participate in the returns of that investment. Instead of a payout of the peace of God, these will receive worry for worry. This cyclical pattern will bear down heavier and heavier, draining the participant of strength and vigor.

The moment anxiety enters the life of a believer; it asphyxiates the life of God. Strength leaves and the fear of the world comes in. Those that are gripped in fear cannot walk in the Spirit. Weighed down by natural things, it is impossible for such a person to receive a miracle, for they have given the prominent place in their life to the enemy.

There is nothing that you can do *naturally* that will produce *supernatural results*. Rather, only those that walk in faith and walk in the Spirit can participate in the benefits of that realm. Worry will never produce performance, *but faith will do the impossible.*

Watch and Pray

Be sober, be vigilant; because your adversary the devil, as a roaring lion, walketh about, seeking whom he may devour.

1 Peter 5:8

Be sober and vigilant for the enemy is after your victory. Even Jesus told Peter, *"Satan has desired to sift you as wheat"* (Luke 22:31). You are a threat to the kingdom of darkness. As such, your adversary the devil, walks about seeking *whom* he may devour.

Be sober. Be watchful.

You have an enemy who has committed himself to clipping your wings in God. If he can keep you grounded in the natural, you will be ineffective for the Kingdom. Therefore, he seeks to steal God's Word from within your heart and to weigh you down with ungodly burdens. A saint without a Word, is a saint without direction or vision.

Satan has a strategy against your life. He has a strategy against your church. He has a strategy against your family. However, if you will release your care to God and give His Word priority, He will care for you. He will see to it that His Word performs in your life.

The world will load you down, but God will lift you up!

When you hear thoughts that
REHEARSE ANXIETY…
recognize that it's
a STRATEGY of the enemy.

When you hear…
"I don't know what we're going to do,"
CAST YOUR CARE UPON JESUS.

When the enemy says…
"But the doctor said it was incurable,"
ENCOURAGE YOURSELF IN THE LORD.

When your mind is racing with…
"Do you think God is going to do anything?"
REHEARSE THE PROMISES OF GOD.

Do not let the suggestions of demonic propaganda cycle within your meditations. Submit to God and give no place to the devil!

The moment you hear a thought, deal with it in God.
Cast your care upon the Lord.

God is raising up a generation that will refuse to live under the heel of their adversary. They will say, *"I won't live one day depressed! I won't live one day full of wrath! I won't live one day under care! I refuse to be bound up by fear! I have made up my mind to contend for God's best in all things!"*

CHOOSE to live free.

> **Stand fast therefore in the liberty by which Christ has made us free, and do not be entangled again with a yoke of bondage.**
>
> **Galatians 5:1 NKJV**

The Way of a Champion | 329

Jesus told Peter, *"Satan has desired to sift you"* and then again He warned him once more, *"Watch and pray, that ye enter not into temptation"* (Luke 22:32; Matthew 26:41).

Leaving Peter and the other disciples, Jesus went off to pray by Himself in the Garden of Gethsemane. The hour of His betrayal was at hand. Returning to His disciples sometime later, He *"found them asleep again for their eyes were heavy"* (Matthew 26:43). Jesus had told them to watch and pray; yet they grew weary and slept instead. While they slept, a great campaign had been launched against their souls. The enemy sought to scatter the sheep.

When the mob finally came to take Jesus away, the disciples were caught off guard. Unprepared for the actions of their adversary, some fled and others fought. Peter drew his sword. The Bible says, *"Then all the disciples forsook Him, and fled"* (Matthew 26:56b). Had they watched and prayed as Jesus commanded, they would not have fallen at the moment of temptation. If they had obeyed Jesus, they would not have been caught unawares by the stratagem of their adversary.

Jesus was taken to be interrogated before the counsel, but Peter followed from afar. Waiting on the wayside, a handmaid approached him in the darkness and said, *"Hey, you're one of His disciples, aren't you?"* Peter denied it vehemently and said, *"I have no idea what you're talking about."* After this, he denied the Lord two more times, once with cursing and swearing. On the third time, Peter was suddenly jarred to his senses by the remembrance of His Master's words, and the Bible records, that he wept bitterly. He realized that he had *slept instead of prayed*. When the enemy was strategizing against him, he slept on his faith and thereby bowed the knee to his adversary.

> *"Be sober, be vigilant; because your adversary the devil, as a roaring lion, walketh about, seeking whom he may devour."*

Hours earlier, Jesus had warned Peter. He had said, *"Simon, Simon, behold, Satan hath desired to have you, that he may sift you as wheat: But I have prayed for thee, that thy faith fail not"* (Luke 22:31-32a). Once more, He warned Peter in the Garden of Gethsemane. *"Pray Peter!*

Pray that you don't enter into temptation!" Jesus, as the Shepherd of his soul, knew what was coming by the Holy Ghost. He prayed for him and that his faith would not fail. Jesus told Peter, *"When you have turned from your ways, strengthen your brethren"* (Luke 22:32b).

Don't let the devil knock the wind out of your sail. *Pray!*

Consistency in God

There is *consistency* in God. You can arrive at a place where your walk is consistent with His promises. This is a place of agreement around the Word of God. It is a place that is without division or schism.

The first step toward this place of consistency and stability is to cast your cares upon Jesus. If He is really the Lord of your life, *then allow Him to run it.*

Does He care about your health?
Then PUT YOUR BODY in the hands of Jesus.

Does He care about your finances?
Then PUT YOUR LIFE and your financial success in the hands of Jesus.

Does He care about your family?
Then PUT YOUR RELATIONSHIP and your children in the hands of Jesus.

Those that desire to walk as *mature* Christians, should incorporate two very important *decisions* into their daily walk. If you will practice these things on a daily basis, you will make great strides in your growth in God:

1. Once and for all, make the decision to stop worrying, repent and put your life in His hands. Cast your cares on Jesus and take *His yoke* upon your shoulders. Submit to His authority

in your life. Meditate on His thoughts. Guard the Seed in your heart. Speak His Word always. Act in faith. Expect His best. Rest in Him.

2. Be sober. Be watchful. Be vigilant. The Christian that is not sober will cycle in life. They will not go anywhere new, but only around the mountain, time and time again. Therefore, *pray*. Commit to your connection in God. Tap into His power. Rehearse His Word. Practice your delegated authority. Take dominion. Exercise your divine rights. Enforce His influence in your jurisdiction.

> **Finally, my brethren, be strong in the Lord and in the power of His might. Put on the whole armor of God that you may be able to resist the wiles of the devil.**
>
> **Ephesians 6:10-11 NKJV**

God has given you power to be consistent in Him. His nature is not subject to the world system, therefore, He remains unmoved in the face of contradiction. As an heir of the Kingdom, your nature is as His. You have the *power of consistency*. You have the authority to walk in SUPERNATURAL STABILITY.

With the dominion that you've been given, you can stand in the face of the wind and declare your authority. There on the rock of revelation, you can stand steadfast in the Word of Truth, declaring the confidence of your faith.

When the winds blows and the waters swell, recognize that your war is not against flesh and blood, but against principalities of darkness. Casting aside the heavy burden of a lower realm, rest in God's divine ability and embrace the *consistency* of His nature.

Always remember this:

Those that do not walk in consistency of direction will be without sobriety. Without sobriety, accuracy will miss its mark. In its place will be confusion, strife and every evil work (James 3:16). God is not the author of such things. His nature is consistent with His Word.

When God tells you something, He will not change His mind a week later. If He does "change His mind," it's only because you were either deceived the first time around *or* you were in disobedience the second time around. God's voice is not hard to understand, neither is He is an author of confusion. His Word is not "yes" and "no," but it is always consistent with His promises. *The nature of God is never changing.*

> **Jesus Christ is the same yesterday, and today and forever.**
>
> **Hebrews 13:8**

Putting Your Life in His Hands

The word "adversary" comes from two Greek words. One is translated *anti* or *opposite*. Therefore, your adversary is an anti-Christ. He is everything that opposes Christ and the anointing. The second Greek word is translated as *judgment*. It means *opponent*, just as if someone faced an *archenemy* in a court of law.

Have you ever seen a witness on the stand in court? After the attorney has heard and questioned the witness, the opposite side will approach the stand. The *adversary* will take his turn. His mission is to discredit the witness. To do so, he will employ confusion and double talk.

The devil is a specialist in confusion and inconsistency. Those that confront him in the realm of the flesh will be confounded and confused. It is impossible for the child of God to beat the adversary in *his* playing field. They must rise above him to overcome him. Victory comes to those who will walk in the high places with God.

Be sober. Be vigilant.

Your adversary's only weapon is his *words*. Do not let him speak into your life. Do not let him meddle with your meditations. Cast down the tormenting thoughts. Dismiss the mental warfare. Douse the fiery dart.

Remember, the thoughts that you allow or disallow can mean either life or death. What you meditate on, will grow and produce fruit in your life. If you meditate on the wrong thoughts, *those thoughts will produce a harvest after their kind.* However, if you meditate on God's thoughts and speak His Words, you will grow in grace and strength before Him.

This is why you have been given the mind of Christ (1 Corinthians 2:16). Therefore, meditate on His Word day and night. Put His Word in your mouth. Speak His opinion and as you do, God will begin to grow in your life. His power will work its way into every facet of your existence.

Put your life in the hands of God. What you do not place in His hands, *you will become responsible to defend.* Those who are bearing this burden will stay up late worrying. They will toss and turn and battle within their sleep, defending the things that God has offered to protect.

Put your life into the Lord's hands and free yourself from this battle. Those who are watchful and diligent to this end will instead, fight the good fight of faith. They will not be heavy laden with care, but they will be empowered in God to take on higher heights, while claiming greater victories.

"My yoke is easy, My burden is light."

Waging a War of Words

The devil seeks to distract the child of God from the walk of faith. By means of a diversion, he will attempt to sidetrack the believer and gain access into their life. He will inundate them with suggestions of care and concern. He will whisper his meditations and lie in wait, hoping that the child of God will consider his thoughts and then speak them.

He is seeking whom he may devour. He is looking for the one that he can consume with his words. Just as a person uses their mouth to eat, Satan uses his mouth to devour. This is why he is called the *devourer* and the *eater*. Through accusation, intimidation and cursing he slanders God's elect.

The majority of the world is rehearsing *fear thoughts* and speaking *fear words*. The source of their meditations originates from the pit of Hell. Darkness spoke and they listened. A *suggestion* came from the wrong realm and they received it.

God's Word is never a suggestion.
His Word is a command.

Know this: The devil can't read your mind and he can't tell your future. In fact, the devil and his cohorts don't know what tomorrow brings. They can, however, suggest a future. They can inspect your life and come up with plausible outcomes and predictions of doom and loss. If you accept the future that the devil suggests, then the power of darkness will prevail in your life. That *power* will go to work to bring the suggestions of your adversary into fulfillment.

The devil is an illusionist. He is a fraud.

He will send his representative to you. He will send a lying mouth, *a devouring mouth*. It is written that the devil is as a *"roaring lion, walking about, seeking someone to devour"* (1 Peter 5:8). He's a copycat! The only roaring lion is the Lion of the Tribe of Judah. Only the King of Kings and the Lord of Lords is sovereign!

Nevertheless, the devil will use his mouth. With his mouth, he wages war against the saints. The Bible, however, says that the Lord shall consume the devil *"with the breath of His mouth and the brightness of His coming"* (2 Thessalonians 2:8). God also uses words, but His Words do not devour the *righteous*. They devour the powers of *darkness*.

> **These things says He who has the sharp two-edged sword...I will come to you quickly and will fight against them with the sword of My mouth.**
>
> **Revelation 2:12b,16b NKJV**

The Word of God is Spirit and life. Those that pick up the Sword of the Spirit will always prevail in the strength and power of God. They will fight the good fight, *and win*.

Guard your ears. Listen to the voice of God.

Those that listen to the words of their enemy, will receive weakness into their body. Turning from the simplicity of the Gospel, life will become complicated. Instead of *"God will supply all my needs and by His stripes I am healed,"* these will begin to confess, *"I'm just so tired. I'm so exhausted."*

The devil, having solicited a verbal affirmation from the believer, will then move in further, suggesting a physical symptom. Already in a weakened state from their meditations, they will succumb to the second suggestion as they did to the first. Instead of going to pray, they will go to sleep, hoping that the dawn of a new day will bring relief.

The Word of God is the Sword of the Spirit. Those that make confession of that Word safeguard their freedom. Those that are bound need only to submit to the Word and commit to prayer.

Freedom is as close as their next breath.

Refusing Meditations of Defeat

Stay free and do not allow the enemy to bind you. Confess the Word. Cast your cares. Walk in the Spirit. Be sober. Be watchful. As you do these things, you will become proficient in detecting a word or a spirit that is not of God. When Satan uses the mouth of another and something hits your spirit the wrong way, you will know immediately. Always ready with the *Sword of the Spirit* and your *shield of faith*, you will use the occasion to WIELD YOUR AUTHORITY and defeat every adversary.

Did you know that the Christian is not defeated *after* they backslide?

A person who backtracks in God *sowed* for their defeat. They didn't become defeated *after* they committed a certain act, but rather, the defeat started back when their meditations were merely seeds of suggestion. Little by little, they gave the enemy greater place in their life. In turn, they lost their joy, their sobriety, their testimony, their focus and finally their hope.

When the lying word came, they received it as truth, and fear gained entry. Fear gave the hearer the expectation of the outcome. In the same way that faith comes by hearing the Word of God, *fear comes by hearing the word of the devil.* When the substance of their fearful hope was realized, an outward manifestation took place.

The one that meditates on the lies will develop an expectation in the lies.

> **No weapon that is formed against thee shall prosper; and every tongue that shall rise against thee in judgment thou shalt condemn. This is the heritage of the servants of the Lord, and their righteousness is of Me, saith the Lord.**
>
> **Isaiah 54:17**

No weapon that is formed against you will prosper. If you will keep your mind stayed on the Lord, He will keep you in perfect peace (Isaiah 26:3). In fact, the peace of God that passes all understanding will guard your heart and mind through Christ Jesus (Philippians 4:7).

As you keep your mind on the Word of God, no serpent or roaring enemy will be able to devour you. Every weapon that is formed against you will fail. Speaking to the demonic suggestions, you will say, *"Shut up and get out of my life. I refuse to meditate on you because I believe the report of the Lord."*

Today, MAKE A SOBER DECISION to refuse every demonic suggestion. Willfully disregard the thoughts that are not sanctioned by the mind of Christ. Declare your faith and say, *"No weapon formed against me will prosper and the joy of the Lord is my strength. I will not cave to lying words or meditations of defeat."*

Answer the Devil

Be sober, be vigilant; because your adversary the devil, as a roaring lion, walketh about, seeking whom he may devour: Whom resist steadfast in the faith, knowing that the same afflictions are accomplished in your brethren that are in the world.

1 Peter 5:8-9

"Whom resist steadfast in the faith…" Resist the devil, steadfast in your convictions. In the Greek, "steadfast" is translated as "strong," "stable," and "sure." Those that walk in faith can be *sure*. They can be *confident* and *strong* in what God has promised. The one that resists the devil can do so with certainty.

You have been called to GREATNESS IN GOD and the land of promise is before you. In this life, you will encounter *giants*. However, do not be moved by the size of your opposition, but with the confidence of faith, triumph over your adversary. Like David and the heroes of old, you too will subdue kingdoms, work righteousness, obtain promises, shut lying mouths and prevail over every Goliath.

> And what more shall I say? For the time would fail me to tell of Gideon and Barak and Samson and Jephthah, also of David and Samuel and the prophets: who through faith subdued kingdoms, worked righteousness, obtained promises, stopped the mouths of lions, quenched the violence of fire, escaped the edge of the sword, out of weakness were made strong, became valiant in battle, turned to flight the armies of aliens.
>
> **Hebrews 11:32-34 NKJV**

"...who through faith subdued kingdoms..."

Goliath looked at David with contempt and said, *"Come to me, and I will give your flesh to the birds of the air and the beasts of the field!"* The devil, seeking to strike terror in the heart of David, used a GIANT MOUTH to utter threats of doom and demise.

Unmoved by the suggestions, David replied with the Word of the Lord: *"You come to me with the sword, with a spear, and with a javelin, but I come to you in the name of the Lord of hosts, the God of the armies of Israel... This day I will take your head from you"* (1 Samuel 17:44b,45b,46a).

Always answer the devil. Never allow him to have the final word. In the natural, you might not feel like taking up your authority, but refuse to go by what you feel. Instead, rise up and do what the Lord has told you to do. Do what you have been trained to do and the devil will flee.

There will be mountains, and storms will inevitably come. However, when the devil says, *"This storm is going to kill you,"* the one that is certain in the Word will say, *"No, God is with me in the middle of the storm and I have the peace that passes understanding."* When the devil challenges, *"But this giant mountain is in your way,"* faith will speak its confidence, *"Yes, but I have a Word that will move the mountain!"*

The devil will preach impossibility, but you serve the One who has said, *"With men it is impossible, but with God all things are possible"* (Matthew 19:26b).

Those that resist the devil, will see him flee (James 4:7). He will flee from the presence of the Name. He will flee from the one that knows their authority and power. The one that resists him steadfast will outlast the attack and prevail in every way.

Victory for Today, Victory for Tomorrow

Do not sorrow, for the joy of the Lord is your strength.

Nehemiah 8:10

Resist the devil joyfully. Laugh hysterically at his prophecies of doom and *rest in the One* that has promised to carry your burdens. When he launches a fiery dart at you, express amusement and say, *"Devil, that's the funniest thing I've ever heard! Have you forgotten WHO you're talking to? Do you know WHAT God has said about ME?"* As the situation calls for it, remind your adversary of all that God has said about you. Speak the promises and resist his devouring. Remind him, *"I'm not the one you devour. I'm the one you flee from!"*

God will lead you from triumph to triumph.

There is VICTORY FOR TODAY
and
VICTORY FOR TOMORROW.

There is strength in God. There is strength for everyday. This *spiritual might* that is part of your new nature, finds its source in the joy of the Lord. The joy of the Lord, of course, is in the *report* that comes from the Lord! When you know what God has said, you will know joy unspeakable and full of glory.

As Peter, you will say:

> **... yet believing you rejoice with joy inexpressible and full of glory, receiving the end of your faith...**
>
> **1 Peter 1:8b-9a**

When you know what God has promised, the walk of faith is all joy. The author of Hebrews wrote, *"Let us run with endurance the race that is set before us, looking unto Jesus, the author and finisher of our faith, WHO FOR THE JOY SET BEFORE HIM, endured the cross, despising the shame, and has sat down at the right hand of the throne of God"* (Hebrews 12:1b-2).

There is joy in the *journey* and *victory* of faith.
There is joy in both the *expectation* and the *fulfillment* of hope.

"Do not sorrow..."

Those who have lost their strength are those who have misplaced their joy. Turning their eyes from the report of the Lord to a *distraction on the wayside*, they became encumbered by the care and inconsistencies of a lower realm. Instead of standing on the foundation of the Word and looking into the *horizon of promise*, they turned their gaze from the *expectation of hope*.

Therefore, resist the devil with the joy of the Lord. Run with endurance the race that has been set before you. Run, *expecting to win*. There is championship in your blood, for Jesus has already pioneered your victory. Consider Him and despise the things that would distract you from purpose. Remain steadfast in your course and run the race that is set before you. Resist the enemy and the *lying diversion* with the strength of the Lord. Resist him, steadfast in the promise.

Resist him steadfast in the faith knowing that

> **the same sufferings are experienced by your brotherhood in the world.**
>
> **1 Peter 5:9 NKJV**

Stand firm with all patience and joy. Know that the persecution and the affliction is not unique to you. Neither is it unique to your era or your region in the world, for the devil has NOTHING NEW. They are the *same afflictions* that have come against *"your brotherhood in the world."* Those that know this, will realize that the strategies of the adversary are age old. The devil would like the child of God to think that their giant/situation/mountain is so unique that it supersedes the ability of the Word of God.

The TEMPTATION is not new.
The CHALLENGE is not new.
The LIE is not new.

Therefore, know that the Word of God has the SAME POWER TODAY to lead you into the joy and triumph of faith. The enemy's fiery darts have been launched at the children of promise for ages and generations. There is nothing unique about his warfare.

Always remember: The challenge is nothing more than an occasion to overcome. Therefore, do not neglect so great a salvation, but contend for the victory that you have been assured.

Fight the good fight of faith.
The good fight is the fight that you win.

DOMINION *is yours.*

ABOUT THE AUTHOR

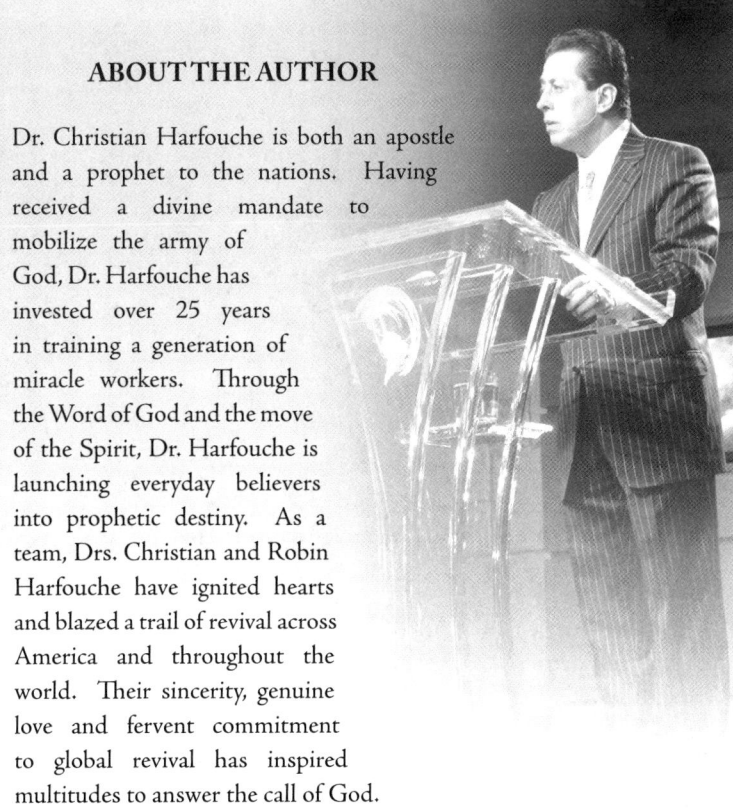

Dr. Christian Harfouche is both an apostle and a prophet to the nations. Having received a divine mandate to mobilize the army of God, Dr. Harfouche has invested over 25 years in training a generation of miracle workers. Through the Word of God and the move of the Spirit, Dr. Harfouche is launching everyday believers into prophetic destiny. As a team, Drs. Christian and Robin Harfouche have ignited hearts and blazed a trail of revival across America and throughout the world. Their sincerity, genuine love and fervent commitment to global revival has inspired multitudes to answer the call of God.

Drs. Christian and Robin Harfouche are committed to training New Testament disciples at The World Center in Pensacola, Florida. The World Center is home to both the International Miracle Institute Bible Training Center and a vibrant, multi-cultural, cross-denominational church. People from around the world move to Pensacola for training and impartation from a major miracle ministry. Drs. Christian and Robin Harfouche continue to travel worldwide, conducting Miracle Soul-Winning Crusades and imparting their lives to the Body of Christ. Their influence and the miracle testimonies of their disciples can be seen daily on the highly acclaimed television program, *Miracles Today*.

International Miracle Institute (IMI)
Equipping A Generation Of Miracle–Workers!

The Lord has given Drs. Christian and Robin Harfouche a mandate to train and equip over 400,000 miracle–workers for the great end–time harvest of souls.

Through the integrity of the Word of God and the move of the Spirit, IMI is empowering a generation to live in victory and to walk in power.

Invest yourself in a supernatural training program.

Allow revelation from the Word of God and impartation from a major miracle ministry to supernaturally equip you for your end–time purpose!

IMI offers two training options!

IMI In–Residence Training (Pensacola, Florida)
IMI Correspondence Program (home study program)

IMI Training At A Glance

- Receive training by Drs. Christian and Robin Harfouche.
- Grow in a practical revelatory understanding of the Word of God.
- Learn how to have continual supernatural results in God.
- Impact the world with signs, wonders and miracles following.
- Fully accredited to confer both undergraduate and graduate degrees.

For More Information:
Visit: www.globalrevival.com
Email: IMI@globalrevival.com
Phone: 850–439–6225

Year One of IMI powerfully equips those called to walk on the cutting edge in the Word of God. This foundation enables you as a believer to live and operate in the supernatural and fulfill the call of God on your life. **Year One is an accredited year of bible college, containing over 100 hours of teaching on 96 CD's.**

Your Authority:
Become all that you can be by knowing, understanding, and exercising your authority in Jesus Christ.

Heavenly Identity:
Understand your identity in Christ.

The God Man:
Learn all about the unlimited abilities invested in you.

Great Faith:
Find out how you can grow to be a wonder worker by building your faith in God.

The Anointing:
Find out about the Anointing in you and how you can cooperate with this unction.

Miracles:
Step into a place in the Lord where nothing is impossible.

Year Two of IMI continues where Year One left off, helping you unlock the deep truths and revelation in the Word of God. Building on the foundation of Year One, **Year Two further enables you as a believer to live and operate in the supernatural** and fulfill the call of God on your life. **Year Two is an accredited year of bible college, also containing over 100 hours of teaching on 96 CD's.**

Advanced Studies in Faith:
A study to build your faith from level to level.

Understanding the Supernatural:
Learn to operate in the highest dimension of life in the spirit.

Healing in the Atonement:
Understand your divine right to the provision and benefits of healing in the atonement.

Ministry Gifts:
"And God gave gifts unto men…" A study of the Call-The Office.

Prophets and Prophecy:
A study of Old and New Testament Prophets; recognize the spirit of error, develop the spirit of pioneer, study the predictive future Word, and learn to cooperate with the Anointing.

Demons & Demonology:
Understand the origin, operation, strategies, and the believers' dominion over the powers of darkness.

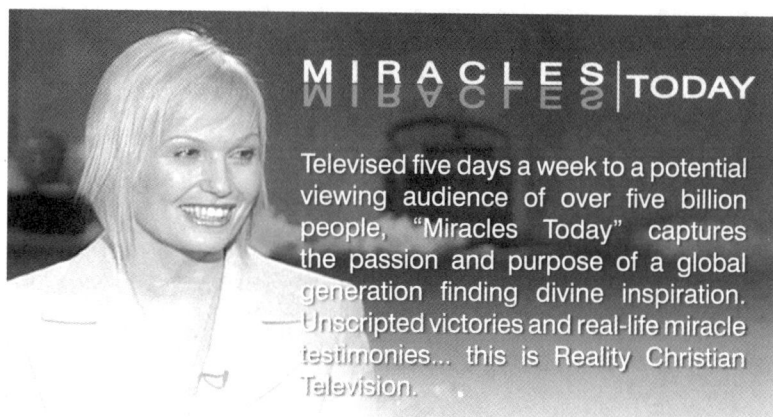

Real people living extraordinary lives – Miracle's Today celebrates the voice of the disciple. Televised daily around the world, Miracles Today captures the passion and purpose of a generation with a divine mandate. Embracing the promises of God and the triumphant walk of faith, Miracle's Today is the celebration of unscripted victories and real life miracle testimonies. Trained and mentored by Drs. Christian and Robin Harfouche, these disciples have answered a global call to broadcast the creative expression of God throughout the Earth. Miracle's Today is God's method of stirring a generation into destiny.

For broadcast times and stations, please visit:
www.globalrevival.com

For further information:
Christian Harfouche Ministries
421 N. Palafox St. • Pensacola, FL 32501

Office: 850–439–6225

Website: www.globalrevival.com
Email: info@globalrevival.com

Remember, miracles don't just happen. By the Word of God and the power of the Spirit, the IMI Correspondence Program will train and equip you to be a miracle worker for this end-time harvest of souls.

"Study to show yourself approved unto God, a workman that needs not to be ashamed, rightly dividing the Word of Truth." 2 Timothy 2:15

For More Information:
Visit: www.globalrevival.com
Email: IMI@globalrevival.com
Phone: 850–439–6225

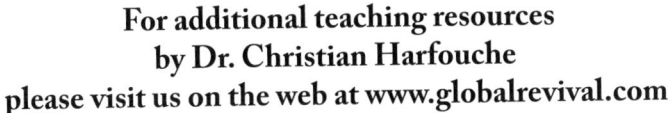

**For additional teaching resources
by Dr. Christian Harfouche
please visit us on the web at www.globalrevival.com**

or contact:

Global Revival Distribution
421 North Palafox St., Pensacola, Florida 32501
Email: info@globalrevival.com
Order Line: 850–439–9750